Adobe® PageMaker® 7.0

Classroom in a Book®

Adobe

Contents

Getting Started

Adobe® PageMaker® 7.0 is the ultimate software tool for producing professional-quality business communications for print, press, or online distribution as Adobe® PDF. With PageMaker, you can integrate text and graphics from many sources into virtually any kind of publication, from newsletter and brochures to color catalogs and magazines to Web pages, with maximum precision and control.

About Classroom in a Book

Adobe PageMaker 7.0 Classroom in a Book® is part of the official training series for Adobe graphics and publishing software developed by experts at Adobe Systems. The lessons are designed to let you learn at your own pace. If you're new to PageMaker, you'll learn the fundamental concepts and features you'll need to master the program. And if you've been using Adobe PageMaker for a while, you'll find that Classroom in a Book teaches many advanced features. The enhanced Export Adobe PDF command is covered in detail.

The lessons in this edition show how to assemble a flyer, letterhead, booklet for a CD jewelcase, pamphlet, newsletter, catalog, and book. Although each lesson provides step-by-step instructions for creating a specific project, there's room for exploration and experimentation. You can follow the book from start to finish or do only the lessons that correspond to your interests and needs. Each lesson concludes with a review section summarizing what you've covered.

Prerequisites

Before beginning to use Adobe PageMaker 7.0 Classroom in a Book, you should have a working knowledge of your computer and its operating system. Make sure you know how to use the mouse and standard menus and commands and also how to open, save, and close files. If you need to review these techniques, see the printed or online documentation included with your Windows® or Mac® OS system.

Installing Adobe PageMaker

Before you begin using *Adobe PageMaker 7.0 Classroom in a Book*, make sure that your system is set up correctly and that you've installed the required software and hardware. You must purchase the Adobe PageMaker 7.0 software separately.

You must install the application from the Adobe PageMaker 7.0 CD onto your hard disk; you cannot run the program from the CD. For system requirements and complete instructions on installing the software, see the How_to_Install.wri (Windows) or How_to_Install.txt (Mac OS) file on the application CD.

Note: Be sure to install Adobe Acrobat® Distiller® 5.0, Adobe Acrobat® Reader® 5.0, Adobe PostScript® Driver from the application CD unless you have installed Adobe Acrobat 5.0 separately, and Adobe Type Manager®(ATM®).

Make sure your serial number is accessible before installing the application; you can find the serial number on the registration card or CD sleeve.

Installing the Classroom in a Book fonts

To ensure that the lesson files appear on your system with the correct fonts, you may need to install the Classroom in a Book font files. The fonts for the lessons are located in the Fonts folder on the Adobe PageMaker Classroom in a Book CD. If you already have these on your system, you do not need to install them. If you have ATM (Adobe Type Manager), see its documentation on how to install fonts. If you do not have ATM, installing it from the Classroom in a Book (CIB) CD will automatically install the necessary fonts.

You can also install the Classroom in a Book fonts by copying all of the files in the Fonts folder on the Adobe PageMaker Classroom in a Book CD to:

• Program Files/Common Files/Adobe/Fonts (Windows)

• System Folder/Application Support/Adobe/Fonts (Mac OS)

If you install a Type 1, TrueType, OpenType, or CID font into these local Fonts folders, the font appears in Adobe applications only.

Note: The Birch font can be found on the PageMaker application CD.

Creating and printing lesson projects

The lesson projects in this Classroom in a Book are designed to be printed on black-and white-printers, desktop color printers, and four-color presses. Some projects are designed to be distributed on the Web in HTML or PDF format rather than printed. If you do not have access to any or all of these types of printers, or if you don't have access to a Web server, you can still complete the projects.

Although these projects are composed for a specific printer, you can print them on your own printer by selecting your printer and its PPD in the Print dialog box when it is time to print. (If your printer is not a PostScript printer, you do not have the option to select a PPD.) Alternatively you can export the project files to Adobe PDF and create an Adobe PDF version of the finished piece using the Export Adobe PDF command.

When you export to Adobe PDF, PageMaker creates a PostScript file, and then automatically starts Acrobat Distiller to convert the PostScript file into Adobe PDF. If you do not have enough free RAM to run Acrobat

Distiller simultaneously with PageMaker, you will need to close all open applications other than PageMaker. For most of the lesson projects, you can use the default options for Export Adobe PDF, as described in Lesson 1 "Creating an Adobe PDF version of the flyer" on page 41. For information on using Export Adobe PDF to create separations, see Lesson 7 "Creating separations using Adobe PDF" on page 239. For information on customizing the options associated with Export Adobe PDF command—changing the file size or image quality, for example, see Lesson 9, "Setting PDF Options" on page 277.

Installing PPDs (Windows only)

In Windows, you need to install the PPDs for the AGFA-ProSet9800 and the HP LaserJet 5Si printers. These PPDs are included on the Classroom in a Book (CIB) CD in the folder WinPPDs. Even though you may never print to these printers, you will specify these printers as the final output device in several projects.

Before you begin any project that you plan to take to a service provider, you must know which final output device the provider will use and, from the start, select that device for Compose to Printer in the Document Setup dialog box, even if you plan to print drafts on your own printer. (You'll learn how to do this in the lessons.) In PageMaker for Windows, font choices and sizes, resolution of text and graphics, and the print area depend on the device you select.

To ensure that you get the expected results in these lessons, install these PPDs now.

The PPDs for the two printers used in this Classroom in a Book are on the Classroom in a Book (CIB) CD. Follow these steps to install them:

1 Insert the Classroom in a Book (CIB) CD, and navigate to the folder containing the two PPD files, AGPRO981.PPD and HPLJ5SI1.PPD.

2 Using Windows Explorer, open the folder Program Files/Adobe/PageMaker 7.0/ Rsrc/Usenglsh/Ppd4 on your hard drive.

3 Drag the two files, AGPRO981.PPD and HPLJ5SI1.PPD, from the Classroom in a Book (CIB) CD to the Ppd4 folder on your hard drive.

You have successfully installed the drivers and printers required to complete the lessons in this book.

Copying the Classroom in a Book files

The Adobe PageMaker Classroom in a Book CD includes folders containing all the electronic files for the lessons. Each lesson has its own folder, and you must copy the folders to your hard drive to do the lessons. To save room on your drive, you can install only the necessary folder for each lesson as you need it, and remove it when you're done.

To install the Classroom in a Book files:

1 Insert the Adobe PageMaker Classroom in a Book CD into your CD-ROM drive.

2 Create a folder named PM70_CIB on your hard drive.

3 Copy the lessons you want to the hard drive:

• To copy all of the lessons, drag the Lessons folder from the CD into the PM70_CIB folder.

• To copy a single lesson, drag the individual lesson folder from the CD into the PM70_CIB folder.

If you are installing the files in Windows, you need to unlock them before using them. You don't need to unlock the files if you are installing them in Mac OS.

In Windows, unlock the files you copied:

• If you copied all of the lessons, double-click the unlock.bat file in the PM70_CIB/Lessons folder.

• If you copied a single lesson, drag the unlock.bat file from the Lessons folder on the CD into the PM70_CIB folder. Then double-click the unlock.bat file in the PM70_CIB folder.

Note: If as you work through the lessons, you overwrite the Start files, you can restore the original files by recopying the corresponding Lesson folder from the Classroom in a Book CD to the PM70_CIB folder on your hard drive.

Additional resources

Adobe PageMaker Classroom in a Book is not meant to replace documentation that comes with the program. Only the commands and options used in the lessons are explained in this book. For comprehensive information about program features, refer to these resources:

The Adobe PageMaker 7.0 User Guide. Included with the Adobe PageMaker 7.0 software, this guide contains a complete description of all features.

Online Help,

an online version of the user guide, which you can view by choosing Help > Help Topics (Windows) or Help > PageMaker Help Topics (Mac OS).

The Adobe Web site (www.adobe.com),

which you can view by choosing Help > Adobe Online if you have a connection to the World Wide Web.

Adobe Certification

The Adobe Training and Certification Programs are designed to help Adobe customers improve and promote their product proficiency skills. The Adobe Certified Expert (ACE) program is designed to recognize the high-level skills of expert users. Adobe Certified Training Providers (ACTP) use only Adobe Certified Experts to teach Adobe software classes. Available in either ACTP classrooms or on-site, the ACE program is the best way to master Adobe products. For Adobe Certified Training Programs information, visit the Partnering with Adobe Web site at http://partners.adobe.com.

Lesson 1
Flyer

In this project you'll assemble a single-page, black-and-white flyer from start to finish. The photograph and most of the text featured in this flyer are ready for you to import into PageMaker. You'll also learn how to type text directly into a publication and you'll draw several graphic elements (square, circle, and line).

For this lesson, you will open and view the final version of the flyer, and follow the step-by-step instructions that introduce some of the basic features and tools of PageMaker. Even if you have experience using the PageMaker application, this introduction may reveal some useful tips and techniques.

This project covers the following topics:

• Restoring default PageMaker settings

• Changing the view of a publication

• Creating a new publication

• Opening an existing publication

• Setting up the horizontal and vertical rulers

• Displaying and hiding guides

• Positioning the zero point

• Using the pointer tool, the text tool, and the zoom tool

• Specifying multiple columns

• Locking the guides

• Creating, placing, formatting, and positioning text and graphic elements

• Creating a drop cap

• Applying a tint to text

• Specifying a hanging indent

• Creating ruler guides

• Drawing circles, rectangles, and lines

• Adjusting the stacking order of elements on the page

• Range kerning text

• Using the Snap to Guides option

• Printing the flyer on a desktop laser printer

• Exporting the flyer to Adobe PDF

If this is your first time using PageMaker, it should take about 2 hours to complete this lesson. If you have some experience using PageMaker, it should take about 90 minutes to complete this lesson.

Locating files and fonts

All files and fonts needed for this lesson are found on the *Adobe PageMaker Classroom in a Book* CD-ROM in the folders 01Lesson and Fonts, respectively.

Restoring default settings

Before starting PageMaker, delete the PageMaker 7.0 preferences file to ensure all settings are returned to their default values.

1 If PageMaker 7.0 is running, choose File > Exit or Quit.

2 Locate the PageMaker preferences file in the following location, depending upon your system:

Windows \PageMaker 7.0\rsrc\usenglsh\ PM70.cnf

Note: If Windows is set to hide filename extensions, the preferences file will instead appear without the .cnf extension.

Macintosh System Folder: Preferences: Adobe PageMaker 7.0P Prefs

3 Drag the preferences file to the Recycle Bin (Windows) or Trash (Macintosh).

The PageMaker preferences settings are returned to their default values.

To preserve your preference settings, drag the preferences file to a different folder. When you are ready to restore the settings, drag the file back to its original folder and click Yes when asked whether to overwrite the existing file.

Starting PageMaker

After verifying that the correct fonts are installed on your computer, you will start the PageMaker application.

1 In addition to the commonly used fonts identified in the Getting Started chapter, make sure the following fonts are installed on your computer: AGaramond, AGaramond Italic, and Myriad Roman.

Windows only: *Because of the way Windows handles fonts, AGaramond Italic does not appear in font menus in Windows applications. You must apply italic to AGaramond to use AGaramond Italic.*

Myriad, a multiple master typeface, is a sans serif design. Myriad makes a good text face as well as providing flexibility for filling display needs in all sizes and media.

Note: *Serifs are the small strokes at the top and bottom of a letter. Typefaces without serifs are generally called sans (without) serifs.*

2 Depending on the platform, start PageMaker as follows:

• In Windows, choose Start > Programs > Adobe > Adobe PageMaker 7.0 (your menus may differ depending upon your installation).

• In Mac OS, open the Adobe PageMaker 7.0 folder and double-click the Adobe® PageMaker® 7.0 icon.

Adobe® PageMaker® 7.0

Once launched, PageMaker displays the menus and tool box. If necessary, close the Template and Picture palettes (Windows).

Opening an existing publication

Opening the final version of the publication and following the step-by-step instructions will help you become acquainted with PageMaker.

Note: Windows users need to unlock the lesson files before using them. For information, see Copying the Classroom in a Book files on page 4.

1 Choose File > Open, and, in the Open Publication dialog box, locate and double-click the 01Final.pmd file in the 01Lesson folder.

PageMaker opens the final version of the publication you will create in this lesson, with horizontal and vertical rulers extending along the top and left edges of the publication window.

2 If the publication window does not fill the screen, click the Maximize button in the right corner of the title bar to expand the window.

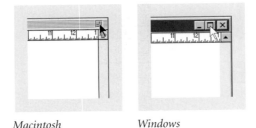

Macintosh   *Windows*

As you look at the publication window, notice the following elements:

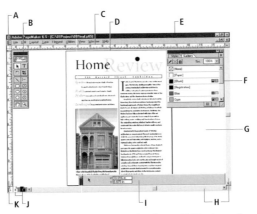

A. Zero point marker B. Tool palette C. Horizontal ruler D. Page E. Publication window F. Styles and Colors palettes G. Pasteboard H. Scroll bars I. Control palette J. Page icons K. Vertical ruler

Toolbox Displays tools that you use for drawing, entering or editing text, selecting and dragging objects on the page, panning the page, and zooming in and out of the page. You click to select a tool. The toolbox appears in the upper left corner of the publication window.

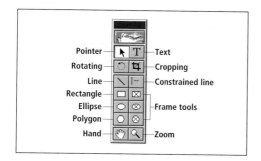

Pointer, Rotating, Line, Rectangle, Ellipse, Polygon, Hand, Text, Cropping, Constrained line, Frame tools, Zoom

Control palette Lets you make precise changes to text and graphics without selecting a tool or choosing a menu command. The Control palette appears in the lower portion of the publication window, and changes modes depending upon what is currently selected.

Page Defines the print area of a publication. Whenever you create a new publication, you specify the dimensions of the page. Only text or graphics on the page will print.

Pasteboard Provides a workspace outside the page where you can store and manipulate elements before positioning them on the page. The term pasteboard, like many of the terms in this course, comes from traditional publishing, where layout artists assemble text and graphics on a physical pasteboard. The extra space on the board serves as a work space for elements not yet placed on the page.

Styles and Colors palettes Displays the predefined paragraph styles and colors. PageMaker also has palettes for layers, master pages, and hyperlinks (more about these in later lessons). To save screen space, PageMaker lets you group the palettes you regularly use, or you can drag a palette out of the group if you want to display it independently. To activate a palette, you click its tab. Each palette also includes: a menu; a Maximize button to expand and minimize the palette; and buttons to create or delete a style, color, layer, etc.

A. Palette tab B. Maximize button C. Palette menu D. Trash button E. New button

Page icons Indicates the currently displayed page (page one in this case). PageMaker displays an icon for every page in the publication. To view a page, you click its page icon. The L and R page icons represent the left and right master pages.

Changing the view of a publication

PageMaker opens a publication in the view that was selected when it was last saved. This publication was saved in the Fit in Window view.

Note: *When the size of this page is reduced to fit within a 13-inch (or smaller) monitor, the 10-point text is displayed as gray bars (an effect known as* greeking).

1 Choose View > Actual Size.

The view of this publication is magnified to its actual size (its size when printed), making it possible to read the text.

2 To toggle between the Fit in Window and Actual Size views, while holding down the Ctrl key (Windows) or the Command and Option keys (Macintosh), click the page (use the right mouse button in Windows). Toggle back to the Actual Size view.

3 Click the scroll arrows or drag the scroll bars on the right and bottom edges of the publication window to scroll the page.

You may find it easier to use the following method to scroll in your publication.

4 Hold down the Alt key (Windows) or Option key (Macintosh), position the pointer on the page or pasteboard, hold down the mouse button until the pointer changes to a grabber hand, and drag in any direction to scroll the view of the page.

5 Click the zoom tool (🔍) in the toolbox to select it.

The pointer changes to a magnifying glass. The zoom tool makes it easy to magnify and reduce the view of selected portions of the page. With the zoom tool selected, you can magnify the view of a specific portion of the page by either clicking or dragging over the area.

6 With the zoom tool selected, hold down Ctrl (Windows) or Option (Macintosh).

The plus sign in the zoom tool changes to a minus (–) sign.

7 Click the page to reduce the view of the page.

8 With the zoom tool still selected, drag over any portion of the page. Notice how PageMaker displays a rectangle with a dashed line as you drag the tool. When you release the mouse button, the selected portion of the page fills the publication window.

9 Double-click the zoom tool in the toolbox to switch to the Actual Size view. Using a similar shortcut, jump to the Fit in Window

view by holding down the Alt key (Windows) or Option key (Macintosh), and double-clicking the zoom tool in the toolbox.

Working with the toolbox and palettes

As you work, you may find the toolbox and palettes are in your way, especially if you have a small screen. PageMaker gives you several options to minimize the impact of the toolbox and palettes, while still keeping them handy. You can move the toolbox or palettes, minimize the palettes so just the title bar and tabs show, temporarily hide all the palettes at once, or hide each group of palettes individually.

Throughout these lessons, feel free to move or hide the toolbox and palettes as necessary.

1 Select the hand tool (✋).

2 Position the pointer over the title bar of the Styles and Colors palette window, hold down the mouse, and drag the palette to the right edge of the publication window.

You can drag the toolbox or any palette anywhere within the publication window. You can even let part of the palette or toolbox extend outside the publication window.

You'll now see how small a palette can be while still visible.

3 Click the Maximize button in the Styles and Colors palette window until the palette window jumps to its minimum size (just the title bar and palette tabs display).

Maximize   *Minimize*

4 Click the Maximize button in the palette window again to return the palette to its full size.

If you like the palettes handy, but out of the way, you can move them to the bottom of the screen. You'll try this next.

5 Drag the Styles and Colors palette window until its bottom edge aligns with the bottom of the publication window. (In Mac OS, you may need to drag the palette window until its bottom edge aligns with the bottom edge of the monitor screen.) Click the Maximize button in the palette window.

PageMaker reduces the palette to its minimum size and automatically drops it to the bottom of the screen. (Normally when you minimize a palette the titlebar remains stationary.)

6 Click the Maximize button in the palette window again to return the palette to its full size.

If you need to see the full screen, you can temporarily hide all the palettes and the toolbox at once.

7 Press the Tab key.

The toolbox, Control palette, and Styles and Colors palettes disappear.

Note: Be careful using this shortcut when the text tool is selected. If you have text selected with the text tool, pressing Tab replaces the text with a tab character. If you have an insertion point in text, pressing Tab inserts a tab character into the line.

8 Press Tab again to redisplay the toolbox and palettes.

Finally, you can hide and show the toolbox, Control palette, or other palettes using the hide or show options on the Window menu. The Window menu has a hide or show option for the toolbox and every palette. The options change from show to hide depending upon whether the toolbox or palette is displayed or, for palettes that are grouped, whether the palette is active.

9 Choose Window > Hide Colors.

Because the Colors and Styles palettes are grouped together, PageMaker hides both palettes.

10 Choose Window > Show Styles to redisplay the palettes.

Notice that both palettes are displayed, but now the Styles palette is the active palette.

11 Click the Colors palette tab to make it the active palette (or choose Window > Show Colors).

Using the rulers

The rulers along the top and left borders of your publication window can help you position text and graphic elements on a page.

1 Click the pointer tool ( ) in the toolbox to select it.

2 Without clicking in your publication, move the pointer around the publication window, and notice how the hairline indicators in the vertical and horizontal rulers correspond to the position of the pointer.

Also notice how when no text or graphic elements are selected in your publication, the Control palette displays the horizontal and vertical position of the cursor as X and Y coordinates, respectively.

Note: Since inches is the unit of measure established for this publication, the Control palette and the horizontal and vertical rulers display in inches.

Positioning the zero point

The point on your page (or pasteboard) that aligns with zero on both the horizontal and vertical rulers is known as the *zero point*. By default, the zero point of single-sided publications is located at the upper left corner of the page. To make it easier to measure distances from specific areas of your page, you can move the zero point to any location.

1 Without clicking in your publication, move the pointer to the upper left corner of the page. Notice how the zeros on the horizontal and vertical rulers are aligned at this location. (If necessary, click the scroll bars along the right and bottom edges of the publication window to view the upper left corner of the page.)

2 With the pointer tool selected, position the pointer on the intersection of the rulers in the upper left corner of your publication window (on the zero point marker as shown below), and hold down the mouse button.

Zero point marker

3 With the mouse button still held down, drag the zero point down and right until the horizontal and vertical guides are roughly aligned with the upper left edge of the letter **H** in the display text **Home Review**, and release the mouse button.

The horizontal and vertical rulers indicate the new location of the zero point.

4 Double-click the crosshair of the zero point to restore the zero point to its default location at the upper left corner of the page.

Setting up the rulers

You can set the horizontal and vertical rulers to the measurement system you prefer. In general, it's a good idea to choose a measurement system before you assemble a publication.

1 Choose File > Preferences > General.

The Preferences dialog box lets you customize PageMaker. If a publication is open, the options you select in the Preferences dialog box apply to that publication only. If no publication is open, the options you choose apply to all new publications you create.

Notice how Inches is selected for both the Measurements In and Vertical Ruler options. PageMaker lets you set the horizontal and vertical rulers to different units of measurement.

2 Choose Picas for Vertical Ruler and click OK.

The horizontal ruler reflects the unit of measure (Inches) originally selected for the Measurements In option. The vertical ruler indicates picas as the unit of measure.

Note:: Derived from an old term for metal type of that size, a pica is a measure of type (approximately equal to 1/6 of an inch), divided into 12 points (each point equal to .0138 (1/72) of an inch).

Notice how the text and graphic elements remain in the same position on the page. Even though you usually work with one unit of measure throughout a publication, you can see it is possible to change to another unit of measure at any time without altering the positioning of elements.

3 As a shortcut to the Preferences dialog box, double-click the pointer tool in the tool box. For Vertical Ruler, choose Inches, and click OK to restore the original measurement system.

Sometimes you will want to hide the rulers so you have more room on the screen to view your publication.

4 Choose View > Hide Rulers to hide the rulers.

5 Choose View > Show Rulers to once again display the rulers.

Displaying guides

Nonprinting guides make it easier to assemble a publication like this.

1 Choose View > Show Guides to display all nonprinting guides used to create this publication.

Notice the cyan horizontal and vertical lines positioned at various locations on the page. These *ruler guides* are used to position text and graphics on the page accurately. It is possible to have as many as 120 ruler guides on the page, in any combination of horizontal and vertical.

The pink horizontal lines at the top and bottom of the columns are the top and bottom margin guides. The darker blue vertical lines indicate the columns. Column guides help define areas for text to flow into automatically.

Note: Column guides overlap the left and right margin guides.

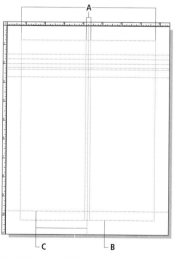

A. Column guides B. Bottom Margin guide C. Ruler guides

2 If you have altered 01Final.pmd, choose File > Revert, and when prompted, click OK to revert to the original version of the file.

Note: If you have saved any changes made to the 01Final.pmd file, copy the original 01Final.pmd file from the 01Lesson folder on the Adobe PageMaker 7.0 Classroom in a Book *CD-ROM.*

Planning to print this flyer

It's a good idea to gather all printing require-ments before you start to work. Designed to be printed on a 300 dpi (dots per inch) desk-top laser printer, this flyer (including the grayscale TIFF image scanned at 100 dpi), can print successfully on a wide variety of PostScript and non-PostScript printers.

Most printers do not print to the very edge of the page. You need to determine the max-imum printable area your printer can print, and adapt your designs accordingly. If the documentation that came with your printer does not provide the dimensions of the maximum printable area, you can manually determine it. To do so, draw a shaded box in a PageMaker publication that covers an entire page, and print the page. (By the end of this lesson you'll know how to draw and fill objects.) The resulting printed page will show you the print area, also known as the *imageable area.*

Note: If you do not have the required printer, you can still create the project as directed and then print it on your own printer by selecting your printer and its PPD (if it is a

PostScript printer) in the Print dialog box when it is time to print. You can also use the Export Adobe PDF command to create an Adobe PDF version of the project rather than a printed copy, as described in Creating an Adobe PDF version of the flyer on page 41.

Assembling a two-column flyer

After creating a new publication, you will place and format text and graphics to assem-ble this two-column flyer.

So that you can use the 01Final.pmd publi-cation as a reference, leave it open as you assemble the flyer.

Creating a new publication

After setting the options in the Document Setup dialog box, you will name and save your publication.

1 Choose File > New.

The Document Setup dialog box prompts you to establish some of the specifications for the flyer.

2 In the Document Setup dialog box, click Double-sided to deselect it and type .75 for the left margin. Make sure the Right, Top, and Bottom options display a value of 0.75 (to establish a .75-inch margin around the entire page).

3 In the Document Setup dialog box, choose 300 for Target Output Resolution and choose (Windows only) the printer that matches your printer for Compose to Printer (or HP LaserJet 5Si if you don't have a 300 dpi printer). Then click OK.

By default, every publication has at least one column that spans the area between the left and right margin guides. For this reason, the dark blue vertical column guides overlap the pink left and right margin guides.

4 With the pointer tool selected, position the pointer on either vertical dark blue column guide, hold down the mouse button until the cursor becomes a double-headed arrow, and drag the column guide left or right. When you release it, you can view the pink margin guide behind it.

PageMaker lets you adjust the size of a single column to a different width than the area between the left and right margin guides.

5 Drag the column guide back to its original position over the margin guide.

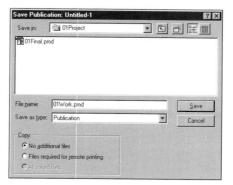

Note: Unlike many word-processing applications, PageMaker makes it possible to print text and graphics positioned between the edge of the page and the margins.

6 Choose File > Save As, and in the dialog box type **01Work.pmd** for the file name and make sure Publication is selected for Save as Type (Windows) or Save As (Macintosh). Locate and select the 01Lesson folder and click Save.

PageMaker saves the 01Work.pmd publication.

💡 The .pmd filename extension is required in PageMaker for Windows and will be added to a filename if you don't include it. PageMaker on the Macintosh does not require the filename extension, nor will it add it to filenames. However, if you transfer files to a Windows computer, the extension lets PageMaker for Windows recognize and open the file.

Specifying column guides

With the .75-inch margins already established using the Document Setup dialog box, you are ready to add column guides and ruler guides. For this flyer, you will divide the page into two columns.

1 Choose Layout > Column Guides, and, in the Column Guides dialog box, type **2** for Number of Columns and **.25** for the Space Between Columns (Windows) or Space Between (Mac OS), and click OK.

When you specify two or more (up to twenty) columns, PageMaker automatically creates columns of equal width, filling the

entire area between the left and right margin guides. The vertical space between the columns is called the *gutter*.

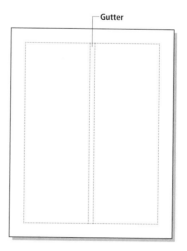
Gutter

To create columns of varying width, you can drag the column guides, manually resizing the columns.

2 With the pointer tool selected, position the pointer on any column guide, and drag the column guide to the left or right.

3 Choose Layout > Column Guides, and, in the Column Guides dialog box, notice how Number of Columns is set to Custom. Type **2** for Number of Columns to restore the two columns of equal width, and click OK.

4 Choose File > Save.

Locking the guides

Once you have established the final design grid, it is a good idea to lock the guides, preventing column and ruler guides being moved accidentally.

1 Choose View > Lock Guides to select the option.

2 Attempt to move the column guides.

Note: If you want to move or delete a guide (margin, column, or ruler) when the guides are locked, choose View > Lock Guides to deselect the option. After you move or delete a guide, relock the guides.

Placing a graphic

You will use the Place command to import a photograph into the flyer. PageMaker lets you import, link, and export text and graphic elements that are saved in a PageMaker-compatible format. For more information on placing graphics, refer to the *Adobe PageMaker 7.0 User Guide*.

This particular photograph was scanned on a flatbed scanner, imported into Adobe Photoshop® to be sized for the flyer, and saved as a grayscale TIFF image at a resolution of 100 dpi.

1 Choose File > Place. Locate and open the 01Lesson folder, and then double-click the 01ArtA.tif file.

The pointer changes to a loaded graphic icon. You will position the graphic icon where you want the upper left corner of the graphic to appear.

To cancel importing when the loaded graphic (or text) icon is displayed, click the pointer tool in the toolbox.

2 With the loaded graphic icon (▧ Windows or ▦ Mac OS), click anywhere on the page to place the photograph.

PageMaker positions the photograph so that its top left corner is aligned with the position of the top left corner of the loaded graphic icon where you clicked to place the photograph.

The eight square graphics handles displayed at the corners and edges of the photograph indicate the graphic is selected, and make it possible to resize the graphic vertically, horizontally, or both. The Control palette reflects the attributes of the selected graphic, and offers another way to manipulate objects. You can move and resize objects precisely by entering values in the Control palette.

Now that the photograph is placed in the flyer, you will position the photograph in the lower left portion of the page, reduce the size of the photograph, and then undo the resizing operation.

3 With the pointer tool selected, click in the center of the photograph, and hold down the mouse button until the pointer changes to an arrowhead (▶).

4 With the mouse button still held down, drag the photograph beyond the bottom edge of the page.

PageMaker automatically scrolls the page when the pointer reaches the edge of the publication window. If you drag outside the publication window, PageMaker stops scrolling.

5 With the mouse button still held down, drag the photograph until its left and bottom edges are aligned with the left and bottom margin guides, respectively, and release the mouse button.

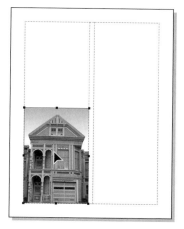

After placing and aligning text in column 2, you will reposition the photograph to be aligned with the text. For now, take this opportunity to experiment with resizing the photograph.

6 With the pointer tool still selected, click on one of the corner handles, and drag toward the center of the photograph, reducing its size.

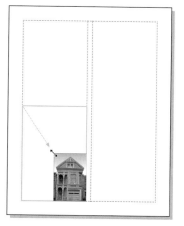

Even though it is possible to resize bitmap images in PageMaker, you will get the best printing results if your images are accurately sized before you import them into PageMaker.

7 If necessary, choose Edit > Undo Stretch to restore the photograph to its original size.

Important: *PageMaker lets you undo only a single level of modification. Any subsequent action, even just clicking the mouse, disables the Undo command.*

If you are unable to restore the photograph to its original size, click the photograph with the pointer tool to select it, press the Delete key, and re-import the 01ArtA.tif file as explained in steps 1 and 2.

8 With the pointer tool still selected, hold down Shift and drag the top-center handle of the photograph up towards the top of the page.

Normally when you drag a top or side center handle, PageMaker resizes only in a vertical (or horizontal) direction. However, resizing with the Shift key maintains the proportions of the image, regardless of the handle you use.

9 Choose Edit > Undo Stretch to restore the photograph to its original size or place it again (as described in steps 1 and 2).

10 Choose File > Save.

Note: Choosing the Save command deselects all objects in a publication.

Placing text in column 2

You can insert text created in other word-processing applications into a PageMaker publication. PageMaker supports a wide variety of word-processing applications and text-file formats, including Rich Text Format (.rtf). You can also import text from documents created using earlier versions of PageMaker.

For information on installing filters for importing different file types into PageMaker, see the Adobe PageMaker 7.0 online Help.

1 Choose File > Place, and, in the dialog box, double-click the 01TextA.doc file in the 01Lesson folder.

The pointer changes to a loaded text icon.

2 Position the loaded text icon (▤) in column 2 below the top margin guide. Click to place the text (avoid clicking outside of the column).

The text flows into the column automatically.

Note: If you click outside of the column, the text will not flow into the column. If this is the case, make sure the pointer tool is selected, click the placed text, press the Delete key, and import the 01TextA.doc file again.

The *windowshades* that stretch horizontally across the top and bottom borders of the text indicate the text is selected as a text block. A *text block*, like a graphic, is an object that you can move, resize, and reshape. In addition to the loops in the center, a selected text block has square corner handles at each end of the windowshade. With the pointer tool selected, you can drag a corner handle to adjust the size of a text block.

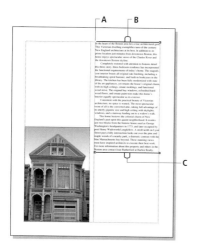

*A. Corner handle **B.** Top windowshade handle **C.** Bottom windowshade handle*

The empty windowshade handle at the top of a text block indicates the beginning of a story. The empty windowshade handle at the bottom of a text block indicates the end of a story. A *story* is text recognized by PageMaker as a single unit. A story can be one letter or several hundred pages of text, and can be contained in a single text block or threaded through many different ones.

3 Position the pointer on the bottom windowshade handle (bottom loop), and drag up to reduce the size of the text block.

A red triangle appears in the bottom windowshade handle, indicating the end of the story is not displayed.

4 Position the pointer on the bottom windowshade handle (bottom loop), and drag down, making sure the entire story is displayed.

Note: *Clicking, rather than dragging, the red triangle loads the remaining text, causing the cursor to be displayed as a loaded text icon. If you clicked the triangle by mistake, click the pointer tool in the toolbox to cancel. Then click the text again to select it as a text block.*

Much like adjusting the height and width of a graphic element, you can adjust the height and width of a text block by dragging a corner handle (at the left and right ends of the windowshade).

5 With the pointer tool selected, position the pointer on the bottom left corner handle of the text block in column 2, hold down the mouse button until the pointer changes to a double-headed arrow, drag it in any direction, and release the mouse button, adjusting the width and the height of the text block.

PageMaker automatically reflows the text within the text block. Depending on the size of the text block, the red triangle in the bottom windowshade handle may indicate the entire story is not displayed.

6 Choose Edit > Undo Stretch to restore the text block to its original size.

If you are unable to restore the text block to its original size, click the text block with the pointer tool to select it, press the Delete key, and import the 01TextA.doc file again as described in steps 1 and 2.

7 Choose File > Save.

Formatting the text in column 2

You will apply character specifications (such as size, typeface, and type style) to the text in column 2 using the Control palette.

Note: To create, edit, or format text, the text tool must be selected.

1 Choose View > Actual Size.

2 Click the text tool (**T**) in the toolbox to select it.

The pointer changes to an I-beam, and the Control palette displays frequently used character specification options, providing quick access to most of the options that are available from the menus.

You can select a single character or the entire contents of a text block by dragging the text tool across the target text. To select a word, double-click it with the text tool. To select a paragraph, triple-click it with the text tool.

For this flyer, you need to change the font and size of all the text in the column. The next step shows you the easiest way to select the entire story.

3 With the text tool, click the text in column 2 to establish an *insertion point* (a blinking vertical bar where you can begin typing). Choose Edit > Select All.

The character specifications you select in the Control palette apply to selected text only. You will change the font, point size, and leading.

The *point size* of a font is the height of the font from the bottom of the descenders (such as p) to the top of the ascenders (such as h), but does not indicate the height of each letter. For example, a lowercase "a" set in 12-point type is not 12 points high.

Leading is the vertical space in which text is placed. Like type size, leading is measured in points. Unlike type size, which varies with each letter, leading is an exact measurement.

12-point leading is always 12 points high. This vertical space for type is also referred to as the *slug* or the *leading slug*.

4 In the Control palette, choose Myriad Roman for Font, type **9.5** for Size and **17** for Leading, and click the Apply button.

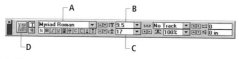

A. *Font pop-up menu* **B.** *Size* **C.** *Leading*
D. *Apply button*

When formatting text using the Control palette, it is possible to apply the specification by pressing Enter or Return, rather than clicking the Apply button. However, if the Control palette is not active, pressing Enter or Return instead replaces the selected text with a hard carriage return.

5 Choose File > Save.

Creating a drop cap

A *drop cap* is a large initial letter that spans two or more lines of text.

1 Select the zoom tool (Q) in the toolbox, and drag over the first paragraph in column 2 to magnify its view.

2 Select the text tool (**T**), and drag to select the first letter of the first paragraph in column 2.

> n the heart of the Boston area lies a true arch
> This Victorian dwelling exemplifies turn-of-th
> England architecture at its best. In addition to
> tion just minutes from downtown Boston, th

3 In the Control palette, choose AGaramond (Regular) for Font.

When you choose from a pop-up menu or click a button in the Control palette, PageMaker automatically applies the formatting or effect to the selection. In contrast, when you type a value in the Control palette you must click the Apply button or press Enter or Return for the change to take effect.

4 Choose Utilities > Plug–ins >Drop Cap, type **4** for Size, and click OK.

5 Press Ctrl (Windows) or Command (Macintosh) together with the Shift and F12 keys to force PageMaker to redraw the screen at the current screen view.

6 Choose View > Fit in Window to view the entire page.

7 Choose File > Save.

Positioning the text block in column 2

You will position the text block in column 2, aligning its bottom edge with the bottom margin guide.

1 Select the pointer tool, and click the text in column 2 to select it as a text block.

You can use the Shift key as you drag objects to move them in a straight line horizontally or vertically.

2 With the text still selected as a text block, position the pointer on the text in the middle of the text block. Hold down Shift, and drag the text block until its bottom edge

snaps to the bottom margin guide, with its left and right edges still aligned with the column guides.

3 Choose File > Save.

Positioning the graphic

Aligning text and graphic elements within a publication is one of the keys to successful page layout. To allow for a two-line caption under the photograph, you will align the bottom of the photograph with the *baseline* of the text in the column 2. The baseline is the imaginary line on which the text (letters) rests. Descenders (such as y) fall below the baseline.

1 Magnify the view of the lower third of the page.

2 Position the pointer on the horizontal ruler, hold down the mouse button until the pointer becomes a double-headed arrow.

3 Drag down to create a horizontal ruler guide that is aligned with the baseline of the third to last line of text in column 2, and release the mouse button.

Because you locked the guides earlier in this lesson, once you release the mouse you cannot adjust the guide. To move or delete the guide, temporarily unlock the guides (choose View > Lock Guides to deselect the option). So that you don't accidentally move the graphic or the text block, position the pointer over the guide in the margin or between columns. Then, either drag the guide to the correct location, or drag it off the page to delete it. Then, relock the guides.

4 With the pointer tool selected, hold down Shift (to constrain the movement to 90°), and drag the photograph until its bottom

edge snaps to the horizontal ruler guide (that you just created), with its left and right edges still aligned with the column guides.

The photograph is aligned with the text in column 2, and you are ready to create the caption for the photograph.

5 Choose File > Save.

Creating the caption

Rather than importing existing text into PageMaker, you will type the two-line caption below the photograph and position it so the text block snaps to the bottom margin guide.

PageMaker has all the word-processing capabilities you need to type and format your text from scratch. While it is possible to create and edit text in layout view, you may find many advantages to using Story Editor, the full-featured word processor included with PageMaker. For more information about the Story Editor, refer to the *Adobe PageMaker 7.0 User Guide.*

Just as with formatting text, you must select the text tool to enter or edit text.

1 Select the text tool (**T**), and click in column 1 below the photograph to establish an insertion point.

The blinking cursor on the left margin guide indicates the position of the insertion point.

2 Type the following sentence:

Close to the beautiful Charles River, this home shares the historic charm of its Cambridge neighborhood.

Because you established an insertion point within column 1, the width of the text block automatically equals the width of the column.

3 With the text tool still selected, triple-click the caption to select it. Triple-clicking text selects a single paragraph.

4 In the Control palette, choose AGaramond (Regular) for Font, type **11** for Size (⁑T) and **17** for Leading (t⁂), and click the Italic button (*I*).

Note: When you apply italic to AGaramond, PageMaker uses AGaramond Italic. On the Macintosh, you can get the same result if you select AGaramond Italic directly.

5 Select the pointer tool, click the caption to select it as a text block, hold down Shift (to constrain the movement to 90º), and position the pointer over the text. Drag the text

block until its bottom edge snaps to the bottom margin guide, with its left and right edges still aligned with the column guides.

Because the caption and the text in column 2 both have the same leading value and are snapped to the same guide, their baselines align.

6 Choose File > Save.

Placing text in column 1

Again, you will place text created and saved with a word-processing application, automatically flowing it into column 1.

1 Choose View > Fit in Window.

2 Choose File > Place, and in the Place Document dialog box, double-click the 01TextB.doc file in the 01Lesson folder.

The pointer changes to a loaded text icon.

3 With the loaded text icon displayed, click in column 1 a little below the top margin guide to place the text.

The text flows into the column automatically.

4 Select the zoom tool ( ) in the toolbox and drag over the entire left column above the photograph.

5 Select the text tool (**T**), click anywhere in the new text block to establish an insertion point, and choose Edit > Select All to select the entire story.

6 In the Control palette, choose Myriad Roman for Font, type **10** for Size and **26** for Leading, click the Bold button (**B**).

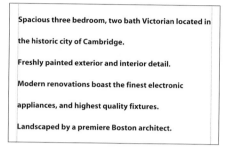

7 Choose File > Save.

Applying a tint to text

A tint is a lightened color. For this lesson, you will use the Colors palette to apply a 40% tint of black (gray) to the first word in each paragraph above the photograph.

In addition to applying colors and tints to text, you can apply colors and tints to lines, rectangles, ellipses, polygons, and monochrome or grayscale bitmap images (such as TIFF images) that you import into PageMaker.

1 If not already displayed, click the Colors palette tab to activate the Colors palette.

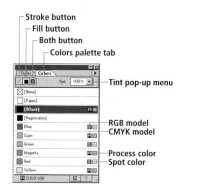

- Stroke button
- Fill button
- Both button
- Colors palette tab
- Tint pop-up menu
- RGB model
- CMYK model
- Process color
- Spot color

PageMaker groups the Styles and Colors palettes together. (You'll learn more about styles in Lessons 3 and 4.) The Colors palette displays a list of available colors with icons that indicate the model used to define the color (such as CMYK or RGB) and the type of color (such as Spot or Process). You select the Stroke, Fill, or Both button when you want to tint or color the *stroke* (the line or outline) or *fill* (the interior) of an object you've drawn in PageMaker.

To apply color (or a tint of a color) to text, you must select the text with the text tool.

2 With the text tool selected, double-click the first word (in the first paragraph) in column 1 to select it.

Double-clicking text with the text tool selects an entire word.

Spacious three bedroom, two bath Victorian located in the historic city of Cambridge.

Freshly painted exterior and interior detail.

Modern renovations boast the finest electronic

appliances, and highest quality fixtures.

Landscaped by a premiere Boston architect.

3 In the Colors palette, make sure [Black] is selected in the list of colors, and choose 40% from the Tint pop-up menu to apply a 40% tint of black to the text.

In addition to applying a tint, you will format the first word of each paragraph to display a 20-point italic font.

4 With the first word still selected, in the Control palette choose AGaramond for Font, type **22** for Size, and click the Italic button (*I*).

5 Repeat steps 2 to 4 for the first word in each paragraph of this text block.

Spacious **three bedroom, two bath Victorian**

located in the historic city of Cambridge.

Freshly **painted exterior and interior detail.**

Modern **renovations boast the finest electronic**

appliances, and highest quality fixtures.

Landscaped **by a premiere Boston architect.**

6 Choose File > Save.

Indenting the text

You can use the Indents/Tabs command to set tab stops (up to 40 per column), the indent levels of paragraphs, and the leader style (such as dots or dashes) for the spaces between tab stops. In this example, you will indent all lines that follow the first line of each paragraph by setting a hanging indent.

Note: Indents move text inward from the left and right edges of a text block, and tabs position text at specific locations in a text block.

1 With the text tool selected, click the text in column 1 to establish an insertion point, and choose Edit > Select All to select the text.

2 Choose Type > Indents/Tabs.

The Indents/Tabs dialog box displays a ruler. The zero point of the Indents/Tabs ruler corresponds with the left edge of the column, not with the zero point of the publication window. When you choose the Indents/Tabs command, PageMaker tries to align the zero point of the Indents/Tabs ruler with the left edge of the selected text. However, the current display size, the position of the selected text in the publication window, together with the monitor size, may force PageMaker to center the dialog box in the publication window.

3 In the Indents/Tabs dialog box, position the pointer on the bottom black triangle at the zero point on the ruler, and drag it to the ½-inch mark on the ruler. (0.5 inches displays for Position.) Note that the top triangle moves with the bottom triangle.

To move the bottom triangle independently, hold down Shift as you drag.

4 Drag the top black triangle back to its original position aligned with the zero point on the ruler. (−0.5 inches displays for Position.) Click OK.

5 Click outside the text to deselect it.

The text in column 1 displays a ½-inch hanging indent.

6 Choose File > Save.

Creating a ruler guide

Now that the text in column 1 is placed and formatted, you are ready to align it with the text in column 2. You will create a ruler guide that touches the baseline of the text in column 2, and then align the baseline of the text in column 1 with this guide.

1 Click the hand tool (✋) in the toolbox.

The pointer changes to a hand icon. The hand tool lets you move or *pan* the page within the publication window.

You will shift the page over a little so you can see some of the text in column 2 as well.

2 Position the hand tool in the middle of the text block in column 1, hold down the mouse button, and drag left until some of the text in column 2 is displayed. (You want to be able to see a portion of the first line of text in both columns.)

3 From the horizontal ruler, drag to create a horizontal ruler guide that aligns with the baseline of the first line of text in column 2.

As you drag down from the horizontal ruler, the Y indicator in the Control palette displays the precise position of the pointer.

4 Select the pointer tool, and click the text in the top portion of column 1 to select it as a text block.

5 Position the cursor on the text block, hold down Shift (to constrain the movement), and hold down the mouse button until the pointer changes to an arrowhead.

🔆 If you click on the object or text block and hold the mouse button down until the pointer changes to an arrowhead, PageMaker displays the object or text while you drag it. On the other hand, if you move a selection immediately, PageMaker displays only the bounding box of the object or text block.

6 With the Shift key still held down, drag the text block until the baseline of the first line of text is aligned with the horizontal ruler guide you just created. Its left edge should still be aligned with the left guide of column 1.

The baselines of the text in both columns are now aligned.

7 Choose File > Save.

Creating the display text

You will create the display text (heading) and position it above the columns of text. Display text, by its size, weight, or font design, is used to attract attention. After typing the heading and assigning text attributes, you will align the heading text on a ruler guide.

1 Choose View > Actual Size.

2 Select the text tool (**T**) in the toolbox.

3 Click the pasteboard above the page to establish an insertion point. (If necessary, shift the page down to view the pasteboard.)

To pan the page without changing tools, hold down Alt (Windows) or Option (Macintosh), and drag the page as needed. When you release the mouse button, the pointer returns to the selected tool.

Before typing the text, you will specify the character formatting.

4 In the Control palette, select AGaramond for Font, type **82** for Size (**!T**), and click the Apply button ( ).

5 Type **Home Review**.

Note: When you create or place text on any part of the pasteboard (except the pasteboard to the left of the page), the width of the text block automatically equals the width of the area between the left and right margin guides.

6 From the horizontal ruler, drag to create a horizontal ruler guide at 1.5 inches.

You will align the baseline of the text with this horizontal ruler guide.

7 Select the pointer tool, click the words **Home Review** to select it as a text block, position the pointer on one of the right corner handles, hold down the mouse button until the pointer changes to a diagonal double-headed arrow, drag it until it is roughly aligned with the right edge of the text, and release the mouse button, reducing the width of the text block.

8 With **Home Review** still selected as a text block, position the pointer on the text block, and hold down the mouse button until the pointer changes to an arrowhead.

9 With the mouse button still held down, drag the text block until the baseline of the display text is aligned with the 1.5-inch horizontal ruler guide, with the left edge of the text aligned with the left margin guide, and release the mouse button.

10 Choose File > Save.

Cutting and pasting text

You will cut the word **Review**, paste it back into a separate text block, and then increase its point size.

1 Select the text tool (**T**), and double-click the word **Review** to select it.

2 Choose Edit > Cut to cut the selected text.

3 Select the pointer tool, click the word **Home** to select it as a text block, and drag the bottom right corner handle until it is roughly aligned with the right edge of the text, reducing the width of the text block to better organize your work space.

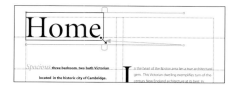

To toggle between the selected tool and the pointer tool, hold down Ctrl (Windows) or Command (Macintosh), and press the spacebar. As you press the spacebar, the tool changes to the zoom tool. However, when you release the spacebar, the tool switches to either the pointer or the previously selected tool. (Holding down Ctrl or Command and the spacebar while you click or drag is a zoom tool shortcut.)

4 Select the text tool, and choose Edit > Paste.

The pasted text appears as a selected text block.

5 Select the text tool again, and double-click the word **Review** to select it.

6 In the Control palette, type **122** for Size, and click the Apply button.

The word **Review** is set in a larger point size than the word **Home**.

7 Choose File > Save.

Applying a tint to the display text

You will apply a 20% tint of black to **Review**.

1 In the Colors palette make sure [Black] is selected in the list of colors, and choose 20% from the Tint pop-up menu.

Now that you have applied a tint of black to the text, reduce the size of the text block and position it.

2 From the horizontal ruler, drag to create a horizontal ruler guide at 1.75 inches.

3 Select the pointer tool, click the word **Review** to select it as a text block, and drag a right corner handle until it is roughly aligned with the right edge of the text, reducing the size of the text block.

4 With the text still selected as a text block, drag the text block until the baseline of the text is aligned with the 1.75-inch horizontal ruler guide, with the stem of the uppercase **R** in the word **Review** intersecting the lower-case **e** in the word **Home**.

To move a text block (or graphic) in increments, select the text block or graphic with the pointer tool, and either press the arrow keys or click the X and Y nudge buttons in the Control palette.

5 Choose File > Save.

Adjusting the stacking order

Notice how the word **Review** overlaps the word **Home**. Since you just pasted the word **Review** back into the publication, the text object **Review** is positioned at the top of the stack.

As you place, paste, draw, or create text or graphic elements, PageMaker keeps track of their stacking order on the page. Moving or modifying an object does not affect the stacking order.

1 With the pointer tool selected, click the word **Review** to select it as a text block.

2 Choose Element > Arrange > Send to Back to stack the word **Review** behind the word **Home**, at the bottom of the stack.

Since the Send to Back command sends the selected text or graphic element to the bottom of the stack, the word **Home** overlaps the word **Review**.

3 Choose File > Save.

Drawing a circle

PageMaker offers a variety of drawing tools, giving you more options for creating graphics. You will use the ellipse tool to draw a circle, accentuating the dot above the letter **i** in the word **Review**.

1 Select the zoom tool (🔍), and drag over the letter **i** in the word **Review**.

💡 Your Adobe PageMaker 7.0 Quick Reference Card and the PageMaker online help list keyboard shortcuts for selecting tools and menu commands. To access shortcuts in online help, choose Help > Help Topics, and select Windows Shortcuts from the Contents listing (Windows), or choose Help > PageMaker Help Topics, and select Macintosh Shortcuts from the Contents listing (Macintosh).

2 Click the ellipse tool (◯) in the toolbox to select it.

The pointer changes to a crosshair icon.

You can make the ellipse tool draw a circle by holding down Shift as you drag.

3 Hold down Shift and drag to draw a circle approximately twice the size of the dot above the letter **i**, and release the mouse button.

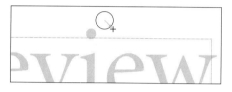

If you are not satisfied with the size of the circle, make sure the graphic handles are displayed around the circle (indicating it is selected), press the Delete key, and draw another circle.

4 In the Colors palette, make sure the Both button (▨) is selected, and click [Black] to apply the color black to the stroke and fill of the circle.

5 Select the pointer tool, click the circle to select it, and drag it until it is centered on the dot above the letter **i**.

6 Choose File > Save.

Drawing a box

After drawing a box, you will assign a width to the stroke around the box, and manually position it below the words **Home Review**.

1 Choose View > Actual Size, and scroll to view the page just below the display text **Home Review**.

2 From the horizontal ruler, drag once to create a horizontal ruler guide at 2 inches and again to create one at approximately 2.3 inches.

3 Click the rectangle tool (☐) in the toolbox to select it.

The pointer changes to a crosshair. Using the rectangle tool, you can draw rectangles or squares of any size.

4 Position the crosshair on the intersection of the left margin guide and the 2-inch horizontal ruler guide. Hold down the mouse button, and drag to the intersection of the right margin guide and the 2.3-inch horizontal ruler guide. Release the mouse button to complete the box.

If you are not satisfied with the rectangle, make sure the rectangle is selected, and either drag a graphic handle to the correct location or press the Delete key, and draw another rectangle.

5 Choose Element > Stroke > Hairline to assign a stroke style and weight to the stroke of the box.

Note: Even though you will not perceive a difference in stroke width on most monitors, the stroke will print correctly on printers with 600 dpi or greater. Most monitors cannot display fractional stroke widths in the Actual Size view.

Notice that after you release the mouse button, part of the box is obscured by the ruler guide. By default, the ruler guides appear in front of all text and graphics.

6 Choose View > Send Guides to Back to display the guides behind the text and graphics.

The hairline is displayed on the page.

7 Choose File > Save.

Dragging to define a text block

After creating the address text, you will center the text in the hairline box using the paragraph view of the Control palette.

To create the display text **Home Review**, you may recall selecting the text tool, clicking the pasteboard to establish an insertion point, and typing the display text. Now, to create the address text, you will use a different approach that involves selecting the text tool, dragging to define a text block (rather than just clicking), and then typing the address text.

1 Select the text tool (**T**) and position the I-beam on the bottom left corner of the box (let it snap to the left margin guide). Hold down the mouse button, drag diagonally up across the box to the right margin guide (exact height is not important), and release the mouse button.

This defines a text block that spans the area between the margin guides. When you release the mouse button, the blinking cursor is displayed on the left margin guide, indicating the text insertion point.

Before you type the address, you'll choose the font and point size, and scale the width of the characters using the Horizontal scaling option.

2 In the Control palette, choose Myriad Roman for Font, type **10** for Size (**⬆T**), click the Bold button (**B**), and choose 130% from the Horizontal Scaling pop-up menu.

Horizontal scaling pop-up menu

3 Type the following address:

322 Harvard Street, Cambridge

You are ready to use the Control palette to apply the paragraph specifications to the address.

Note: *When applying one or more paragraph specifications to a single paragraph, you must establish an insertion point in the paragraph. When applying paragraph specifications to multiple contiguous paragraphs, you must select some text in each paragraph you want to format.*

4 With an insertion point still established in the address, click the Paragraph-view button (¶) in the Control palette.

As with character specification options, the paragraph view of the Control palette provides quick access to frequently used paragraph specification options available in the menus.

5 Click the Center-align button in the Control palette to center the text in the text block.

Center-align button

PageMaker centers the text within the text block.

6 Choose File > Save.

Range kerning the address

In addition to the fonts you use, the spacing between letters, words, and lines can have tremendous impact on the look of a publication. Range kerning is one of the available techniques for increasing or decreasing the space between letters.

PageMaker's kerning is measured in *ems*. An em is a horizontal space as wide as a font's point size. In 12-point type, an em is 12 points wide, while in 48-point type, an em is 48 points wide.

PageMaker accepts kerning values between -1 and 1 (1 equals 1 em space), accurate to .01 em space. Negative values move characters closer together, and positive values move characters further apart.

To kern the address, you will select the entire range of address text, and enter a precise value in the Control palette to increase the original letter spacing of the text.

1 With the text tool selected, triple-click the address to select it.

As you learned earlier, triple-clicking text with the text tool selects an entire paragraph. Also, notice how the Control palette still displays the options for formatting paragraphs.

Note: You can apply range kerning only to a selected range of text. For example, you cannot set a range kerning value before typing text.

2 Click the Character-view button in the Control palette, type **.75** for Kerning, and click the Apply button to apply range kerning to the address.

A. Apply button B. Character-view button C. Kerning

3 From the horizontal ruler, drag to create a horizontal ruler guide at approximately 2.2 inches.

The baseline for the address is established.

4 Select the pointer tool, click the address to select it as a text block, press the Up or Down Arrow key on the keyboard until the baseline of the text is aligned with the 2.2-inch horizontal ruler guide.

5 Choose File > Save.

Drawing a vertical line

As a finishing touch to the flyer, you will use the constrained-line tool to draw a vertical line that will be centered in the gutter (the vertical space between the columns). The constrained-line tool makes it possible to draw straight lines that are constrained to 45º angles.

1 Choose View > Snap to Guides to deselect it, making sure it is unchecked.

Activated when you create a publication, the Snap to Guides option causes the guides to exert a magnetic-like pull on text and graphics objects.

2 From the vertical ruler, drag to create a vertical ruler guide at 4.25 inches.

The vertical ruler guide appears in the center of the gutter.

3 Choose View > Fit in Window.

4 Drag to create a horizontal ruler guide aligned with the baseline of the last line of text in both columns.

5 Click the constrained-line tool (|−) in the toolbox to select it.

The pointer changes to a crosshair icon.

6 Align the crosshair with the intersection of the bottom edge of the address box and the 4.25-inch vertical ruler guide, and drag down to the new horizontal ruler guide at the bottom of the page to draw the line.

7 With the vertical line still selected, choose Element > Stroke > Hairline to apply a stroke style and weight to the line.

You have completed assembling the flyer, so take a moment to view your work.

8 Choose View >Hide Guides to hide the guides.

9 Choose File > Save to save the 01Work.pmd publication.

Producing the flyer

Given the specifications and requirements of this black-and-white publication, you can print it successfully on any 300 dpi desktop laser printer, and then photocopy the number of copies you want as needed. You can also create an Adobe PDF version of the flyer that you can post on the Web or send to colleagues as an e-mail attachment.

Printing the flyer

1 If you are planning on printing this project, turn on your printer now and check the printer setup on your computer

For information on setting up your printer and selecting the appropriate printer driver, see the *Adobe PageMaker 7.0 User Guide.*

2 Choose File > Print to open the Print Document dialog box for the type of printer you selected.

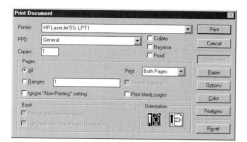

In addition to displaying the most frequently used settings, the Print Document dialog box contains buttons that let you set additional print options.

3 Select the correct printer (Windows) and PPD for your printer.

Note: *The PPD option is not available if you are printing to a non-PostScript printer.*

4 In the Print Document dialog box, click the Color button. In the Print Color dialog box, make sure Grayscale is selected.

5 Click the Print button to print the flyer.

You've created and printed the flyer. You can exit PageMaker now or you can create an Adobe PDF version of the flyer.

Creating an Adobe PDF version of the flyer

First you will re-save the publication from which you will export to Adobe PDF.

1 Choose File > Save, and save the publication 01Work.pmd in the 01Lesson folder.

When you export to Adobe PDF, PageMaker automatically starts Acrobat Distiller, which processes the file and produces an Adobe PDF version.

2 If you do not have enough free RAM to run Acrobat Distiller simultaneously with PageMaker, close all open applications other than PageMaker.

3 Choose File > Export > Adobe PDF.

Note: *In Mac OS, be sure you have already selected a PostScript driver in the Chooser.*

4 In the PDF Options dialog box, select OnScreen for PDF Style and Acrobat for the Printer Style. (The Acrobat printer style is created automatically the first time you export to PDF. For information on creating and editing PDF styles and printer styles, see chapter 12 of the *Adobe PageMaker 7.0 User Guide.*)

In this lesson, you'll use the default settings in the PDF Options dialog box to create your Adobe PDF file. These default settings are designed to create an Adobe PDF file optimized for onscreen viewing.

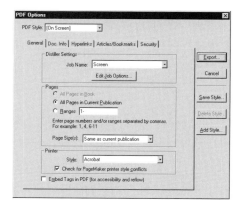

5 Click the Doc Info tab, and enter information for filename, subject, author and keyword. For Title, select and delete the file name. Type **Home Review** in the Title text box. Leave the Subject, Author, and Keyword entries *as is*.

Document information is often used to refine index searches in document collections. For this reason, you should always replace at least the file name with the document title. (Note that this and Security are the only panels in this dialog box in which you can change information without defining a new PDF Style.)

6 Click Export.

7 In the Export PDF As dialog box, make sure the filename is 01Work.pdf. Select the View PDF option (Windows) or View PDF Using option (Mac OS) if you want to open the newly created Adobe PDF file in Acrobat or Acrobat Reader rather than save it and open it at a later time. Click Save to save the PDF version into the 01Lesson folder.

PageMaker creates a PostScript file, and then starts Acrobat Distiller to convert the PostScript into Adobe PDF. This may take a few minutes, depending on the speed of your computer.

Note: On Mac OS, a window opens showing the progress of Distiller. The settings displayed in this window may not match those you selected in the PDF Options dialog box. Your PDF files will be created using the correct settings you specified.

Acrobat or Acrobat Reader will launch automatically and display the Adobe PDF version of your file. Close this PDF file and Acrobat or Acrobat Reader when you have finished reviewing it. (If the PDF file doesn't open automatically, navigate to the 01Lesson folder and double click the 01Work.pdf. Acrobat or Acrobat Reader will launch and open the newly created Adobe PDF file.)

8 Click the close box in the title bar of 01Work.pmd to close it. If prompted to save, click Yes.

9 Click the close box in the title bar of 01Final.pmd to close the publication. If prompted to save, click No.

Since you will reset the PageMaker preferences at the beginning of every lesson, exit the PageMaker application, even if you plan to move on to the next lesson.

10 Choose File > Exit (Windows) or File > Quit (Macintosh) to exit PageMaker.

Review questions

1 What are two ways to change the magnification of a page?

2 How do you create a non-printing guide line on your page?

3 What does a red triangle in a text block's bottom windowshade handle indicate?

4 How do you center the lines in a paragraph?

5 What do you call the space between text columns?

Answers

1 You can do any of the following:

• Select the zoom tool in the toolbox, and click on or drag over the area you want to magnify. To zoom out, hold down Ctrl (Windows) or Option (Macintosh), and click on the page.

• Choose a magnification level from the View menu.

• In Windows, hold down the Ctrl and Alt keys and click the right mouse button to toggle between Fit in Window and Actual Size views.

• Double-click the zoom tool in the toolbox to switch to Actual Size view. Hold down Alt (Windows) or Option (Macintosh) and double-click the zoom tool to switch to Fit in Window view.

• Hold down Ctrl (Windows) or Command (Macintosh) together with the spacebar and click or drag (covered in Lesson 2).

2 First, make sure rulers are visible along the top and left edges of the window. If not, choose View > Show Rulers. Then position the pointer in either ruler, drag away from the ruler, and release the mouse button to create the guide.

3 The text block contains more text that has not been placed on the page or pasteboard.

4 Select the text tool and click an insertion point in the paragraph. Click the Paragraph-view button in the Control palette, and then click the Center-align button.

5 The gutter.

Lesson 2

Architect's letterhead

With Adobe PageMaker, you can create part or all of your letterhead design yourself. This lesson shows how fictitious Madrid architects Braga+Braga used Adobe PageMaker to arrange text and graphics for a simple yet striking letterhead design. The letterhead design incorporates the use of two spot colors (premixed inks printed on a commercial printing press) and tints of spot colors (spot colors that are lightened by printing a dot pattern instead of a solid color).

This lesson also shows you how to save the letterhead design as a custom template. Once the letterhead is printed, it's easy to use the custom template to assemble text to be printed on your own printer. To demonstrate the entire process, you will create the Braga+Braga letterhead template, and then assemble a letter that is meant to be printed on the letterhead stationery. The text featured in the lesson is in Spanish, since Marie Braga is addressing a Spanish-speaking client in her letter.

This lesson covers:

• Establishing an application default measurement system

• Creating, saving, and opening a custom template

• Selecting and applying spot colors

• Creating a tint of a spot color

• Resizing, reflecting, and rotating a text block

• Grouping and ungrouping objects

• Using the Tile command

• Dragging objects from one publication to another

• Using the Lock Position and Non-Printing commands

• Printing on a commercial printing press

It should take you approximately 2-3 hours to complete this lesson.

Before you begin

All the files and fonts needed to assemble the letterhead are found on the *Adobe PageMaker 7.0 Classroom in a Book* CD-ROM in the folders 02Lesson and Fonts, respectively.

Note: Windows users need to unlock the lesson files before using them. For information, see Copying the Classroom in a Book files on page 4.

Starting PageMaker

Before beginning to assemble the publication for this lesson, you will use the Preferences dialog box to establish application defaults, and then you will open the final version of the letterhead you will create.

1 Before launching PageMaker, return all settings to their defaults by deleting the PageMaker 7.0 preferences file. See "Restoring default settings" in Lesson 1.

2 In addition to the commonly used fonts listed in the Getting Started chapter, make sure the fonts AGaramond, AGaramond Italic, AGaramond Semibold Italic, Myriad Bold, and Myriad Roman are installed.

Windows only: Because of the way Windows handles fonts, AGaramond Semibold Italic appears in the ATM Fonts list as AGaramond, Bold Italic (notice the comma). However, neither AGaramond Semibold Italic nor AGaramond, Bold Italic appear in font menus in Windows applications. You must apply bold and italic to AGaramond to use AGaramond

Semibold Italic. You must apply italic to AGaramond to use AGaramond Italic. You must apply bold to Myriad Roman to use Myriad Bold.

Like the Myriad typeface used in the previous lesson, Adobe Garamond is an Adobe Originals typeface.

3 Start PageMaker.

Setting an application default

PageMaker has two kinds of defaults:

• Publication defaults are settings that apply to a specific publication. You set a publication's defaults when it is the currently active publication and has no objects selected. The defaults are stored in the publication when you save the file.

• Application defaults are settings that PageMaker uses each time you create a new publication. These defaults are stored in the PageMaker preferences file. You set application defaults when no publications are open.

Publication defaults override application defaults.

This project uses picas as the measurement system. Picas are the units most commonly used in graphic design. Picas are divided into 12 points. When you specify a measurement in picas and points, you separate the picas and points with the letter p. For example, 22p9 means 22 picas and 9 points.

Because you will be creating letterhead, an envelope, and a business card, it will save time to set the default measurement system once as an application default. Then, each new publication will already have the measurement system set.

1 Choose File > Preferences > General.

The Preferences dialog box displays some of the application defaults that will be applied to any new publication you create. You may recall from the previous lesson that the horizontal and vertical rulers reflect the units of measure selected in the Measurements in and Vertical ruler pop-up menus, respectively.

2 In the Preferences dialog box, choose Picas for Measurements In and Picas for Vertical ruler. Leave all other options at their default values. Click OK.

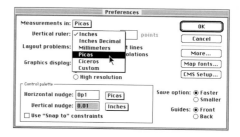

Since no publication is open, this application default will be applied to any new publication you create. Application defaults can be overridden at any time for the particular publication you are working on, setting a publication default. Unlike application defaults, publication defaults have no effect on new publications you create.

Opening an existing document

Let's take a look at the final version of the letterhead you will create in this lesson.

1 Choose File > Open, and locate and double-click the 02FinalA.pmd file in the 02Lesson folder.

The full view of the page displays a single column of text framed on the top and left edges with a letterhead design. The letterhead design features a variety of text and graphics elements and uses two spot colors.

2 If the publication window does not fill the screen, click the Maximize button in the title bar to expand the window.

3 Choose View > Show Guides to display all guides (column, ruler, and margin) used to assemble this publication.

Notice how all guides are displayed behind the text and graphics elements. Even though you just accepted the application default to display guides in front of text and graphics (in the Preferences dialog box), the

publication defaults, set when the letterhead was last saved, take precedence. Again, the application defaults you just set in the Preferences dialog box apply only to new publications you create.

4 Choose View > Bring Guides to Front.

Now the guides are displayed over the text and graphics.

5 Choose File > Open, and locate and double-click the 02FinalB.pmd file in the 02Lesson folder.

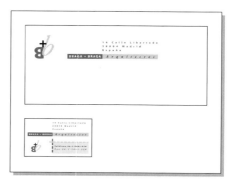

The 02FinalB.pmd publication displays the envelope and business card you will assemble as well.

Talk with your printer

Printing these letterhead publications on a commercial printing press involves delivering files to your prepress service provider (who can perform prepress tasks, and who will ultimately create film separations of your publication on an imagesetter), and then delivering film separations to your printer.

Well in advance of delivering publications to be printed, be sure to review the design with your printer and your prepress service provider. Based on the design, your skills, time, and equipment, your printer and your service provider can evaluate the requirements of the project and the services you require.

Note: In some cases, imagesetting and printing services are provided at the same facility.

In this example, expect a service provider to point out how the adjacent colors featured in the letterhead will require *trapping* (before creating film separations). Art that has not been trapped can easily misregister on the press, causing gaps to appear between adjacent colored elements. Trapping compensates for misregistration by slightly overlapping adjacent colors. For more information on trapping, see Lesson 7, which uses PageMaker trapping options, or refer to the *Adobe PageMaker 7.0 User Guide.*

It is crucial to anticipate this sort of issue, since it will determine how you prepare files to be delivered to your service provider.

Assembling a custom template

Before creating the letter you see in the final publication, you will create and save a custom template that can be opened whenever you want to compose a letter.

Remember: Feel free to zoom in or out and to move or minimize palettes as needed to complete a step.

Creating a new publication

Whenever you create a new publication, the Document Setup dialog box prompts you to specify the page size, orientation, page numbering, margins, and printer type resolution.

1 Choose File > New, and notice that Letter is selected for Page Size.

When you create a new publication, Letter is selected for page size. The page dimensions appear in the application default measurement system, in this case, picas (51 picas by 66 picas equals 8.5 inches by 11 inches).

2 In the Document Setup dialog box, choose Legal for Page Size, and notice how the corresponding page dimensions in picas are displayed (51 picas by 84 picas equals 8.5 inches by 14 inches).

The Legal page size is one of the preset page sizes available in the Page Size pop-up menu. If the page size you want is not available in the Page Size pop-up menu, you can enter precise values for Dimensions to customize the page size. For this lesson, however, you will use the Letter page size.

3 In the Document Setup dialog box, choose Letter for Page Size, and then click the Double-sided check box to deselect it. For Margins, type **10** for Left, **4p6** for Right, **4p6** for Top, and **4p6** for Bottom. (4p6 indicates 4 picas and 6 points, where 1 pica equals 12 points.) You can press the Tab key to jump from edit box to edit box. Choose a Target Output Resolution of **1200** dpi, and choose (Windows only) the AGFA-ProSet9800 for Compose to Printer. Then click OK.

Note: If you do not have the required printer, you can still create the project as directed and then print it on your own printer by selecting your printer and its PPD (if it is a PostScript printer) in the Print dialog box when it is time to print. You can also use the Export Adobe PDF command to create an Adobe PDF version of the project rather than a printed copy, as described in Creating an Adobe PDF version of the flyer on page 41.

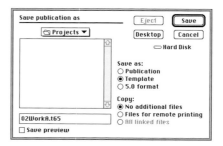

The margin guides form a rectangle enclosing the image area, which is where you will put most of your text and graphics. The horizontal and vertical rulers reflect the currently selected unit of measure, picas.

Saving the publication as a template

Even though the template is not assembled, you will name it and save it as a template. (In PageMaker 7.0, templates have the extension .pmt.) Saving a publication as a template means that when you open this template, PageMaker opens an untitled copy of the template, not the original document.

Choose File > Save As, and type **02WorkA.pmt** for the file name, open the 02Lesson folder, select Template for Save As Type (Windows) or Save As (Macintosh), and click Save.

Establishing a design grid

Horizontal and vertical ruler guides will help you align text and graphics precisely, without printing or restricting the flow of text.

1 Make sure the entire page is displayed. If necessary, choose View > Fit in Window.

2 Position the cursor on the vertical ruler that extends along the left edge of the publication window, and drag to create a vertical ruler guide at 2p (2 picas), referring to the X coordinate value in the Control palette if necessary.

3 Using the same method, create two additional vertical ruler guides at 7p and 8p.

4 From the horizontal ruler, drag to create horizontal ruler guides at approximately 9p, 9p6, 12p, 14p, 15p6, and 64p.

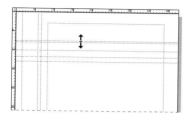

Locking the ruler guides

Now that you have positioned the ruler guides, you will use the Lock Guides command to lock them in place. The Lock Guides command locks ruler guides and column guides in place, preventing you from moving them accidentally.

1 Choose View > Lock Guides.

Note: To reposition or delete a ruler guide, choose the Lock Guides command again to unlock the guides.

2 Choose File > Save.

Creating the display text

With imagination you can use PageMaker to create display text elements that go a long way toward enhancing your publications. Display text, usually 14 points or larger, serves to attract attention.

You'll use the pasteboard to initially assemble the pieces of the letterhead.

1 Select the zoom tool (Q), and click the pasteboard above the page to magnify that area. (To click the pasteboard, you may need to scroll the page using the scroll bar on the right side of the window.)

2 Select the text tool (**T**), and click above the page to establish an insertion point.

Notice the blinking cursor and that the Control palette displays the default type specifications (font: Times New Roman or Times, size: 12 points).

3 With the insertion point already established, type an uppercase letter **B**.

4 With the text tool selected, double-click the uppercase **B** to select it.

5 In the Control palette, choose Myriad Roman for Font, type **65** for Size (!**T**), and click the Bold button (**B**) to apply the type specifications to the selected text.

6 With the text tool still selected, click the pasteboard above the page (a little away from the uppercase **B** to avoid inserting the cursor in the same text block as the **B**), and type + (a plus sign).

7 Double-click the plus sign to select it, and in the Control palette choose Myriad Roman for Font, type **50** for Size, and click the Bold button.

8 With the text tool still selected, click the pasteboard above the page (a little away from the uppercase **B** and plus sign, again, to avoid inserting the cursor in the same text block as the other two characters), and type a lowercase letter **b**.

9 Double-click the lowercase **b** to select it, and in the Control palette choose AGaramond (Regular) for Font, type **110** for Size, and click the Italic button (*I*).

Note: Because of the way fonts are defined, when you apply italic to AGaramond, PageMaker actually uses AGaramond Italic. On the Macintosh, you can get the same result if you select AGaramond Italic directly.

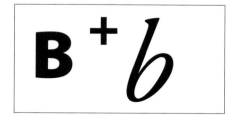

Notice that you did not need to click the Apply button (or press Enter or Return) to apply the new font and size to the letter. When you click a button in the Control palette, PageMaker applies any values you've typed as well as applying the button's style or effect.

10 Choose File > Save.

Resizing text blocks

Since you did not define the text block size of the three text objects just created, take a moment to resize each one.

1 Select the pointer tool, and click the uppercase **B** to select it as a text block.

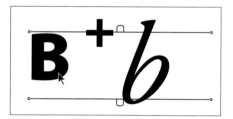

Once a text element is selected as a text block (with the pointer tool), the text block can be resized, positioned, or transformed.

Notice how the windowshades extend well beyond the bounds of the uppercase **B**. Since you did not define the dimensions of this text block, PageMaker defined the width of the text block to equal the image area between the left and right margin guides.

It is easier to work with a text block when its width is close to the width of its content, especially in a design like this where you are manipulating three text blocks close together. The selection area of text includes the text block. So, when a text block is over-sized, you can mistakenly select it even though you are clicking quite a distance from the actual text.

2 With the uppercase **B** still selected as a text block, drag a right corner handle until it is roughly aligned with the right edge of the uppercase **B**, reducing the width of the text block.

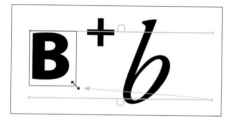

3 Use the same method to reduce the width of the text blocks for the plus sign and the lowercase **b**.

With the width of the text blocks reduced, it is easier to select, view, and manipulate these text blocks.

4 Choose File > Save.

Defining spot colors

Before applying colors to the display text you just created, you will select two pre-defined spot colors from one of the color libraries included with PageMaker.

As mentioned before, spot colors are printed on a printing press using premixed inks. Use spot colors when an element (such as a corporate logo) requires an exact color match, or to add impact to your publication.

Note: Incorporating spot and process colors into a publication created in PageMaker is simple, but to get the best printed results, you need to understand how spot and process colors are printed. Always discuss a project with your service provider and printer.

1 Choose Utilities > Define Colors, and click New.

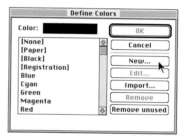

The Color Options dialog box prompts you to select a color. You can specify a spot or process color as RGB (red, green, and blue), HLS (hue, lightness, saturation), or CMYK (cyan, magenta, yellow, and black). Each model represents a different approach to describing color. For more information, refer to the *Adobe PageMaker 7.0 User Guide*.

2 In the Color Options dialog box choose PANTONE® Uncoated from the Libraries pop-up menu.

PANTONE offers 736 spot colors that set the industry standard for reproducible spot-color inks, and 3,006 process colors organized chromatically, including process-color simulations of the spot-color library.

3 In the Color Picker dialog box, scroll through the colors.

Although you can click a color to select it, typing the ink number (if you know it) is often faster than scrolling to locate a color.

4 Type **660** for PANTONE CVU, and click OK.

Note: *CVU stands for Computer Video Uncoated.*

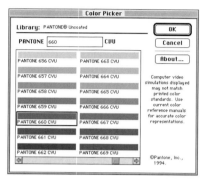

5 In the Color Options dialog box, click OK to accept the default color name displayed for Name.

The Define Colors dialog box displays the color you have just selected. Now you can select or create another color.

6 In the Define Colors dialog box, click New.

7 In the Color Options dialog box, make sure the Spot and CMYK options are selected, and choose PANTONE® Uncoated for Libraries.

8 In the Color Picker dialog box, type **5595** for PANTONE CVU, and click OK.

9 In the Color Options dialog box, click OK to accept the default color name displayed for Name, then click OK to close the Define Colors dialog box.

10 Choose File > Save.

Applying spot colors

After opening the Colors palette, you will apply the spot colors you just selected to the display text. In addition to text, you can apply colors to lines, rectangles, ellipses, and monochrome and grayscale bitmap images.

1 Click the Colors palette tab to activate the Colors palette.

In addition to displaying the two spot colors you selected, the Colors palette displays three spot colors, Blue, Green, and Red; four process colors, Cyan, Magenta, Yellow, and [Black]; and four items you cannot remove, [None], [Paper], [Black], and [Registration].

The Stroke, Fill, and Both buttons apply to objects. When you apply color to text, it doesn't matter which button is selected.

2 Select the text tool (**T**), double-click the uppercase **B** to select it, and in the Colors palette click PANTONE 660 CVU to apply the spot color to the uppercase **B**.

Note: To apply color to text, you must first select the text with the text tool. You won't see the applied color until you deselect the text.

3 With the text tool still selected, double-click the lowercase **b** to select it, and in the Colors palette click PANTONE 5595 CVU.

4 Choose File > Save.

Reflecting a text block

You can reflect any object (text or graphic element) vertically or horizontally, using the Reflecting options in the Control palette.

1 Select the pointer tool, and click the uppercase **B** to select it as a text block.

2 In the Control palette, click the Horizontal Reflecting button (⊞).

The uppercase **B** is reflected horizontally.

3 With the uppercase **B** still selected as a text block, click the Vertical Reflecting button (⊞).

The uppercase **B** is reflected vertically.

4 Choose File > Save.

Positioning text blocks

In order to compose a logo design using the display text, you manually position the text blocks to overlap one another.

First you'll zoom in to the area.

1 Hold down Ctrl (Windows) or Command (Macintosh) together with the spacebar. The pointer changes to the zoom tool. Drag across the three text blocks to magnify the view.

This magnification short-cut lets you quickly zoom in to an area without changing tools.

To align these text elements, you will use the slow-drag method of positioning objects, displaying text as you drag a text block. When you use the quick-drag method, a bounding box indicates the dimensions of the text block as you drag, but no text is displayed.

2 With the pointer tool selected, click the uppercase **B** to select it as a text block, position the cursor on the text block, and hold down the mouse button until the pointer changes to an arrowhead.

3 With the mouse button still held down, drag the text block until the vertical stem of the plus sign is aligned with the vertical stem of the uppercase **B** as shown in the illustration below, and release the mouse button.

4 With the pointer tool still selected, click the lowercase **b** to select it as a text block, and drag the text block until the stem of the lowercase **b** overlaps the uppercase **B** as shown in the following illustration.

5 Choose File > Save.

Adjusting the stacking order of text objects

Notice how the lowercase **b** overlaps the uppercase **B** and the plus sign. Since the lowercase **b** was created last, it is positioned at the top of the stack. You will use the Send Backward command to move the lowercase **b** from the top of the stack to the middle of the stack. Unlike the Send to Back command that moves an object to the bottom of the stack, the Send Backward command moves an object back in the stack in single-position increments.

1 With the pointer tool selected, click the lowercase **b** to select it as a text block.

2 Choose Element > Arrange > Send Backward.

With the lowercase **b** positioned in the middle of the stack, it is overlapped by the plus sign, now positioned at the top of the stack.

3 Choose File > Save.

Grouping text objects

Now that the three text objects are positioned, grouping them together will let you position them as a single entity on the page.

1 With the pointer tool still selected, choose Edit > Select All to select all text and graphics elements in your publication.

2 Choose Element > Group.

The text objects are joined together as a single entity, with handles indicating the group is selected.

3 Position the pointer in the center of the group, and drag the logo design to the upper left corner of the page.

4 Find the intersection of the 9p6 horizontal ruler guide and the 8p vertical ruler guide.

5 Once again, position the pointer in the center of the group, and drag it until the bottom edge of the logo design is aligned with the 9p6 horizontal ruler guide, and until the left edge of the uppercase **B** is aligned with the 8p vertical ruler guide.

6 Choose File > Save.

Using the Control palette to resize a rectangle

After using the rectangle tool to draw a box, you will enter precise values in the Control palette to resize the box. The Control palette lets you make several changes to an object without switching tools and offers a precision that is difficult to duplicate when manipulating an object manually. The Control palette lets you resize, move, scale, crop (imported images), rotate, and skew.

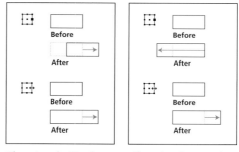

A. *Apply button* B. *Proxy icon* C. *Coordinates* D. *Width and height* E. *Percent scaling* F. *Scaling button* G. *Rotating* H. *Horizontal reflecting* I. *Vertical reflecting* J. *Skewing*

When you select an object, the Control palette displays a *Proxy* icon to the right of the Apply button. The Proxy icon contains nine spots called *reference points*. Changes you make to an object with the Control palette are affected by the reference point you select and the state of that point. Except for the center point, the reference points correspond to handles of the object.

Each reference point in the Proxy icon has two states, represented by a square point or an arrow. To toggle between the states, you click a selected point or double-click an unselected point.

Square When a selected point is a square, the object's corresponding handle remains stationary or serves as an anchor, depending upon the action. For example, if you change W and H, the corresponding handle remains stationary as the width and height change. If instead you change X and Y, the entire object moves until the corresponding handle is at the new location.

Arrow When the point is an arrow, the corresponding handle is the focus of change. For example, if you change W and H, that handle is dragged to establish the new size. In the same way, if you change the X and Y values, PageMaker drags that handle to resize the object. (For more information on the Control palette, refer to the *Adobe PageMaker 7.0 User Guide.*)

Before
After

Before
After

Before
After

Before
After

Changing the X value in the control palette from 2 to 3

Changing the W value in the control palette from 2 to 3

Note: Unless otherwise stated, throughout this book, when a step says to select a point in the Proxy icon, it means a square point.

1 Select the rectangle tool (□) in the toolbox, and drag to draw a box of any dimension near the top of the page.

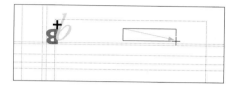

2 With the box still selected, in the Control palette make sure a corner reference point in the Proxy icon is selected (to make it possible to resize both dimensions of an object), type **11p** for W (width) and **1p6** for H (height), and click the Apply button (□).

To create another box, you will copy and paste the first box, and then use the Control palette to resize the pasted box.

3 With the box still selected, choose Edit > Copy to copy the box to the Clipboard.

4 Choose Edit > Paste to paste a second box to be slightly offset from the first box.

5 With the second box selected, in the Control palette type **17p4** for W, and press Enter or Return to increase the width of the second box.

Note: Depending on where you drew the boxes, your artwork may look different from the illustration below.

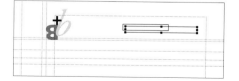

Applying spot colors to the boxes

Using the Colors palette, you will apply spot colors to the stroke and fill of the two boxes. As was mentioned before, the three buttons Stroke, Fill, and Both allow you to apply or change the color of stroke, fill, or both on a rectangle or ellipse. In this example, you want to apply color to the stroke and fill of both boxes.

1 Select the pointer tool, and click the outline of the smaller box to select it.

When a PageMaker-drawn shape has no fill, you select it by clicking its stroke.

2 In the Colors palette click the Both button, and click PANTONE 660 CVU to apply a spot color to the stroke and fill of the box.

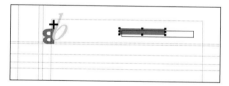

3 With the pointer tool selected, click the outline of the larger box to select it. Make sure the Both button is selected in the Colors palette, and select PANTONE 5595 CVU.

4 Choose File > Save.

Positioning graphics

You will manually position the boxes to be aligned with existing ruler guides.

1 With the pointer tool selected, click the second (larger) box to select it, and drag it until its left edge is aligned with the right edge of the first (smaller) box.

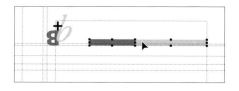

2 Magnify the view of the boxes to see if their edges are precisely aligned. If not, press the Right or Left Arrow keys (or click the X or Y nudge buttons in the Control palette) to move the selected box in 1-pixel increments.

3 With one of the boxes still selected, hold down the Shift key (to select multiple objects), and click the unselected box so that both boxes are selected.

4 Choose Element > Group to group the boxes into a single entity.

5 Drag the boxes until their bottom edges are aligned with the 9p6 horizontal ruler guide, and the right edge is aligned with the right margin guide.

Remember: *If the palettes are in the way, you can move them, minimize them (with the Maximize button in the title bar), or temporarily clear them from the window by pressing the Tab key.*

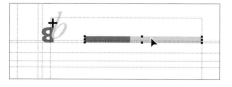

6 Choose File > Save.

Placing, formatting, and positioning the Braga+Braga text

After placing text, you will format it, cut and paste a portion of it, and then position it in the left box.

1 Choose File > Place, and double-click the 02TextA.doc file in the 02Lesson folder.

2 With the loaded text icon displayed, scroll to view the pasteboard above the page, and click the pasteboard to place the text.

3 Magnify the view of the placed text on the pasteboard if necessary.

4 Select the text tool (**T**), and drag to select the words **Braga+Braga** in the first line.

5 In the Control palette, choose Myriad Roman for Font, type **12** for Size (**T**), type **.2** for Kerning ( ), click the Bold button (**B**), and click the All caps button (C).

Note: Because of the way fonts are defined, when you apply bold to Myriad Roman, PageMaker actually uses Myriad Bold. On the Macintosh, you can get the same result if you select Myriad Bold directly.

6 With **Braga+Braga** still selected, choose Edit > Cut.

Before pasting the text you just cut, you will drag to define a text block that spans the width of the left box, making it easier to center the text inside.

7 With the text tool still selected, drag to define a text block in the left box, spanning the width of the left box; the exact height is unimportant.

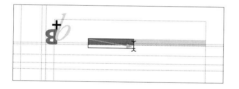

8 Choose Edit > Paste to paste **Braga+Braga** in the text block you just defined.

By default, the text is left aligned in the text block.

9 With the insertion point still in **Braga+Braga**, click the Paragraph-view button (¶) in the Control palette, and click the Center-align button (≡) to center the text in the text block.

Since you defined the text block to span the width of the left box, the text is centered horizontally inside it.

10 With the text tool selected, drag to select **Braga+Braga**, and in the Colors palette click [Paper] to apply the paper color to the text.

Applying [Paper] to text or graphics elements causes the color of the paper on which you print to show through the selected object.

Before aligning **Braga+Braga**, you will turn off the Snap to Guides option.

11 Choose View > Snap to Guides to deselect it, making sure it is unchecked.

12 Select the pointer tool, click **Braga+Braga** to select it as a text block, press the Up or Down Arrow key on the keyboard until the baseline of the text is aligned with the 9p horizontal ruler guide.

13 Choose File > Save.

Formatting and positioning the Arquitectos text

You will follow a similar procedure for **Arquitectos** (meaning architects in Spanish) that fills the right box of the double box.

1 If necessary, scroll to view the placed text on the pasteboard.

2 Select the text tool (**T**), double-click the word **Arquitectos** to select it.

3 In the Control palette, click the Character-view button ([T]), and choose AGaramond (Regular) for Font. Then type **13** for Size (‡T), and click the Bold (**B**) and Italic buttons (*I*).

Note: Because of the way fonts are defined, when you apply bold and italic to AGaramond, PageMaker actually uses AGaramond Semibold Italic. On the Macintosh, you can get the same result if you select AGaramond Semibold Italic directly.

4 With **Arquitectos** still selected, choose Edit > Cut.

5 With the text tool still selected, drag to define a text block in the right box, spanning the width of the right box (exact height is not important).

6 Choose Edit > Paste to paste **Arquitectos** in the text block you just defined.

7 With the insertion point still in **Arquitectos**, click the Paragraph-view button ([¶]) in the Control palette, and type **1p2** for both Left Indent (→≡) and Right Indent, and click the Force-justify button (≡).

In force-justified text, PageMaker *justifies* (aligns) the text with the left and right edges of the text block even if it contains only a few characters, spacing them so that the text fits exactly between the vertical edges of the text block. Since you set 1p2 left and right indents, the text is force-justified 1p2 away from the vertical edges of the text block.

8 Select the pointer tool, click **Arquitectos** to select it as a text block, and press the Down Arrow key on the keyboard until the baseline of the text is aligned with the 9p horizontal ruler guide.

9 Choose File > Save.

Formatting and positioning the address

After cutting the address from the placed text on the pasteboard, you will position it in the upper right portion of the page.

1 If necessary, scroll to view the placed text on the pasteboard.

2 Select the text tool (**T**), and drag to select the first three lines (the address) of the remaining placed text on the pasteboard. (Do not select the telephone and fax numbers.)

3 In the Control palette, click the Character-view button (T), and choose Myriad Roman for Font, type **10** for Size (⭤T), **15** for Leading (⭤▲), **.73** for Kerning (⭤▼), and click the Bold button (**B**).

4 In the Colors palette, click PANTONE 660 CVU to apply a spot color to the text.

5 With the address still selected, choose Edit > Cut.

6 From the vertical ruler, drag to create a vertical ruler guide at 29p2.

7 With the text tool still selected, drag to define a text block that spans from the 29p2 vertical ruler guide to the right margin guide, above **Arquitectos** (exact height is not important).

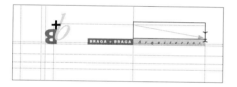

8 Choose Edit > Paste to paste the address into the text block you just defined.

9 From the horizontal ruler, drag to create a horizontal ruler guide at 7p.

Before aligning the address, you will turn the Snap to Guides option back on.

10 Choose View > Snap to Guides to select it.

11 Select the pointer tool, click the address to select it as a text block, and press the Up or Down Arrow key until the baseline of the last line of text is aligned with the 7p hori-

zontal ruler guide, and until the right edge of the text block is aligned with the right margin guide.

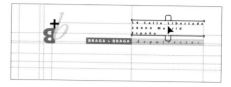

A portion of the address is positioned within the top margin.

12 Choose File > Save.

Drawing lines

The letterhead design includes two dashed-lines that you will create using the con-strained-line tool. The constrained-line tool lets you draw straight lines that are con-strained to 45° angles on the page.

1 Choose View > Fit in Window.

The first line you will draw is a horizontal line aligned with the 14p horizontal ruler guide.

2 Select the constrained-line tool (|−) in the toolbox, position the crosshair on the inter-section of the 14p horizontal ruler guide and the 2p vertical ruler guide, and drag to draw a horizontal line that extends to the right margin guide.

Since the guides (margin, column, and ruler) are in front of the text and graphics, the 14p horizontal ruler guide overlaps the line you just drew.

3 Choose View > Send Guides to Back to display the horizontal line over the horizontal ruler guide.

4 With the line still selected, choose Element > Stroke > 1 pt dashed line to apply a stroke style and weight to the line.

5 In the Colors palette make sure the Stroke button is selected, and click PANTONE 5595 CVU to apply a spot color to the line.

The second line you will draw is a vertical line that is aligned with the 8p vertical ruler guide. So that you can use the control palette to help you position the line, you'll deselect the first line.

6 Select the constrained-line tool again to deselect the line you just drew. Position the crosshair on the intersection of the 12p horizontal ruler guide and the 8p vertical ruler guide, and drag to draw a vertical line that extends to the 64p horizontal ruler guide.

7 With the second line still selected, choose Element > Stroke > 1 pt dashed line, and in the Colors palette click PANTONE 660 CVU.

8 Choose File > Save.

Applying a tint of a spot color to a box

After drawing a box in the left margin, you will use the Colors palette to fill the box with a 30% tint of a spot color.

1 Select the rectangle tool (▢), position the crosshair on the intersection of the dashed lines, and drag to the intersection of the 64p horizontal ruler guide and the 2p vertical ruler guide to draw a box.

2 With the box still selected, make sure the Both button is selected in the Colors palette, click PANTONE 5595 CVU, and choose 30% for Tint.

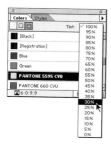

3 Choose File > Save.

Rotating a text block

After using the Control palette to rotate a text block, you will format the rotated text, and then position it in the tinted box.

1 If necessary, scroll to view the remaining line of placed text on the pasteboard and use the zoom tool (🔍) to enlarge the text line.

2 Select the text tool (**T**). Click an insertion point before the letter **T** of **Telefono**. Press the Backspace (Windows) or Delete (Macintosh) key to remove the line above the numbers and any spaces.

3 Select the pointer tool, and click the text to select it as a text block.

4 In the Control palette, make sure the top left corner reference point is selected in the Proxy icon. Type **90** for Rotation (↻), and press Enter or Return.

Teléfono-34-1-5641-918 + Fax-34-1-5641-328

Formatting the rotated text

You will format the text before positioning it in the tinted box, since formatting text after positioning it can alter its alignment.

1 If necessary, hold down Ctrl (Windows) or Command (Macintosh) together with the spacebar, and drag across the rotated text to magnify the view.

2 Select the text tool (**T**), and drag to select the telephone number, **Telefono-34-1-5641-918**.

3 In the Control palette, choose Myriad Roman for Font, type **9** for Size (⁑**T**), type **.6** for Kerning (⇔), and click the Bold button (**B**).

4 Drag to select the remaining rotated text, + **Fax-34-1-5641-328**, and, in the Control palette, choose AGaramond (Regular) for Font, type **11** for Size, type **.6** for Kerning, and click the Bold and Italic (*I*) buttons.

Don't worry if the fax number wraps to the next line. You'll resize the text block in the next procedure.

5 Select the pointer tool, and click the rotated text to select it as a text block.

Rather than drag the text block to the page, you will cut it, zoom in to the bottom left corner of the page, and then paste it.

6 With the text block selected, choose Edit > Cut.

7 Zoom in to the bottom left corner of the page.

8 Choose Edit > Paste.

9 With the rotated text block still selected, position the pointer over the text, hold down the mouse until the pointer changes to an arrowhead. Then drag the text block so that the baseline of the rotated telephone number is aligned with the 7p vertical ruler guide, and the left corner handles (now at the bottom) snap to the bottom edge of the tinted box.

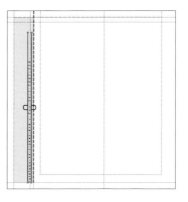

10 Choose File > Save.

Resizing a text block

To center the rotated text between the top and bottom edges of the tinted box, you will manually resize the text block to span the vertical length of the box, and then you will use the Control palette to center the text in the text block.

1 If necessary, with the pointer tool selected, click the rotated text to select it as a text block.

2 Zoom out if necessary to see the entire text block.

3 Position the pointer on the handle shown below, and drag the handle up until it is aligned with the top edge of the tinted box, resizing the text block.

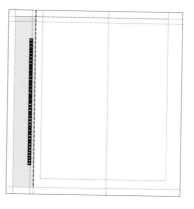

The text block spans the vertical length of the tinted box, and you are ready to apply the paragraph formatting that centers the rotated text in the text block.

4 Select the text tool (**T**), and click an insertion point in the rotated text.

Note: As mentioned earlier, to apply paragraph specifications to a single paragraph, you must click an insertion point in the paragraph or select some portion of the text in the paragraph. To apply paragraph specifications to multiple contiguous paragraphs, you must select text in each paragraph you want to format.

5 In the Control palette, click the Paragraph-view button (⌶), and click the Center-align button (≡).

Since the text block spans the vertical length of the tinted box, the text is horizontally centered in the vertical box.

6 Choose View > Hide Guides to hide the nonprinting guides used to assemble this template.

7 Choose File > Save to save the 02WorkA.pmt template.

The letterhead template is completely assembled. You are ready to create the envelope and business card.

Assembling an envelope

Using the text and graphics elements from the 02WorkA.pmt template, you will create the design for an envelope.

Tiling the publication window

After opening a custom template that includes outlines of a business-size envelope and a business card, you will use the Tile command to display all open publications within the publication window.

1 Without closing the open publications, choose File > Open, and double-click the 02Templt.pmt file in the 02Lesson folder.

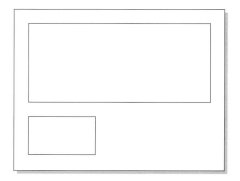

The untitled copy of the template displays outlines of a business-size envelope and a standard-size business card.

2 Choose File > Save As, and type 02WorkB.pmd for the file name, open the 02Lesson folder, and click Save.

3 Choose Window > Tile to tile the PageMaker window with all open publications and templates.

The PageMaker window displays the 02FinalA.pmd and 02FinalB.pmd, and the 02WorkA.pmt and 02WorkB.pmd files.

4 Click the close boxes in the title bar of the 02FinalA.pmd and 02FinalB.pmd publications to close them. If prompted to save before closing, click No.

5 Choose Window > Tile to tile the PageMaker window with two publications.

It will be easier to assemble the envelope with a large view of the publications.

Dragging a group from one publication to another

PageMaker makes it possible to copy text, graphics, and groups from publication to publication by simply dragging the objects. Before you drag and drop a portion of the letterhead design from the 02WorkA.pmt publication to the 02WorkB.pmd publication, you will group the required text and graphic elements.

1 Click the title bar of the 02WorkA.pmt publication to make it the active publication.

2 Select the pointer tool, drag to select all letterhead elements at the top of the page (**B** + **b** logo, double box containing **Braga+Braga** and **Arquitectos**, and address) in the 02Lesson publication. Be careful not to select the dashed lines or the tinted box and rotated text.

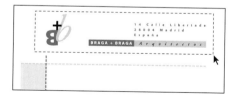

3 If necessary, hold down Shift, and click individual elements to include or exclude them from the selection.

4 Choose Element > Group to group the text and graphics elements into a single entity.

5 Position the pointer in the center of the group in the 02WorkA.pmt publication, hold down the mouse button, drag the group to the center of the 02WorkB.pmd publication, and release the mouse button.

The group is still selected in the 02WorkA.pmt publication (because it's the active publication), and the Control palette displays the available options for modifying a group.

6 With the pointer tool selected, click the group in the 02WorkB.pmd publication to select it, activating the 02WorkB.pmd publication.

7 Drag the text to the upper left corner of the envelope as shown below (approximately 3p from the top and left edges of the envelope outline).

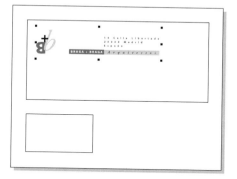

The envelope design is complete.

8 Choose File > Save to save the 02WorkB.pmd publication.

Assembling a business card

In addition to creating text and graphic elements, assembling the business card involves copying and pasting existing elements, and applying new type specifications to the pasted text elements.

Creating a tinted box

After drawing a box, you will use the Control palette to resize the box and the Colors palette to fill the box with a 30% tint of a spot color.

1 Hold down Ctrl (Windows) or Command (Macintosh) together with the spacebar, and drag across the business card outline, magnifying its view.

2 Select the rectangle tool (☐), and drag to draw a box of any dimension.

3 With the box still selected, in the Control palette type **11p2.5** for W and **3p7.5** for H, and click the Apply button (☐).

4 With the box still selected, in the Colors palette make sure the Both button is selected, click PANTONE 5595 CVU, and choose 30% for Tint.

5 From the vertical ruler, drag to create a vertical ruler guide at 13p3.

6 Select the pointer tool, click the tinted box to select it, and drag the box until its left edge is aligned with the 13p3 vertical ruler guide, about one pica (1p) above the bottom edge of the business card as shown in the illustration below.

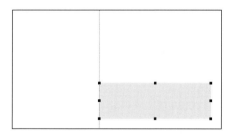

7 Choose File > Save.

Drawing lines

Like the letterhead design, the business card design includes two dashed lines that you will create using the constrained-line tool.

The first line you will draw is a horizontal line that is aligned with the top edge of the tinted box.

1 Select the constrained-line tool (|−), position the crosshair on the top right corner of the tinted box, and drag left to draw a horizontal line that extends about one pica (1p) beyond the left edge of the tinted box.

2 With the line still selected, choose Element > Stroke >1 pt dashed line.

3 In the Colors palette, make sure the Stroke button is selected, and click PANTONE 5595 CVU to apply a spot color to the line.

The second line you will draw is a vertical line that is aligned with the left edge of the tinted box.

4 With the constrained-line tool still selected, position the crosshair on the bottom left corner of the tinted box, and drag up to draw a vertical line that extends about 1p beyond the top edge of the tinted box.

5 With the second line still selected, choose Element >Stroke > 1 pt dashed line, and in the Colors palette click PANTONE 660 CVU.

6 Choose View > Send Guides to Back.

7 Choose File > Save.

Copying text from one publication to another

Since the business card includes some text not found on the envelope, you will copy the telephone/fax text in the 02WorkA.pmt template, and paste it to the 02WorkB.pmd publication.

1 Click the title bar of the 02WorkA.pmt template to make it the active window.

2 Select the text tool (**T**), triple-click the telephone/fax text in the tinted box to select it, and choose Edit > Copy.

3 Click the title bar of the 02WorkB.pmd publication to make it the active publication.

4 Select the text tool, drag to define a text block that spans the width of the tinted box (exact height is not important).

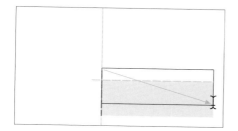

5 Choose Edit > Paste.

The pasted text is not rotated like the copied text, because you copied the text only, not the rotated text block.

6 Click outside the selection to deselect it.

7 Double-click the plus sign between the two numbers to select it, and press Enter or Return, replacing the plus sign with a hard carriage return.

Although it may be hard to tell, the telephone number and the fax number are now separate paragraphs.

8 Triple-click the first paragraph (the telephone number) in the pasted text to select it.

9 In the Control palette, click the Character-view button, and choose Myriad Roman for Font, type **6** for Size (**‡T**), **11.5** for Leading (**‡⚍**), and **.2** for Kerning (**⚌⚍**), and click the Bold button (**B**).

10 Triple-click the second paragraph (the fax number) in the pasted text to select it, and in the Control palette type **7** for Size, **11.5** for Leading, and **.35** for Kerning, and click the Apply button (▦).

11 With the insertion point still in the text block, choose Edit > Select All to select the entire text.

12 In the Control palette, click the Paragraph-view button (¶), and type **p8** for both Left Indent (→≣) and Right Indent (≣←), and click the Force-justify button (≣).

13 Select the pointer tool, click the text to select it as a text block, hold down Shift (to constrain the movement), and drag the text block until the text is vertically centered in the tinted box.

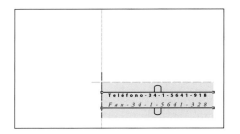

To move a text block (or graphic) in increments, select the text block or graphic with the pointer tool, and either press the arrow keys or click the X and Y nudge buttons in the Control palette.

14 Choose Window > Cascade.

15 Choose File > Save.

Copying, pasting, and formatting the address

After ungrouping the text and graphic elements in the envelope, you will copy the address and drag it to the business card outline, applying new type specifications and aligning it in the upper right portion of the business card.

1 Scroll to view the envelope design in the 02WorkB.pmd publication.

2 With the pointer tool selected, click the group in the envelope outline to select it.

3 Choose Element > Ungroup to ungroup all elements, making it possible to move the text and graphic elements independently.

4 Click the pasteboard (or an empty portion of the page) to deselect all objects.

You can also click the pointer tool in the toolbox to deselect all selected objects.

5 With the pointer tool selected, click the address to select it as a text block, and choose Edit > Copy.

As with text, you can also copy and paste a text block.

6 Choose Edit > Paste to paste a copy of the address text block slightly offset from the original address text block.

7 Drag the pasted address text block into the top half of the business card outline.

8 Hold down both Ctrl (Windows) or Command (Macintosh) together with the space-bar, and drag to magnify the text block.

You are ready to apply new type specifications to the pasted address.

9 Select the text tool (**T**), click an insertion point in the pasted address, and choose Edit > Select All to select all text in the text block.

10 In the Control palette, click the Character-view button, and type **7** for Size (**⬆T**), **12** for Leading (⬆⚍), and **.55** for Kerning (⚋⚊), and click the Apply button (⬚) to apply the new type specifications to the pasted address.

11 Select the pointer tool, click the pasted address to select it as a text block, and drag the top right corner handle until it is roughly aligned with the right edge of the first line of address, reducing the width of the text block.

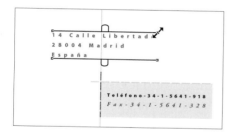

The bottom windowshade handle may display a red triangle, indicating the entire story is not displayed.

12 If the red triangle is displayed in the bottom windowshade handle, drag the bottom windowshade down to display the entire story.

13 With the pasted address still selected as a text block, drag the text block until the left edge of the text is aligned with the 13p3 vertical ruler guide in the upper right portion of the business card as shown in the illustration below.

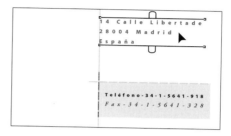

14 Choose File > Save.

Creating the double boxes

After drawing the boxes, you will use the Control palette to resize the boxes, and the Colors palette to fill each box with a spot color.

1 Select the rectangle tool (☐), and drag to draw a box of any dimension to the right of the business card.

2 With the box still selected, in the Control palette type **7p9** for W and **1p2** for H, and press Enter or Return.

3 In the Colors palette, make sure the Both button is selected, and click PANTONE 660 CVU.

4 With the rectangle tool still selected, drag to draw another box of any dimension to the right of the first box.

5 In the Control palette, type **11p3** for W and **1p2** for H, and press Enter or Return.

6 In the Colors palette, click PANTONE 5595 CVU.

7 Select the pointer tool, and drag the second box until its left edge touches the right edge of the first box.

8 Hold down Ctrl (Windows) or Command (Macintosh) together with the spacebar, and drag to magnify the view of the edges to check for precise alignment. Adjust the selected box if necessary.

9 With one of the boxes still selected, hold down Shift and click the adjacent box so both boxes are selected. Then choose Element > Group.

You will slow-drag this group to the business card outline to view the objects as you drag. If you quick-drag a group, the bounding box of the group is displayed as you drag, but not the objects.

10 With the group still selected, position the pointer in the center of the group, and hold down the mouse button until the pointer changes to an arrowhead.

Note: If the ruler guide you are about to drag the boxes to is not on the screen, you can let PageMaker scroll the screen while you drag. Just drag to the edge of the publication window; when the pointer reaches the edge, PageMaker will scroll until you stop the mouse.

11 With the mouse button still held down, drag the group until the vertical edge (where the boxes are joined) is aligned with the 13p3 vertical ruler guide, positioned between the address and the top of the vertical line, and release the mouse button.

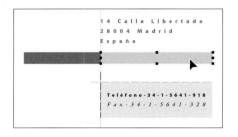

12 Choose File > Save.

Copying, pasting, and formatting the Braga+Braga text

After copying **Braga+Braga** (in the left box of the double boxes in the envelope design), you will drag to define a text block in the left box in the business card design, applying new type specifications and aligning it in the left box.

1 Scroll to view the envelope design.

2 Select the text tool (**T**), triple-click **Braga+Braga** in the envelope design to select it, and choose Edit > Copy.

3 Scroll to view the business card outline.

4 With the text tool selected, drag to define a text block that spans the width of the left box of the double boxes (exact height is not important), and choose Edit > Paste to paste **Braga+Braga** into the text block.

You are ready to apply new type specifications to the pasted text.

5 With the insertion point still in the pasted text, choose Edit > Select All, and, in the Control palette, type **8** for Size (↕T) and **.3** for Kerning (↔), and click the Apply button (▦).

6 Select the pointer tool, click **Braga+Braga** to select it as a text block, and use the arrow keys or Control palette nudge buttons until the text is vertically centered in the left box.

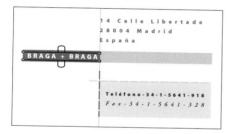

7 Choose File > Save.

Copying, pasting, and formatting the Arquitectos text

You will format and position the word **Arquitectos** in the right box of the double boxes using a similar procedure used to format and position the words **Braga+Braga** in the left box.

1 Scroll to view the envelope design.

2 Select the text tool (**T**), triple-click **Arquitectos** in the right box (of the double boxes) in the envelope design to select it, and choose Edit > Copy.

3 Scroll to view the business card outline.

4 With the text tool selected, drag to define a text block that spans the width of the right box of the double boxes (exact height is not important), and choose Edit > Paste to paste **Arquitectos** into the text block.

You are ready to apply new type specifications to the pasted text.

5 With the insertion point still in the pasted text, choose Edit > Select All to select it, and in the Control palette type **10** for Size (↕T), and click the Apply button (▦).

6 In the Control palette, click the Paragraph-view button (¶), and type **p10** for both Left Indent (→≣) and Right Indent (≣←), and press Enter or Return.

7 Select the pointer tool, click **Arquitectos** to select it as a text block, and use the arrow keys or nudge buttons until the text is vertically centered in the right box.

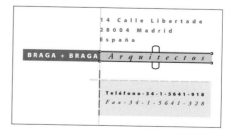

8 Choose File > Save.

Applying new type specifications to the B+b logo

After copying and pasting the three text elements in the **B+b** logo design, you will apply new type specifications to each text object, and realign the text objects into the logo design.

1 Scroll to view the envelope design, with the pointer tool selected, select the **B+b** logo design in the envelope (hold Shift as you click to select multiple objects).

2 Choose Element > Group to group the three text objects, choose Edit > Copy, and then choose Edit > Paste to paste a copy of the grouped **B+b** logo.

3 With the pasted group still selected, drag the group to the right of the business card outline.

4 With the **B+b** logo still selected, choose Element > Ungroup.

5 If necessary, magnify the view of the **B+b** logo.

6 Select the text tool (**T**), and double-click the lowercase **b** to select it.

7 In the Control palette, click the Character-view button, type **55** for Size (‡**T**), and click the Apply button (▦).

8 Double-click the uppercase **B** to select it, and, in the Control palette, type **32** for Size, and click the Apply button.

9 With the text tool still selected, double-click the plus sign to select it, and, in the Control palette, type **25** for Size, and click the Apply button.

Applying new type specifications to the text objects has forced them out of alignment.

10 Select the pointer tool, and align the three text objects of the **B+b** logo, clicking individual text objects to select them as text blocks, and dragging the text blocks until the **B+b** logo looks like the original logo on the envelope.

11 With the pointer tool selected, shift-click to select the three **B+b** logo text objects, and choose Element > Group to group the text objects into a single entity.

12 With the group selected, position the pointer on the **B+b** logo group, and drag it until it is positioned in the lower left portion of the business card outline as shown in the illustration below.

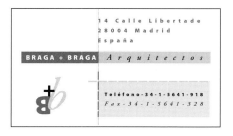

You are finished assembling the business card design.

13 Choose View > Fit in Window.

14 Choose View > Hide Guides to hide the view of the guides.

15 Choose File > Save to save the 02WorkB.pmd publication.

Printing the letterhead

Now that you have assembled all elements for the letterhead (stationery, envelope, and business card), you are ready to prepare these publications to be sent to a service provider. In addition to performing trapping (unless you decide to do it yourself using PageMaker's trapping options) and various prepress tasks, your service provider will create the spot color film separations on an imagesetter that will be delivered to your commercial printer.

Using the Lock Position command

To prepare the individual letterhead publications (letterhead, envelope, and business card) to be sent to your service provider, you will use the Group command to group all text and graphic elements in each publication into a single entity, and then apply the Lock Position command to each publication to lock all text and graphic elements, protecting your work from any accidental changes.

1 With the 02WorkB.pmd publication still activated, choose Edit > Select All to select all text and graphic elements in the publication.

2 Choose Element > Group to group all elements into a single entity.

3 With the group still selected, choose Element > Lock Position to lock the group.

4 Choose File > Save to save the 02WorkB.pmd publication.

5 Choose 02WorkA.pmt from the Window menu to activate the template you assembled.

6 With the 02WorkA.pmt publication displayed, select the pointer tool in the toolbox. Then choose Edit > Select All.

7 Choose Element > Group to group all elements into a single entity.

8 With the group still selected, choose Element > Lock Position to lock the group.

9 Choose File > Save to save the 02WorkA.pmt template as a PageMaker file.

You are ready to deliver these letterhead publications to your service provider. In addition to verifying the correct trapping specification with the printer, your service provider will expect you to verify the line screen frequency with the printer. For this example, a suitable line screen frequency could range from 80 lpi (lines per inch) to 150 lpi. Knowing the line screen frequency, your service provider will create film separations that range from 1200 dpi (dots per inch) to 2400 dpi. Once the film separations are complete, you are ready to deliver them to your printer.

Assembling a letter

Using the 02WorkA.pmt template you assembled, you will place and align the letter text, and prepare the letter publication to be printed on a desktop laser printer.

Using the Non-Printing command

Since the letterhead stationery includes the text and graphics for the letterhead design, you will use the Non-Printing command to designate all text and graphics in the letterhead template to be nonprinting.

1 With the 02WorkA.pmt publication activated, choose Edit > Select All to select all text and graphics in the publication.

2 Choose Element >Non-Printing if it is not already checked.

All text and graphic elements are still displayed, allowing you to view them as you assemble the letter.

3 Choose View > Show Guides.

4 Save the file.

Opening the letterhead template

Now that all text and graphics in the 02WorkA.pmt template have been designated to be nonprinting, you are ready to open a copy of the template.

1 With 02WorkA.pmt template activated, click the close box in the title bar to close the letterhead template.

Closing the 02WorkA.pmt template before you reopen it better demonstrates how you would use a custom template.

2 Choose File > Open, and select the 02WorkA.pmt file in the 02Lesson folder.

The Open Publication dialog box indicates a copy of the template will be opened. Even though you will open a copy of the template, it is possible to open the original template by clicking the Original button.

3 In the Open Publications dialog box, click Open (Windows) or OK (Macintosh).

Because you have saved 02WorkA.pmt as a template, PageMaker opens an untitled copy of the template, preserving the contents of the template.

4 Choose File > Save As, and type 02WorkC.pmd for the file name. Make sure the 02Lesson folder is selected, and click Save.

Placing the letter text

After placing the letter text in this single-column publication, you will align it with an existing horizontal ruler guide.

1 Choose File > Place, and double-click the 02TextB.doc file in the 02Lesson folder.

2 With the loaded text icon displayed, click between the margin guides, below the letterhead design, to place the text.

The left-aligned text flows between the margins of the page. Since the desired type specifications have been applied to the letter text already, you are ready to position the letter text on the page.

Note: The empty top and bottom window-shade handles indicate the entire story is displayed.

3 With the letter text still selected as a text block, drag it until the baseline of the first line of text is aligned with the 15p6 horizontal ruler guide, with the left edge of the text aligned with the left margin guide.

The letter publication is complete.

4 Choose View > Hide Guides to hide the nonprinting guides.

5 Choose File > Save to save the 02WorkC.pmd publication.

If the preprinted letterhead stationery were available, you could print the 02WorkC.pmd publication on a desktop laser printer.

6 Load the letterhead stationery in a 300 dpi desktop printer, choose File > Print, select the desired options in the printing dialog boxes, and click the Print button to print the letter.

7 Close all open publications, and choose File > Exit (Windows) or File > Quit (Macintosh) to exit the PageMaker application.

Review questions

1 What is the difference between a spot color and a tint?

2 What's the difference between opening a normal publication and a template?

3 What can you do if an object appears on top of others in an order you don't want?

4 What is the easiest way to keep multiple objects together in the same arrangement?

5 When dragging an object, how do you ensure that it moves in a straight line?

Answers

1 A spot color is a premixed ink applied to specified areas of the page on a commercial printing press. A tint is a spot color that is lightened by printing a dot pattern instead of the solid color.

2 When you open a template, a new, untitled publication is created by default.

3 Select the object, and choose Element > Arrange. Then choose one of the commands on the Arrange menu.

4 Select the objects and choose Element > Group. If you simply don't want the objects to be moved, select them and choose Element > Lock Position.

5 Hold down the Shift key as you drag.

Lesson 3

Project proposal

The project proposal you'll create in this lesson presents an architect's plan for the development of a community facility within the town of Bella Coola, British Columbia. This three-page, black-and-white publication uses the same framework and design elements on each page. So that you'll only have to create them once, you'll build a master page containing the text, graphics, column guides, and page-numbers that you want to appear on every page.

In addition to assembling a master page, this lesson introduces you to using styles to apply character and paragraph formatting attributes to paragraphs. More than ensuring consistency in a publication, styles free you from repeatedly selecting and applying individual formatting attributes to each paragraph in a publication. Although the PageMaker application provides a collection of styles (style sheet), you will create and edit styles to build a style sheet specific to this publication.

This lesson covers:

• Establishing a master page

• Adding tints to the Colors palette

• Using the Control palette to resize objects proportionally and to move objects

• Specifying automatic page numbering

• Establishing a publication default stroke style and weight

• Using page icons to turn pages

• Displaying and hiding master-page elements

• Overriding the default leading method

• Autoflowing text

• Adjusting the tracking (the spacing between words and letters)

• Varying the number of columns on a page

• Overriding type and paragraph specifications

• Creating, editing, and applying styles

• Creating a custom text wrap

It should take you approximately 2 hours to complete this lesson.

Before you begin

All files and fonts needed for this lesson are found on the *Adobe PageMaker Classroom in a Book* CD-ROM in the folders 03Lesson and Fonts, respectively.

Note: *Windows users need to unlock the lesson files before using them. For information, see Copying the Classroom in a Book files on page 4.*

Opening an existing document

Let's take a look at the final version of the proposal you will create in this lesson.

1 Before launching PageMaker, return all settings to their defaults by deleting the PageMaker 7.0 preferences file. See "Restoring default settings" in Lesson 1.

2 In addition to the commonly used fonts listed in the Getting Started chapter, make sure the following fonts are installed: AGaramond, AGaramond Bold, AGaramond Bold Italic, Birch, Myriad Bold, and Myriad Roman.

Windows only: *Because of the way Windows handles fonts, AGaramond Semibold Italic appears in the ATM Fonts list as AGaramond, Bold Italic (notice the position of the comma), while AGaramond Bold Italic appears as AGaramond Bold, Italic. However, neither AGaramond Bold Italic nor AGaramond*

Bold, Italic appear in font menus in Windows applications. You must apply italic to AGaramond Bold to use AGaramond Bold Italic. You must apply bold to Myriad Roman to use Myriad Bold.

All fonts used in this publication are Adobe Originals fonts. Birch is a particularly legible condensed display typeface and is notable for its angled serifs.

3 Launch PageMaker.

4 Choose File > Open, and double-click the 03Final.pmd file in the 03Lesson folder to view the proposal you will create.

The full view of the first page displays a variety of text and graphic elements, with a single column of text positioned above two columns of text. The page icons in the lower left corner of the publication window indicate this document consists of three pages.

5 If the publication window does not fill the screen, click the Maximize button in the title bar to expand the window.

6 Click the page 2 icon in the lower left corner of the publication window to view the second page.

To move forward one page, press the Page Down key. To move backward one page, press the Page Up key.

The left margin of the second page displays the rotated display text, page number, and graphics that appear on each page of this document.

7 Click the page 3 icon to view the third page.

Again, the left margin displays the graphics and rotated display text.

8 Click the page 1 icon to return to the first page.

9 Choose View > Show Guides to display the guides used to assemble this proposal.

Defining printing requirements

This project proposal was designed to be printed on a 300 dpi or 600 dpi desktop laser printing device. As mentioned in the first lesson, you need to determine the maximum printable area of the target printing device before assembling a publication.

When printed on a 300 dpi or 600 dpi desktop laser printing device, grayscale photographic images scanned at a resolution of 100 dpi will meet the print quality requirements of this publication. Grayscale illustrations, however will print more clearly

if scanned at 300 dpi. However, to save disk space, all the images in this project have been scanned at 100 dpi.

Assembling a master page

Every PageMaker publication contains at least one body page and one master page. While body pages contain the actual text and graphics of the publication, master pages contain repeating elements, such as margin and column guides, page numbers, headers, and footers. In PageMaker, the default master page is called Document Master. You can create and name additional master pages if your publication contains more than one page design. For example, in a book the table of contents, chapter divider, first page of a chapter, body of the chapter, and index all may have separate master pages.

To produce a more cohesive design for this multipage publication, you will establish a master page that will contain a variety of design elements, such as guides, repeating text, page numbering, and graphic elements that will be common to all its pages.

Creating a new publication

To create a master page, create a new or open an existing publication, and then display the master page itself.

1 Choose File > New. Make sure Letter is selected for Page Size. Click Double-sided to deselect it. To set the margin guides, type **2.5** for Left, **.75** for Right, **.75** for Top, and **.75** for Bottom. Choose 600 dpi for Target

Output Resolution and choose (Windows only) HP LaserJet 5Si for Compose to Printer. Then click OK.

Note: If you do not have the required printer, you can still create the project as directed and then print it on your own printer by selecting your printer and its PPD (if it is a PostScript printer) in the Print dialog box when it is time to print. You can also use the Export Adobe PDF command to create an Adobe PDF version of the project rather than a printed copy, as described in Creating an Adobe PDF version of the flyer on page 41.

The publication window displays the untitled publication with the specified page dimensions and margin guides.

2 Choose File > Save As, and type **03Work.pmd** for the file name, open the 03Lesson folder (if not already open), and click Save.

The page 1 icon is highlighted, indicating page 1 is selected. To import, create, and modify text and graphic elements on a master page, you must select the master page.

3 Click the R master-page icon in the lower left corner of the publication window.

PageMaker displays the master page, and highlights the R icon. The page still displays the margin guides you specified in the Document Setup dialog box.

Note: A single-sided publication has only one master-page icon. In a double-sided publication, you would see master-page icons L and R (for the left and right master pages).

Creating column guides

With the margins already defined using the Document Setup dialog box, you are ready to specify the column guides. Even though it is possible to vary column guides from page to page, placing column guides on master pages provides a consistent look throughout a publication. In addition, specifying column guides on the master page saves you the effort of specifying column guides on individual pages.

1 Choose Layout > Column Guides. Type **2** for Number of columns, and click OK.

PageMaker automatically creates columns of equal width, filling the entire image area between margin guides. Any column guides or ruler guides you create on a master page are automatically displayed on publication pages.

2 Choose File > Save.

Adding tints to the Colors palette

In previous lessons, you used the Colors palette to apply tints (lightened colors) to text and graphic objects. In this lesson, you will add two tints of black to the Colors palette, providing a shortcut to applying the same tint to multiple objects.

1 Choose Utilities > Define Colors, and click the New button.

2 In the Color Options dialog box, type **20% Gray** for Name, choose Tint for Type, choose Black for Base Color, type **20** for Tint, and click OK to close each dialog box.

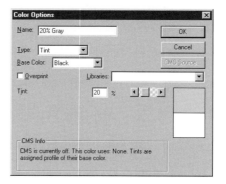

You need to define another color, but this time you'll use the Colors palette.

3 In the Colors palette, either click the new color button at the bottom of the palette or choose New Color from the palette menu.

— Palette menu

— New color button

4 In the Color Options dialog box, type **10% Gray** for Name, choose Tint for Type, choose Black for Base Color, type **10** for Tint, and click OK.

The Colors palette displays the tints 10% Gray and 20% Gray in its list of colors and adds a % sign to the right of each tint name.

5 Choose File > Save.

Using the Control palette to resize an object proportionally

After drawing a circle, you will use the Control palette to resize and position it. This circle will serve to frame the page numbers.

1 Select the zoom tool (🔍), and magnify the view of the upper left corner of the page.

2 Select the ellipse tool (○), hold down Shift (to constrain the ellipse to a circle), and drag to draw a circle of any diameter in the upper left corner of the page.

3 In the Control palette, click the Scaling button to toggle it to proportional scaling (🔳) so that the circle stays round. Then type **.85** for W, and press Enter or Return.

Proportional-scaling button ⌐

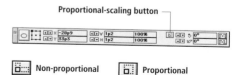

Non-proportional   Proportional

By default, the Scaling button is set to non-proportional scaling, letting you scale an object's height and width independently. When set to proportional scaling, you can enter a single value and PageMaker resizes the object evenly in both directions.

4 In the Colors palette, click the Both button (⊠), and select 20% Gray to apply the 20% tint of black to the stroke and fill of the circle.

5 Choose File > Save.

Specifying automatic page numbering

To automatically number all pages in this publication, you will place a page-number marker on the master page.

Note: *With PageMaker, you can number the pages of a multiple-publication document consecutively from the first publication through the last, restart the page numbering in each publication, or combine the two* *methods. You can also tell PageMaker to begin each successive publication on the next odd or even page number.*

1 Select the text tool (**T**), and drag to define a text block over the gray circle that is wider and taller than the gray circle (exact dimensions are not important).

You'll set the text attributes before you type the page-number marker.

2 In the Control palette, choose AGaramond Bold for Font. Type **50** for Size (↕**T**) and **70** for Leading (↕↔). Click the Paragraph view button (¶), and click the Center-align button (≡).

3 Hold down Ctrl and Alt (Windows) or Command and Option (Macintosh), and press **p**.

The center-aligned page-number marker RM (right master) is displayed on the gray circle, indicating where page numbers will appear.

Note: If your publication had facing pages, you would add a page-number marker on both the right and left master pages.

4 Select the pointer tool, and click the page-number marker. Then hold down Shift together with Ctrl (Windows) or Command

(Macintosh) and click again to select the circle. (Holding down Ctrl or Command lets you select an object underneath an object.)

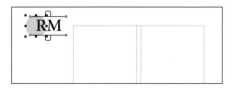

5 With both objects selected, choose Element > Align Objects (Windows) or Element > Align (Macintosh). Click both the vertical and horizontal Center-Align buttons, and click OK.

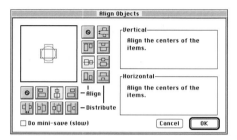

6 With both objects still selected, select the center reference point in the Control palette Proxy icon. Type **1** for X and **.75** for Y, and press Enter or Return to align the center of the two objects with the specified coordinate position.

Remember: Unless otherwise stated, the reference point in the Control palette Proxy icon should be a square point, not an arrow.

7 Select the text tool, and double-click the page-number marker to select it.

8 In the Colors palette, click [Paper] to apply the paper color to the page number.

9 Choose File > Save.

Establishing a publication default stroke style and weight

Before drawing lines (to be printed) over ruler guides and column guides (which don't print), you will set a default stroke style and weight for the publication. If you know ahead of time that several elements in your publication will share certain characteristics (such as stroke style and weight), selecting default settings can save you time. For example, once you set a stroke style and weight, PageMaker will use those default settings each time you draw a line, ellipse, rectangle, polygon, or frame.

1 Click the pointer tool in the toolbox to deselect all objects.

2 Choose Element > Stroke > .5-pt line to establish a publication default.

3 Choose View > Send Guides to Back.

4 From the horizontal ruler, drag to create a horizontal ruler guide at approximately 2.16 inches.

Note: Use the Control palette to help you position ruler guides. It displays the pointer location as you drag.)

5 From the vertical ruler, drag to create a vertical ruler guide at 1 inch.

The first line segment you will draw is a vertical line.

6 Select the constrained-line tool (|−), position the crosshair on the intersection of the bottom edge of the gray circle and the 1-inch

vertical ruler guide, and drag down to the 2.16-inch horizontal ruler guide to draw a line.

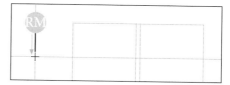

Rather than creating a new vertical ruler guide, you will reposition an existing guide that is no longer needed.

7 Select the pointer tool, and position the pointer over the existing 1-inch vertical ruler guide. Hold down the mouse button until the pointer changes to a double arrow, drag it until it is aligned with the 2.25-inch mark on the horizontal ruler, and release the mouse button to reposition the guide.

The second line segment you will draw is a horizontal line.

8 Select the constrained-line tool, position the crosshair at the ending point of the line you just drew, and drag right to the intersection of the 2.16-inch horizontal ruler guide and the 2.25-inch vertical ruler guide to draw a second line.

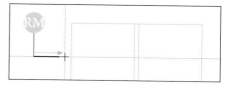

9 Choose View > Fit in Window to view the entire master page.

10 From the horizontal ruler, drag to create a horizontal ruler guide aligned with the bottom margin guide at 10.25 inches.

The 10.25-inch horizontal ruler guide extends beyond the bounds of the bottom margin guide, facilitating precise alignment across the entire page.

The final line segment you will draw is a vertical line.

11 With the constrained-line tool still selected, position the crosshair at the right ending point of the second line you just drew, and drag down to the 10.25-inch horizontal ruler guide to draw a third line.

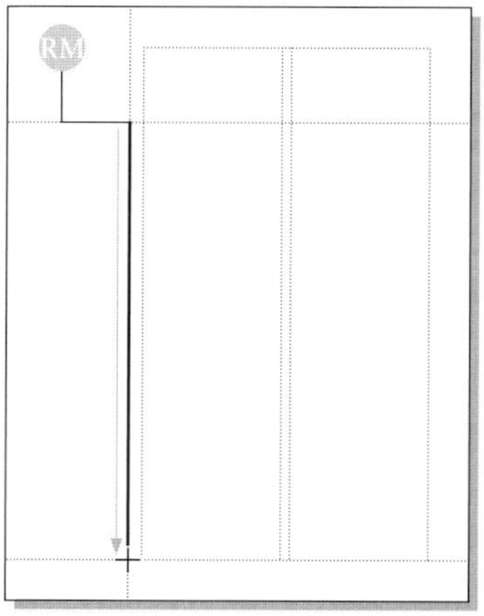

12 Choose File > Save.

Creating the rotated display text

You will create, rotate, and align the display text that is positioned in the left margin of the master page.

1 Select the text tool (T), drag to define a text block that spans the width of the image area (between the left and right margin guides).

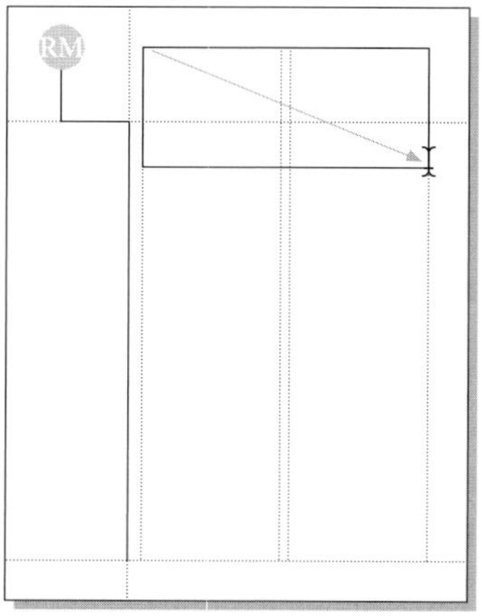

Before typing the text, you will use the Control palette to format the text.

2 In the Control palette, press the Character-view button. Then, choose AGaramond (Regular) for Font, type **130** for Size (↕**T**), and click the Apply button ( ).

3 Type **Project**.

4 With the text tool selected, double-click **Project** to select it. In the Colors palette, click 10% Gray to apply the 10% tint of black to the text.

5 Select the pointer tool, and click the text to select it as a text block. In the Control palette, make sure the center point of the Proxy icon is selected, type **90** for Rotation (↺), and click the Apply button (T).

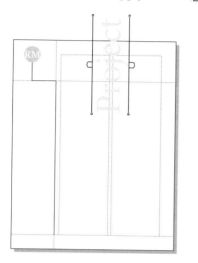

The text is rotated on the center point of the text block.

6 From the horizontal ruler, drag to create a horizontal ruler guide at approximately 9.12 inches.

7 From the vertical ruler, drag to create a vertical ruler guide at approximately 1.57 inches.

8 Choose View > Snap to Guides to deselect (uncheck) the option.

9 With the pointer tool still selected, click the text Project to select it as a text block, and drag it until its baseline is aligned with the 1.57-inch vertical ruler guide, with the bottom edge of the letter P aligned with the 9.12-inch horizontal ruler guide.

Remember: *If you drag immediately after pressing the mouse button, you see the bounding box of the text block. If you pause before you drag, you see the characters in the text block as you drag, making it easier to align the baseline to a ruler guide or to align characters to each other.*

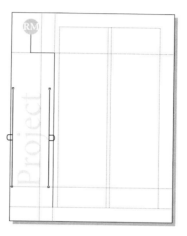

10 Choose File > Save.

Replacing selected text

You can save a bit of time if you copy and paste the word **Project** to create a new text block, and then replace **Project** with the word **Plan**. The new word will already be rotated and have the correct font applied.

1 With the pointer tool still selected, click the word **Project** to select it as a text block, and choose Edit > Copy, and then choose Edit > Paste.

The pasted text block is rotated like the copied text block, and the text is formatted like the copied text.

2 Select the text tool (**T**), double-click the pasted text to select it, and type **Plan** to replace the pasted text.

3 Double-click the word **Plan** to select it, and in the Colors palette click 20% Gray.

This design calls for the word **Plan** to use a smaller font size.

4 With **Plan** still selected, in the Control palette type **100** for Size (**⬍T**), and click the Apply button.

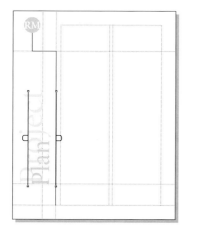

5 Select the pointer tool, and drag the existing 2.25-inch vertical ruler guide to approximately 2.15 inches.

6 With the pointer tool still selected, click the word **Plan** to select it as a text block, and drag it until its baseline is aligned with the 2.15-inch vertical ruler guide, with the stem

of the letter **P** in the word **Plan** aligned with the stem of the letter **t** in the word **Project** as shown below.

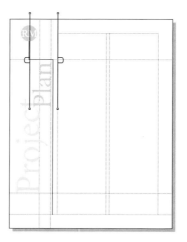

7 With the pointer tool selected, drag the top right handle to conform to the word **Plan**.

Plan overlaps **Project**, and the master page is complete.

8 Choose Edit > Select All and then Element > Lock Position to prevent accidentally modifying the master-page elements.

9 Choose File > Save.

Displaying and hiding master-page elements

You can display master-page elements on a page-by-page basis, making it possible to create a publication that makes use of master-page elements on certain pages.

1 Click the page 1 icon in the lower left corner of the publication window to view the first page.

Since master-page elements are automatically displayed on each page of the publication, the first page of the publication is displayed along with all master-page elements. The master page elements are at the bottom of the stacking order on the page and cannot be moved.

Notice that this page displays an actual page number instead of the page number marker.

2 Choose Edit > Select All, and notice how none of the master-page elements are selected.

Since the first page is displayed, it is not possible to select text and graphic elements on the master page.

You can easily hide master-page elements on a particular page in your publication, provided it is the current page.

3 With the first page still displayed, choose View > Display Master Items to deselect the option.

The text and graphic elements that you created disappear, and the nonprinting guides (margin, column, and ruler) are not affected. If you were to print this page, none of the master-page elements would be printed.

4 Choose View > Display Master Items to again display the master page items.

The first page of the publication is displayed, along with all master-page elements.

Assembling the first page

To assemble the first of three pages of the proposal, you will begin by creating and modifying text. Once the text is formatted, you will create new styles and edit existing styles that you will use throughout the rest of this publication.

Creating the title

After establishing the character and paragraph specifications for the title (Bella Coola) that spans the top of the first page of the proposal, you will type the text and apply a 75% tint of black using the Colors palette.

1 Select the text tool (**T**), and drag to define a text block that spans the width of the two columns (exact height is not important).

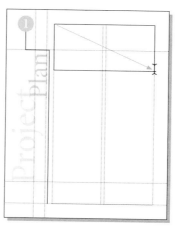

2 In the Control palette, choose Birch for Font, type **100** for Size (⬍T), and click the All Caps button (C).

Note: By default, PageMaker automatically sets the leading to 120% of the font size (as indicated in the Control palette).

3 Type **bella coola**.

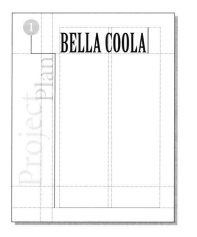

Because you had selected the All Caps button in the Control palette, the text is displayed in uppercase letters.

4 With the text tool still selected, drag to select the letter **B** in the word **BELLA**, and in the Control palette type **120** for Size, and click the Apply button.

Note: If different leading amounts occur within a single line, PageMaker uses the largest leading amount for the entire line.

Since leading is a character attribute, you can apply more than one leading amount within the same paragraph.

5 Drag to select the letter **C** in the word **COOLA**, and, in the Control palette, type **120** for Size, and click the Apply button.

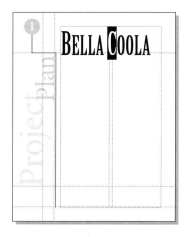

6 With the text tool still selected, triple-click the title text to select it.

7 In the Control palette, click the Paragraph-view button (⬚) and then click the Force-justify button (≡) to force the title text to spread across the width of the text block (which spans the two columns).

8 With the text still selected, make sure [Black] is selected in the Colors palette, and choose 75% for Tint to apply a 75% tint of black.

To make the text easier to work with, you will change the leading method used for the title. The leading method controls where text sits in the slug. (As mentioned in Lesson 1, a slug is the vertical space used by each line of type.)

PageMaker lets you choose three different leading methods: proportional (the default method), top of caps, and baseline. Proportional and baseline leading are the most common methods.

A. *Proportional leading* B. *Top of Caps leading*
C. *Baseline leading*

The proportional leading method (the method currently applied to the title) aligns the baseline of the text one-third of the slug height above the bottom of the slug. The baseline leading method, on the other hand, aligns the baseline of the text with the bottom of the leading slug.

When using baseline leading, the baseline of the last line of text in a text block aligns with the bottom of the text block. Because you'll be placing text underneath this title, it will be easier to work with other text blocks if the bottom of the title text block is not in the way.

9 With the text still selected, notice where the text sits in the highlighted leading slug. Choose Type > Paragraph.

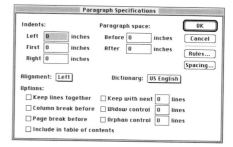

10 In the Paragraph Specifications dialog box, click the Spacing button.

The Spacing Attributes dialog box (Windows) and Paragraph Spacing Attributes dialog box (Mac OS) lets you to control the amount of space inserted between letters and words, the leading method, and the percentage of autoleading. In this example you will use the Spacing Attributes dialog box to override the proportional (default) leading method with the baseline leading method.

11 In the Spacing Attributes dialog box (Windows) or Paragraph Spacing Attributes dialog box (Mac OS), select Baseline for Leading Method. Hold down Shift (Windows) or Option (Macintosh), and click OK to close all the dialog boxes at once.

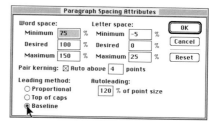

Notice that the slug has shifted in the title so that the baseline touches the bottom of the slug.

12 Select the pointer tool, click the title text to select it as a text block, hold down Shift (to constrain the movement to 90°), and drag the text block to align the top edge of the smaller letters with the top margin guide.

The 120-point letters overlap the top margin.

13 Choose File > Save.

Placing text using the Autoflow command

Use the Autoflow command when you have a lot of text to place. Flowing text automatically means PageMaker will create new pages until all text is placed, eliminating the need for you to add individual pages.

1 Choose File > Place, and double-click the 03TextA.doc file in the 03Lesson folder.

2 Choose Layout > Autoflow.

The pointer changes to an automatic text-flow icon.

PageMaker has three text flow modes, each represented by a different text-flow icon:

Manual flow Flows one column or text block at a time.

Automatic flow Flows text column to column until the entire story is placed, adding pages if needed.

Semiautomatic flow Flows text one column or text block at a time, ending with the loaded text icon if more text remains to be placed.

Whenever you have a loaded text icon, you can switch temporarily between manual and automatic text flow by pressing Ctrl (Windows) or Command (Macintosh). To switch temporarily to semiautomatic flow, hold down Shift when the loaded text icon is displayed.

3 Making sure the automatic text-flow icon does not overlap the margin guides or column guides, click in column 1 below the title text.

The last lines of text in the story are displayed on page 3 of your publication, indicating PageMaker has automatically inserted two pages.

4 With the pointer tool selected, click the text in column 1 to select it as a text block.

The plus sign in the top windowshade handle indicates that text from the same story is contained in another text block, and the empty bottom windowshade handle indicates the end of the story.

5 Click the page 2 icon to view the second page of the publication.

6 With the pointer tool selected, click the text in either column to select it as a text block.

Note: *Depending upon your monitor size and the zoom level, the text in both columns may be grayed-out.*

The top and bottom windowshade handles of the selected text block display plus signs (⊞). As just mentioned, a plus sign in the windowshade handle indicates that text from the same story is contained in another text block.

Plus sign

In previous lessons you placed and created stories that were contained in a single text block. Since the story in this lesson is contained in five text blocks, the text in this publication is *threaded* (through multiple text blocks).

7 Click the page 1 icon to view the first page of the publication.

8 With the pointer tool selected, click the text in column 1 to select it as a text block.

The first line of text in column 1 is positioned where you clicked to place the text, with the empty top windowshade handle (◻) indicating the beginning of a story.

Do not worry if the tops of the two text blocks are not aligned at this point. You will be resizing these later to make room for an introductory paragraph that spans both columns.

Note: If no text had been positioned in the top portion of column 2, the entire right column would have been filled with text.

9 Choose File > Save.

Adjusting the tracking

After formatting the text, you will use the Expert Tracking command to adjust the spacing between letters and words (tracking) in the proposal text. This command is useful for darkening or lightening a page—type with tight tracking darkens a page, and type with loose tracking lightens a page. You can also use Expert Tracking to adjust the spacing of selected lines of very large or very small type (headlines and captions), or to make text fit in a defined space on a page.

1 Select the text tool (**T**), click the proposal text to establish an insertion point, and choose Edit > Select All to select the entire threaded story.

Note: Once the entire story is formatted, you can apply specific styles to a few specific paragraphs (such as headlines, subheads, etc.) to override the original formatting, saving you the effort of formatting all paragraphs individually.

2 In the Control palette, click the Character-view button. Choose Myriad Roman for Font, type **8.7** for Size (⬡T) and **13** for Leading (⬡), and click the Apply button (⬡).

3 With the text still selected, click the Paragraph-view button (⬡) in the Control palette. Then type **.25** for First-line Indent (⬡), and click the Justify button (≡).

The first line of each paragraph is indented, with the left and right edges of the text aligned with the edges of the text block.

Now that the text is formatted, you will use the Expert Tracking command to adjust the spacing between letters and words (tracking) in the proposal text.

4 Hold down Ctrl (Windows) or Command (Macintosh) together with the spacebar, and drag diagonally across the text in column 1 to enclose half the text block.

In this magnified view, notice how the spacing between letters and words in the proposal text is fairly tight.

5 With the entire story still selected, choose Type > Expert Tracking > Very Loose.

The Expert Tracking menu displays six tracking options. The default tracking option No Track means no tracking has been applied to the text.

Because Very Loose tracking increases letter spacing for this point size (of this typeface), the loosened tracking makes the page appear lighter.

Note: It is also possible to select a tracking option from the Tracking pop-up menu in the character view of the Control palette.

6 Choose File > Save.

Varying the number of columns on a page

You can have a different number of columns on different parts of a single page. In this example, you will create a single column of text below the title text, above the two existing columns of text.

You will begin by reducing the size of the text blocks in the left and right columns to make room for a text block that spans the image area (between the left and right margins).

1 Scroll to view the middle portion of the page.

2 From the horizontal ruler, drag to create a horizontal ruler guide at approximately 4.17-inches. (Use the Control palette to verify its location as you drag.)

You will drag the top of the text blocks in the two columns down to this horizontal ruler guide. To help you align the text block, you'll first turn the Snap to Guides option back on.

3 Choose View > Snap to Guides to select (check) the option.

4 Select the pointer tool, click the text in column 2 to select it as a text block, and drag the top windowshade handle down until it snaps to the horizontal ruler guide you just created.

5 With the pointer tool still selected, click the text in column 1 to select it as a text block, and drag the top windowshade handle until it snaps to the ruler guide.

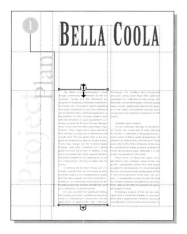

PageMaker automatically flows the text when you resize the text blocks, displaying the first line of text in the threaded story at the top of the first text block.

6 If the baseline of the last line of text in column 2 is not aligned with the bottom margin guide, select the text block and drag the windowshade handle to expose one more line of text. (You can leave column 1 as is; you'll be adding a photograph and caption to it.)

With the size of the text blocks reduced, you have space to create a single column of text below the title text.

7 Select the text tool (**T**), drag to select the first three and a half lines in column 1 (up to and including the word **Bella**), and choose Edit > Cut.

8 Position the insertion point at the beginning of the remaining text in column 1 (before the word **Coola**), and if necessary press the Backspace key to delete the letter space.

9 With the text tool selected, drag to define a text block above the text in the left and right columns, spanning the width of the two columns (exact height is not important), and choose Edit > Paste.

No longer part of the threaded story, the pasted text is a separate story and will serve as an introductory paragraph. Once formatted with a larger font, this introductory text will serve to draw the reader's eye from the larger text into the smaller text of the proposal.

10 Choose File > Save.

Creating and applying a style

A style is a set of character and paragraph formatting attributes. Once you define a style, you can select one or several paragraphs and apply the style. In just one step, all formatting defined for that style is applied to the text. Styles are especially useful when you repeat formatting characteristics in several places or are still experimenting with the layout of a publication.

As with other paragraph attributes, you need only an insertion point in the paragraph to apply a style. A style affects the entire paragraph, regardless of how much text is selected. However, you can override a style by selecting text within the paragraph and applying other attributes to the selected text.

PageMaker lists the styles of a publication in three different places: in the Styles palette, in the Control palette, and on the Styles submenu of the Type menu. You can apply a style to text from any of these style lists.

Earlier you specified the first line of each paragraph in the proposal text to be indented .25 inch. You'll now create a style that has no indent, so you can quickly change the formatting of select paragraphs.

1 Make sure the insertion point is still in the pasted introductory text.

2 In the paragraph view of the Control palette, type **0** for First-line Indent (⁺≣), and press Enter or Return.

The introductory paragraph is no longer indented. To make it easier to remove the first-line indent from a few other paragraphs in this publication, you will create a style where the first line of text in a paragraph is aligned to the left edge of the text block. Once created, you will apply this style to selected paragraphs in the proposal text.

3 With the insertion point still in the pasted introductory text, choose Type > Define Styles, and then click the New button.

4 In the Style Options dialog box, type **No Indent** for Name. Hold down Shift (Windows) or Option (Macintosh), and click OK to close the dialog boxes.

The No Indent style has the type and paragraph specifications assigned to the introductory text.

5 Click the Styles palette tab to display the Styles palette.

Collectively, a publication's styles are called a style sheet, and are listed in the Styles palette. In addition to displaying numerous default styles, the Styles palette displays the No Indent style.

You don't have to re-create styles each time you create a publication. You can copy styles from other PageMaker publications or from other word-processing applications. For more information, see the *Adobe PageMaker 7.0 User Guide.*

Now that you have created the No Indent style, you can apply it to the first paragraph in column 1 below the introductory text.

6 With the text tool selected, click the first paragraph in column 1 (below the introductory text) to establish an insertion point.

Note: When applying a style to a single paragraph, you must establish an insertion point in that paragraph. When applying a style to multiple, contiguous paragraphs, you must select some text in all target paragraphs.

7 In the Styles palette, click No Indent to apply the style to the paragraph.

Since the introductory text is meant to draw the reader's eye into the proposal text, the first paragraph of proposal text looks best without an indentation in the first line of text.

8 Choose File > Save.

Formatting the introductory text

After formatting the introductory text, you place it in its final position on page 1.

1 With the text tool selected, triple-click the introductory text below the title text to select it.

2 In the Control palette, click the Force-justify button (≡) to align the left and right edges of the text with the edges of the text block, including the last line of text.

3 In the Control palette, click the Character-view button ([T]). Choose AGaramond Bold for Font, type **22** for Size (⚹T) and **39** for Leading (⚹≜), and click the Italic button (*I*).

Note: Because of the way fonts are defined, when you apply italic to AGaramond Bold, PageMaker actually uses AGaramond Bold Italic. On the Macintosh, you can get the same result if you select AGaramond Bold Italic directly.

4 With the introductory text still selected, click the Colors palette tab to display the Colors palette. Make sure [Black] is selected in the Colors palette, and choose 65% for Tint to apply a 65% tint of black to the introductory text.

The formatted text is ready to be aligned.

5 Select the pointer tool, click the introductory text to select it as a text block, hold down Shift (to constrain the movement), and drag the text block until its bottom edge snaps to the 4.17-inch horizontal ruler guide.

6 Choose File > Save.

Placing a graphic

After placing and aligning a photograph in column 1, you will reduce the size of the text block in column 1.

1 Scroll to view the bottom of the page.

2 In column 2, locate the fourth line of text above the bottom margin guide. From the horizontal ruler, drag down to create a horizontal ruler guide aligned with the baseline of this line of text.

To allow for a 3-line caption, you will use this horizontal ruler guide to align the bottom edge of the photograph with the baseline of text in column 2.

Note: *Unless you want to place an inline graphic (a graphic attached to text), it's a good idea to make sure the text does not contain an insertion point when importing a graphic.*

3 Select the pointer tool to ensure that the text doesn't contain an insertion point.

4 Choose File > Place. Double-click the 03ArtA.tif file in the 03Lesson folder.

5 With the loaded graphic icon displayed, click in column 1 to place the photograph.

Depending on where you clicked, the photograph overlaps the text in one or both columns.

6 With the photograph still selected, drag it until its bottom edge snaps to the horizontal ruler guide you just created, with its right edge snapped to the right edge of column 1.

The photograph extends into the left margin.

With the photograph aligned, you are ready to resize the text block in column 1.

7 With the pointer tool selected, click the text above the photograph in column 1 to select it as a text block, and drag the bottom windowshade handle to display the last line of text to be approximately one line space above the photograph.

Column 1 displays 14 lines of proposal text.

8 Choose File > Save.

Editing the default Caption style

Once the caption text is placed below the photograph, you will edit the default Caption style and apply it to the text.

1 Choose Layout > Autoflow to deselect it.

2 Choose File > Place, double-click the 03TextB.doc file in the 03Lesson folder.

3 With the loaded text icon displayed, click in column 1 below the photograph to place the text.

If a red triangle appears in the bottom windowshade handle, some of the caption remains to be placed. You will fix this later.

Since all captions in this publication will be formatted identically, you will save time by editing the existing Caption style to create a custom style. Once created, this style can be applied to each caption in your publication.

4 Choose Type > Define Styles.

The Define Styles dialog box displays the default styles that you can apply to text. In addition to creating new styles as you have already done, you can use this dialog box to edit an existing style, creating a custom style.

5 In the Define Styles dialog box, click Caption for Style, and click the Edit button.

6 In the Style Options dialog box, click the Char button.

Even though you can use the character view of the Control palette to format text, the Character Specifications dialog box provides the most complete set of character-formatting options in PageMaker.

7 In the Character Specifications dialog box, choose AGaramond Bold for Font, type **10** for Size and **13** for Leading, and then make sure Italic is selected for Type style. Hold down Shift (Windows) or Option (Macintosh), and click OK to close the dialog boxes.

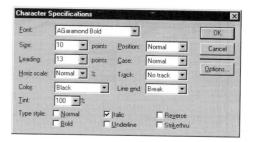

8 Select the text tool (**T**), click the caption text under the photograph to establish an insertion point.

9 In the Styles palette, click Caption to apply a style to the selected paragraph.

10 Select the pointer tool, click the caption text to select it as a text block, and drag the bottom windowshade handle until the entire story is displayed. Then hold down Shift (to constrain the movement), and drag the text block until the baseline of the last line of text is aligned with the bottom margin guide.

11 Choose File > Save.

Editing the default Subhead style

After editing the existing Subhead style to create a custom style for the subheads in this publication, you will apply it to the subhead on the first page.

1 Choose Type > Define Styles, select Subhead 1 for Style, and click Edit.

2 In the Style Options dialog box, click Char. Choose Myriad Roman for Font, type **11** for Size and **13** for Leading, choose Small Caps for Case, and select Bold for Type Style. To close the dialog boxes, hold down Shift (Windows) or Option (Macintosh), and click OK.

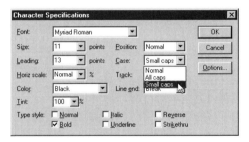

3 Select the text tool, and click the subhead **Available Space Analysis** in column 2 of the first page to establish an insertion point.

4 In the Styles palette click Subhead 1 to apply the style to the subhead text.

5 With the text tool still selected, click the first paragraph below the subhead text you just formatted to establish an insertion point in the paragraph.

6 In the Styles palette click No Indent to apply the custom style to the selected paragraph.

The paragraph following the subhead is no longer indented.

7 If necessary, select the pointer tool, click the text in column 2 to select it as a text block, and drag its bottom windowshade handle down just below the margin guide so the last line of text is aligned with the bottom margin guide.

The first page is complete.

8 Choose File > Save.

Assembling the second page

After applying character specifications to the text on the second page, you will place two graphics with captions.

Applying styles

The styles you created earlier will simplify your work on the second page.

1 Click the page 2 icon to view the second page of the publication.

All master-page elements display on the second page.

2 Magnify the view of the text in the lower half portion of column 1.

3 Select the text tool (**T**), click the subhead **Light and View Considerations** in column 1 to establish an insertion point

4 In the Styles palette, click Subhead 1.

5 With the text tool still selected, click the first paragraph below the subhead text you just formatted to establish an insertion point in the paragraph.

6 In the Styles palette, click No Indent to apply the style to the selected paragraph.

7 Choose File > Save.

Placing a drawing

You will place and position a drawing in the lower portion of column 1.

This drawing was scanned, then resized in Adobe Photoshop and saved in TIFF format with a resolution of 100 dpi.

1 From the horizontal ruler, drag to create a horizontal ruler guide aligned with the baseline of the third line of text above the bottom margin guide.

To allow for a 2-line caption, you will use this horizontal ruler guide to align the bottom edge of the drawing with the baseline of text in column 2.

2 Choose View > Fit in Window.

3 Choose File > Place, click (do not double click) the 03ArtB.tif file in the 03Lesson folder to select it. Make sure As Independent Graphic is selected, and click Open (Windows) or OK (Macintosh).

4 With the loaded graphic icon displayed, click in column 1 to place the drawing.

5 With the drawing still selected, drag it until its bottom edge snaps to the horizontal ruler guide you just created, and its left edge snaps to the left column guide.

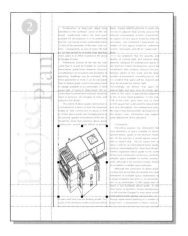

With the drawing aligned, you are ready to resize the text block in column 1.

6 With the pointer tool selected, click the text in column 1 to select it as a text block, and drag the bottom windowshade handle to display the last line of text to be one line space above the drawing.

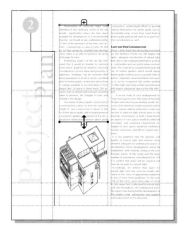

Now that the drawing and text are aligned, you are ready to place the caption text.

7 Choose File > Place, and double-click the 03TextC.doc file in the 03Lesson folder.

8 With the loaded text icon displayed, click in column 1 below the drawing to place the text.

9 Select the text tool (**T**), and click the caption to establish an insertion point.

10 In the Styles palette, click Caption to apply a style to the text.

11 Magnify the view of the caption text.

12 Select the pointer tool, click the caption text to select it as a text block, drag the bottom windowshade handle until the entire story is displayed.

13 Hold down Shift (to constrain the movement), and drag the text block until the baseline of the last line of text is aligned with the bottom margin guide.

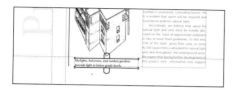

14 Choose File > Save.

Using the Control palette to position a graphic

After placing a second illustration on the second page, you will enter precise values in the Control palette to move it.

The illustration you are about to place and position was created in Adobe Dimensions®, sized in Adobe Photoshop, and saved in TIFF file format with a resolution of 100 dpi.

Note: Adobe Dimensions is a design tool that lets you create and edit 2D Bézier paths and text directly within the program and then extrude, revolve, bevel, and manipulate them for a 3D look.

1 Scroll to view the upper right portion of the page.

2 Choose File > Place, and double-click the 03ArtC.tif file in the 03Lesson folder.

3 With the loaded graphic icon displayed, click in column 2 to place the illustration.

4 With the illustration still selected, select the top left reference point in the Control palette Proxy icon. Type **4.316** for X and **.417** for Y, and press Enter or Return.

The top left corner of the illustration is aligned with the specified coordinate position (4.316, .417).

In addition to overlapping the text in column 2, the illustration overlaps text in column 1.

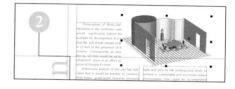

5 Choose File > Save.

Creating a custom text wrap

Since this nonrectangular illustration extends into column 1, you will create a custom text wrap that makes the text flow around the edges of the illustration.

1 With the pointer tool selected, click the illustration to select it, and choose Element > Text Wrap.

The Text Wrap dialog box lets you specify how you want the text to flow around the graphic boundary of the selected object.

2 In the Text Wrap dialog box, click the second icon (rectangular wrap) for Wrap option. For Text Flow, make sure the third icon (wrap all sides) is selected. Type **0** for Bottom (leave the other Standoff values at their default setting), and click OK.

A rectangular graphic boundary (dotted line) frames the illustration, with the text flowing around the edges of the graphic boundary within both columns. You will customize the shape of this graphic boundary to allow the text to flow around the illustration with greater precision.

3 Position the cursor at the bottom edge of the graphic boundary (dotted line) and the right edge of column 1, and click.

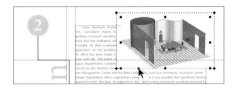

An additional handle is displayed on the graphic boundary. (If you do not see a new handle, click again more quickly.)

4 Position the pointer on the bottom left corner handle of the graphic boundary, hold down Shift (to constrain the movement),

and drag the corner graphic handle up until it is aligned with the baseline of the fourth line of text in column 1.

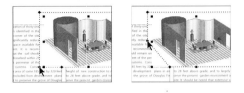

The custom text wrap allows the text to flow around the text wrap boundary. However, although the text is wrapping to the boundary, a portion of the graphic (its white background) is on top of the text, obscuring it. You will send the graphic to the back of the stacking order.

5 Choose Element > Arrange > Send to Back to stack the illustration behind the text and graphic elements.

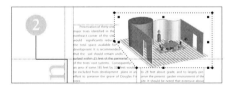

6 Choose File > Save.

Placing, formatting, and aligning a caption

You will place, format, and align a caption to be displayed below the illustration at the top of column 2. Before placing the caption text, you will reduce the size of the text block in column 2 to make some space for the 3-line caption.

1 In column 1, locate the third line of the second paragraph. Then, from the horizontal ruler, drag to create a horizontal ruler guide that is aligned with the baseline of that third line (Y equals approximately 3.4 inches in the Control palette).

To make room for the caption, you'll align the first line of proposal text in column 2 with this baseline. You'll start by dragging its top windowshade handle down, below the text wrap boundary, so the text block is easier to position.

2 With the pointer tool selected, select the proposal text in column 2 as a text block, and drag the top windowshade handle down until one line of text displays above the horizontal ruler guide you just created. Then, holding down Shift (to constrain the movement), drag the text block so the baseline of the first line of text aligns with the ruler guide.

You are ready to place the caption text.

3 Choose File > Place, and double-click the 03TextD.doc file in the 03Lesson folder.

4 With the loaded text icon displayed, click in column 2 (below the illustration) to place the text.

Before aligning the caption text, you will apply the Caption style.

5 Select the text tool (**T**), and click the caption text to establish an insertion point.

6 In the Styles palette, click Caption to apply a style to the text.

7 From the horizontal ruler, drag to create a horizontal ruler guide aligned with the baseline of text closest to the 3.02 inch mark in column 1.

You will use this horizontal ruler guide to align the caption text with the text in column 1.

8 Select the pointer tool, and click the caption to select it as a text block. Then drag the text block until the baseline of the last line of text is aligned with the horizontal ruler guide you just created.

9 Select the hand tool ( ), position the tool over the page at the bottom of the publication window, and drag the page up. Keeping dragging until you see the bottom of the page.

10 If the last line of text in column 2 does not rest on the baseline, select the pointer tool, and click the text in column 2 to select it as a text block. Then drag the bottom windowshade handle so it snaps to the margin guide and the last line of text rests on the margin guide.

The second page of this publication is completely assembled.

11 Choose View > Fit in Window.

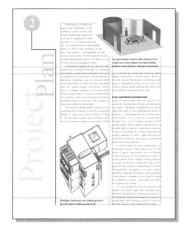

12 Choose File > Save.

Assembling the third page

After formatting and aligning the text on the third page, you will draw a box that will serve to frame an illustration. This boxed illustration and its corresponding caption will span the width of both columns.

Applying styles

You will apply the same styles to the text on the third page as you did on the previous pages.

1 Click the page 3 icon to view the third page of the publication.

As before, all master-page elements are displayed within the bounds of the third page.

2 If there is no text in column 1 on page 3, click the page 2 icon to view the second page, click the text in column 2 with the pointer tool to select it as a text block, and click the red triangle at the bottom of the text block to load the remaining text. Then click the page 3 icon to view the third page. Let the loaded text icon snap to the margin guides in the top left corner of column 1, and then click to place the text.

3 With the pointer tool selected, click the text in column 1 to select it as a text block.

The red triangle in the bottom window-shade handle indicates there is more text to be placed. Before manually flowing the remaining text into column 2, you will format the text in column 1.

4 Select the text tool (**T**), and click the sub-head **Conclusions** to establish an insertion point. (Zoom in first if necessary.) In the Styles palette, click Subhead 1.

5 With the text tool still selected, click the first paragraph below the subhead text you just formatted to establish an insertion point in the paragraph. In the Styles palette click, No Indent.

With the type and paragraph specifications applied to the text, you are ready to align the text.

6 Choose File > Save.

Manually flowing text into a column

Because the illustration and caption will extend across the bottom portion of both columns, you will resize the text block in column 1, and manually flow the remaining text into column 2.

Before reducing the size of the text block in column 1, you will create a horizontal ruler guide aligned with text in column 1. You will eventually use this horizontal ruler guide to align the bottom edge of the box that contains an illustration, allowing enough space for a single-line caption.

1 From the horizontal ruler, drag to create a horizontal ruler guide aligned with the baseline of the second line of text above the bottom margin guide.

After drawing the box that will frame the illustration, you will use this horizontal ruler guide to align the box.

2 From the horizontal ruler, drag to create a horizontal ruler guide aligned with the baseline of text nearest to the 5.9-inch mark on the vertical ruler.

3 Select the pointer tool, click the text in column 1 to select it as a text block, and drag the bottom windowshade handle just below the line of text aligned with the horizontal ruler guide you just created.

As before, the red triangle in the bottom windowshade handle indicates all text is not displayed.

4 Click the red triangle in the bottom windowshade handle to load the remaining text in the story.

5 With the loaded text icon displayed, position the icon in the top left corner of column 2, letting it snap to the column and margin guides. Click to place the text.

The empty bottom windowshade handle of the text block in column 2 indicates the end of the story.

Depending upon how precise you were when you placed the graphics and text throughout this project, the lines may not end in exactly the same spot. Make sure the first line of each text block on this page aligns. Do not worry if one text block is a few lines longer than the other.

6 Choose File > Save.

Drawing a box

After creating a box that will frame the final illustration, you will align it with an existing horizontal ruler guide.

1 Select the rectangle tool (□), and drag to draw a box below the proposal text, spanning the width of the two columns (exact height is not important).

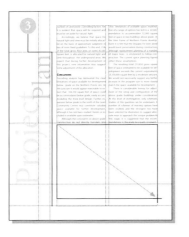

2 In the Control palette, type **3.87** for H, and press Enter or Return to establish the height for the box.

3 With the box still selected, choose Element > Stroke > Hairline to assign a stroke style and weight to the line of the box.

4 Select the pointer tool, position the pointer on the edge of the box, hold down Shift (to constrain the movement), and drag the box until its bottom edge snaps to the

horizontal ruler guide you created, with the left and right edges of the box still aligned with the margin guides.

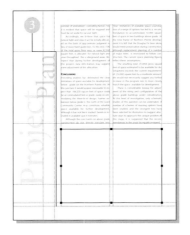

Since the bottom of the box is aligned with what was the baseline of the second line of text above the bottom margin guide, you have provided enough space for the single-line caption.

5 Choose File > Save.

Placing a graphic and caption

After placing the final illustration, you will place, format, and align its corresponding caption.

This illustration was resized in Adobe Photoshop, and saved in TIFF file format with a resolution of 100 dpi.

1 Choose File > Place, and double-click the 03ArtD.tif file in the 03Lesson folder.

2 With the loaded graphic icon displayed, click within the hairline box to place the illustration.

3 With the illustration still selected, drag it until it is visually centered in the hairline box.

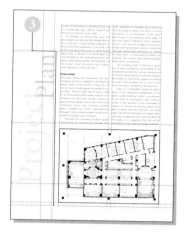

4 Choose File > Place, and double-click the 03TextE.doc file in the 03Lesson folder.

To make the caption text span the image area, you will drag to define a text block that spans both columns.

5 With the loaded text icon displayed, drag to define a text block under the boxed illustration that spans both columns to place the caption (exact height is not important).

6 Select the text tool (**T**), and click the caption text to establish an insertion point. In the Styles palette, click Caption.

7 Select the pointer tool, click the caption text to select it as a text block, and drag the bottom windowshade handle until the entire story is displayed. Then hold down Shift (to constrain the movement), and drag the text block until the baseline of the text is aligned with the bottom margin guide.

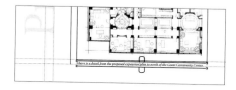

You have completed assembling the entire proposal.

8 Choose View > Fit in Window.

9 Choose View > Hide Guides to hide the column, ruler, and margin guides used to assemble this proposal.

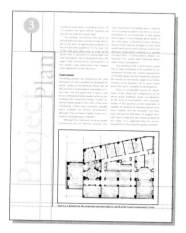

10 Choose File > Save to save the 03Work.pmd publication.

Producing the proposal

As mentioned at the beginning of this lesson, you can print this publication successfully on any 300 dpi or 600 dpi desktop laser printing device, and then photocopy it as needed. Or you can Export to Adobe PDF as described in Creating an Adobe PDF version of the flyer on page 41.

1 Choose File > Print to open the Print Document printing box for the type of printer you selected.

2 In the Print Document dialog box, click Color. Make sure the Composite and Grayscale options are selected.

3 Click Print to print the proposal.

4 Close all open publications, and choose File > Exit (Windows) or File > Quit (Macintosh) to exit the PageMaker application.

Review questions

1 List two advantages to using styles.

2 How do you make every object you will draw in a PageMaker publication have the same stroke width, color, and fill?

3 What is the term that refers to the vertical space used by each line of type?

4 What is a quick way to close multiple dialog boxes with a single click?

5 What is an advantage of placing text with Autoflow on?

Answers

1 Styles let you do the following:

• Maintain a consistent look throughout the publication.

• Ensure accuracy so that different paragraphs all have exactly the same specifications.

• Simplify and speed up formatting.

2 Click the pointer tool to deselect all objects, and then set the stroke and fill options you want using the Element menu and/or the Colors palette. These settings affect all objects you draw in that publication from this point forward but do not affect existing objects.

3 Slug.

4 Hold down Shift (Windows) or Option (Macintosh) and click OK or Cancel.

5 With Autoflow on, PageMaker fills all columns and creates new pages as needed without manual intervention.

Jewelcase booklet

In this lesson you will create the eight-page booklet titled Architecture Treasures of Italy, *featuring eight color photographs of historic Italy. For best results, this booklet needs to be printed on a printing press. To print color art on a commercial printing press, your service provider will separate each page containing composite art into its component colors by creating a film separation on an imagesetter for each ink–cyan, magenta, yellow, black (CMYK), and any spot colors. A commercial printer uses these film separations to create the printing plates used on the press.*

Designed to accompany a CD-ROM, this publication fits in the front cover of a CD-ROM jewelcase. It's easy to get the right dimensions, because the PageMaker application includes a page size already established for this exact purpose. Before printing this booklet on a commercial printing press, you must specify a custom paper size larger than the page size to accommodate the printer's marks (cropping marks) and page information.

This lesson covers:

• Specifying columns of unequal width

• Working with layers

• Creating a bordered frame

• Reversing text out of a frame

• Adding rules to a paragraph

• Flowing text semiautomatically

• Modifying an image using the Image Control command

It should take you approximately 2 hours to complete this lesson.

Before you begin

All files and fonts needed to assemble this booklet are found on the *Adobe PageMaker Classroom in a Book* CD-ROM in the folders 04Lesson and Fonts, respectively.

Note: *Windows users need to unlock the lesson files before using them. For information, see Copying the Classroom in a Book files on page 4.*

Opening an existing document

Let's take a look at the final version of the booklet you will create in this lesson.

1 Before launching PageMaker, return all settings to their defaults, deleting the PageMaker 7.0 preferences file. See "Restoring default settings" in Lesson 1.

2 In addition to the commonly-used fonts listed in the Getting Stated chapter, make sure AGaramond, AGaramond Bold, AGaramond Semibold Italic, and Birch are installed.

Windows only: *Because of the way Windows handles fonts, AGaramond Semibold Italic appears in the ATM Fonts list as AGaramond, Bold Italic (notice the comma). However, neither AGaramond Semibold Italic nor AGaramond, Bold Italic appear in font menus in Windows applications. You must apply bold and italic to AGaramond to use AGaramond Semibold Italic.*

3 Launch PageMaker.

4 Choose File > Open, and double-click the 04Final.pmd file in the 04Lesson folder.

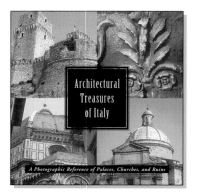

The full view of the first page displays a variety of text and graphic elements. The page icons indicate the booklet consists of eight pages.

5 If the publication window does not fill the screen, click the Maximize button in the title bar to expand the window.

6 Click the page icons to page through the booklet, and then click the page 1 icon to display the first page.

7 Choose View > Show Guides to display the guides used to assemble this booklet.

Talk with your printer

Designed to be printed on a commercial printing press, this booklet features images that were saved as CMYK TIFF files, making it easier to create the film separations.

To reduce the demand for disk space on your system, these images were scanned at a resolution of 100 dpi. Since it is likely that your printer would recommend printing this sort of publication at a line screen frequency of 150 lpi, in a real environment these images would have to be scanned at 300 dpi (double the selected line screen frequency) to meet the printing requirements of this publication.

To successfully print a design like this one, which has images that touch the edge of the page, you must allow the images to extend or *bleed* beyond the trim marks of the page. A bleed allows for inaccuracies of the press and trimming equipment. Your printer can tell

you the optimum bleed size for this job. So that you can better visualize the printed piece, the images in 04Final.pmd do not bleed, nor will they bleed in the version you create.

As discussed in lesson 2, adjacent colored objects in a design require trapping. After verifying the trapping specification, the size of the bleed, and the line screen frequency with your printer, talk with your service provider to determine who will perform the prepress tasks and how you should deliver this publication to your service provider.

Assembling the master page

For these left and right master pages, you will specify column guides, create graphic elements, and specify automatic page numbering.

Creating a new publication

After setting the options in the Document Setup dialog box, you will save and name your publication.

1 Choose File > New, and choose Compact Disc for Page Size. Type **8** for Number of Pages, type **.25** for Inside, **.25** for Outside, **.329** for Top, and **.329** for Bottom to set the margin guides. Set the Target Output Resolution to 2400 dpi, and choose (Windows only) the AGFA-ProSet9800 for Compose to Printer. Then click OK.

Note: If you do not have the required printer, you can still create the project as directed and then print it on your own printer by selecting your printer and its PPD (if it is a PostScript printer) in the Print dialog box when it is time to print. You can also use the Export Adobe PDF command to create an Adobe PDF version of the project rather than a printed copy, as described in Creating an Adobe PDF version of the flyer on page 41.

```
Document Setup                        OK

  Page size:  Compact Disc           Cancel

  Dimensions:  4.722   by  4.75    inches
                                     Numbers...
  Orientation:  ● Tall   ○ Wide

    Options:  ☒ Double-sided    ☐ Adjust layout
              ☒ Facing pages     ☐ Restart page numbering

  Number of pages:  8      Start page #:  1

  ┌ Margins ──────────────────────────────────────
  Inside  .25    inches    Outside  .25    inches
  Top     .329   inches    Bottom   .329   inches

  Target printer resolution:  2400  ▷  dpi
```

The publication window displays the first page of the untitled publication with the specified page dimensions and margin guides. Unless you specify otherwise, page number 1 of a double-sided publication is assigned to the first right page in the publication.

2 Choose File > Save As, and type **04Work.pmd** for Name, open the 04Lesson folder if necessary, and click Save.

3 Click the page 2 icon to view the second and third facing pages.

The zero point is aligned with the intersection of the top, inside edges of the facing pages. (In previous lessons, you assembled

single-sided publications, where the zero point is aligned with the top left corner of the page.)

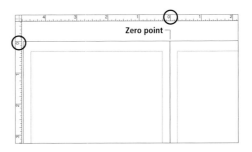

Zero point

Establishing preferences

Because you use the rulers to set up guides, it's a good idea to choose a measurement system before you begin laying out your pages. You'll also reduce the size below which PageMaker displays text as gray lines in layout view.

1 Choose File > Preferences > General.

To open the Preferences dialog box, double-click the pointer tool.

2 In the Preferences dialog box, choose Picas for both Measurements In and Vertical Ruler, and then click More.

Remember: 22p9 means 22 picas and 9 points.

3 In the More Preferences dialog box, set Greek Text Below to **3**. Leave all other settings at their default values. Hold down Shift (Windows) or Option (Macintosh), and click OK to close the dialog boxes.

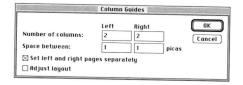

Specifying columns of unequal width

PageMaker automatically creates columns of equal width when you specify multiple columns. In this project you will create unequal columns, using the pointer tool to drag the column guides to the positions you want.

1 Click the master-page icon (⟦L̲R⟧) in the lower left corner of the publication window.

PageMaker displays the facing master pages and highlights the master-page icon. These pages display the margin guides you specified in the Document Setup dialog box, with the zero point aligned with the intersection of the top, inside edges of the facing pages.

2 Choose Layout > Column Guides, and type **2** for Number of Columns, select Set Left and Right Pages Separately (just to see

that you can specify different numbers of columns on the left and right pages), and click OK.

PageMaker automatically creates columns of equal widths, filling the entire image area between the margin guides.

You'll now move the column guides. To maintain the specified space between columns, the guides of adjacent columns move together. It is important that you drag and position the correct guide. The locations specified are for the right guide in column 1, not the left guide of column 2.

3 Select the pointer tool (if necessary). On the right master page, position the pointer on the right column guide of column 1. (See the illustration.) Then drag the column guide until it is aligned approximately with the 15p mark on the horizontal ruler.

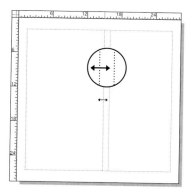

4 On the left master page, drag the right column guide of column 1 until it is aligned approximately with the -13p6 mark on the horizontal ruler.

Note: Since the left page is positioned to the left of the zero point, all X coordinate values for the left page are less than or equal to zero.

5 Choose File > Save.

Drawing a circle

After drawing a small circle, you will use the Control palette to resize it, and the Colors palette to fill it with the color black.

1 Magnify the lower left portion of the left master page.

2 Select the ellipse tool (○) in the toolbox, hold down Shift (to constrain the ellipse to a circle), and drag to draw a small circle of any dimension.

3 In the Control palette, make sure the Scaling button is toggled to proportional scaling (⌗). Type **1p2** for W (width) and press Tab. (Because you selected proportional scaling, PageMaker automatically enters 1p2 for H.) Press Enter or Return to resize the circle.

4 In the Colors palette click the Both button (⊠), and click [Black] to apply the color black to the stroke and fill of the circle.

Placed on the master pages, the circle will serve to frame the page numbers.

5 Choose File > Save.

Setting automatic page numbering

To number all pages in a publication automatically, you can place page-number markers on the master pages. After you place the page number marker in a black circle on the left page, you will copy and paste them to the right page, and reverse the colors.

1 Select the text tool (**T**), and drag to define a text block on top of the black circle, making it approximately the width of the circle (exact height is not important).

If your cursor jumps to the column guide, drag again over the circle.

You need to reverse the text so it will stand out on the black circle. You'll set the text attributes before you type the page-number marker so you can see what you type.

2 In the Control palette, choose AGaramond (Regular) for Font. Type **9** for Size (⬆T), click the Bold (**B**), and Reverse buttons (▣).

Remember that when you click a button in the Control palette, PageMaker applies any values you've typed as well as the action for the button.

Note: Because of the way fonts are defined, when you apply bold to AGaramond, PageMaker actually uses AGaramond Semibold. On the Macintosh, you can get the same result if you select AGaramond Semibold directly.

3 Hold down Ctrl and Alt (Windows) or Command and Option (Macintosh), and press **p**.

The page-number marker LM (left master) is displayed over the black circle, indicating where the page numbers will appear.

You will use the align objects feature in PageMaker to center the text over the circle, but first you need to center the text within the text block. You will both increase the leading, to center the page number within the leading slug, and then change the paragraph alignment from left justified to center.

4 With the cursor still in the text, choose Edit > Select All. In the Control palette, type **15** for Leading (⊤ᴬ). Click the Paragraph-view button (¶) and then click the Center-align button (≡).

5 Select the pointer tool, drag to select both the black circle and the page-number marker.

If you selected only one of the objects, drag again, but start dragging further away so you enclose the bounding boxes of both objects.

6 Choose Element > Align Objects (Windows) or Element > Align (Macintosh). Click both the vertical and horizontal Center-Align buttons, and click OK.

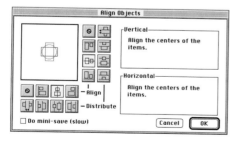

7 With the two objects still selected, select the center reference point in the Proxy icon in the Control palette. Type **-26p3** for X and **26p11** for Y, and press the Apply button (▣) to align the center of the objects with the specified coordinate position.

Remember: *Unless otherwise stated, the reference point in the Control palette Proxy icon should be a square point, not an arrow.*

8 Choose File > Save.

Copying the page-number marker

Since your publication has facing pages, you will copy the left page-number marker, and paste the copy on the right master page.

1 With the pointer tool selected, drag to select both the black circle and the page-number marker. Choose Edit > Copy.

2 Hold down Alt (Windows) or Option (Macintosh) and double-click the zoom tool (🔍) to switch to the fit-in-window view.

Now that both pages are visible, you can zoom in to the area on the right page where you'll paste the page number marker.

3 With the zoom tool still selected, drag across the bottom right quadrant of the right master page.

4 Choose Edit > Paste.

PageMaker pastes the circle and page-number marker on the right master page. Notice that the page-number marker automatically changes to RM (right master).

Note: Page-number markers positioned on the pasteboard display as PB (pasteboard).

5 With the black circle and the page-number marker still selected, in the Control palette make sure the center reference point in the Proxy icon is selected, type **26p3** for X and **26p11** for Y, and press Enter or Return.

Since the circle and the page-number marker will be positioned on a black box, you will reverse the colors of both objects.

6 Select the text tool (**T**), and double-click the page-number marker **RM** to select it. In the Control palette, click the Character-view button (T). Then click the Reverse button (R) to deselect it (and thus change the color back to black).

The Reverse button toggles text between the paper color and black. Until you reverse the circle, the page-number marker will not be visible.

7 Select the pointer tool, hold down Ctrl (Windows) or Command (Macintosh) and click twice to select the black circle. (The first click selects the text block; the second click selects the circle.) In the Colors palette, make sure the Both button (⊠) is selected, and select the color [Paper].

8 Choose File > Save.

Drawing a box

After creating the box that fills the right side of the right master page, you will fill it with the color black and adjust the stacking order to stack the black box behind the circle and the page-number marker.

1 Double-click the hand tool ( ). (This is another shortcut to the fit-in-window view.)

2 Select the rectangle tool (□), and draw a box of any dimension on the right master page.

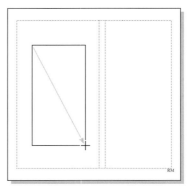

You'll now use the Control palette to both move it to the right edge of the page and to resize it.

3 In the Control palette, select the top right corner reference point in the Proxy icon. Click the Scaling button to toggle it to non-proportional scaling (⊡:). Type **28p4** for X, **0** for Y, **9p6** for W, and **28p6** for H, and then press the Apply button (⊡).

4 In the Colors palette, select the Both button (⊠), and then select [Black] to apply the color black to the stroke and fill of the box.

The black box covers the white circle and page-number marker.

5 With the box still selected, choose Element > Arrange > Send to Back to stack the black box behind the circle and the page-number marker.

The master-page design is complete, and you are ready to assemble the booklet cover.

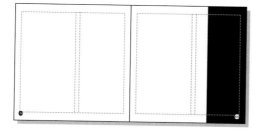

6 Choose File > Save.

Assembling the booklet cover

After hiding the display of the master-page elements on the first page (booklet cover), you will create two layers to separate the art and text. You'll then divide the page into quadrants, place four photographs, and create the boxed title and subtitle.

Looking at layers in the final version

Before you create layers in this booklet, take a look at how layers were used in the final version.

1 Choose Window > 04Final.pmd to switch to the final version of the publication. (In Windows, the path to the file is displayed with the file name on the Window menu.)

2 If necessary, click the page 1 icon to view the front cover of the booklet.

3 Choose Window > Show Layers.

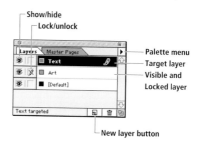

Layers let you separate like elements and treat them like a unit without grouping them. When elements are on a layer, you can display them, hide them, lock them, or even change their stacking order in relation to the rest of the publication. You'll use layers in this booklet to speed up screen redraw and make layout easier. After placing the photographic images on the Art layer, you'll hide that layer as you work on the text layer. When you want to display both layers, you can quickly lock one layer so you don't have to worry about inadvertently moving an object.

4 Click the eye icon (👁) of the Art layer.

PageMaker hides the Art layer throughout the publication, not just on the displayed page. A hidden layer also does not print.

5 Click the page 2 icon, and then click to display the eye icon of the Art layer to again view the images.

You can determine which layer an element is on by selecting the element.

6 Select the image behind the table of contents on page 2.

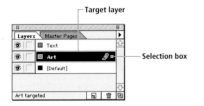

The layer containing the selected element becomes the *target* layer. (It is highlighted and contains the pencil icon.) The small selection box next to the pencil icon indicates that something on that layer is selected. Notice that the color of the graphic handles of the selected image match the color swatch of the layer.

The three palettes you'll use most often in creating this booklet are the Layers, Styles, and Colors palettes. You can combine the three to leave more room to view your page.

7 Drag the Layers tab to the Colors and Styles palette, and then click the Close box of the Master Pages palette.

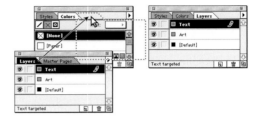

Creating layers

You are now ready to create two new layers in your booklet.

1 Choose File > Close to close 04Final.pmd and to return to your publication. If prompted to save before closing, click No.

Your publication already contains a default layer (called Default). Because that was the only layer when you created the master pages, all the master page elements automatically were placed on the Default layer. You can place master page elements on any layer, and with the exception of stacking order, they will behave like any other element on the layer. However, master page elements always display at the bottom of the stacking order, regardless of the layer they are on.

You will leave the Master Page elements on the Default layer.

2 Click the New Layer button ( ) at the bottom of the Layers palette, type **Art** for Name, and click OK.

Create the next layer using the Layers palette menu.

3 Choose New Layer from the Layers palette menu, type **Text** for Name, and click OK.

The stacking order of layers reflects their order in the palette: the bottom layer in the palette is the bottom layer in the publication. Because the text in the booklet appears on top of the images, you created the text layer as the top layer.

Hiding the display of master-page elements

You can display master-page elements on a page-by-page basis. Because the design doesn't use master-page elements on the cover, you will deselect the display of the master-page elements for the cover.

1 Click the page 1 icon to view the front cover of the booklet.

Since master-page elements are automatically displayed on each page of the publication, the first page of the publication is displayed with all master-page elements found on the right master page.

You can easily hide master-page elements on a page.

2 Choose View > Display Master Items to deselect the option.

The text and graphic elements that you created are not displayed, but the nonprinting guides (margin, column, and ruler) are not affected. If you were to print this page, none of the master-page elements would be printed.

Placing and cropping a graphic

After dividing the front cover into quadrants, you will place a photograph into each quadrant. The photographs were prepared in Adobe Photoshop by applying a single color to a grayscale TIFF image, and then sizing and saving each image in TIFF file format at a resolution of 100 dpi.

1 From the horizontal ruler, drag to create a horizontal ruler guide at 14p3. From the vertical ruler, drag to create a vertical ruler guide at 14p2, dividing the booklet cover into quadrants.

As you learned in Lesson 1, you can move the zero point (the intersection of the horizontal and vertical rulers) to any location on the page. To make it a little easier to align the four photographs on the cover, you will move the zero point from the top-left corner of the page until it is aligned with the center of the page. Each image will have a corner touching the zero point, making it easy to enter their precise location in the Control palette.

2 With the pointer tool selected, position the pointer on the crosshair of the zero point, and drag it until the zero point is aligned with the intersection of the ruler guides you just created. Watch the position in the Control palette; X should be 14p2, and Y should be 14p3.

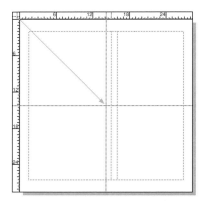

3 Make sure the Art layer is the target layer. If not, click to select it.

4 Choose File > Place, and double-click the 04ArtA.tif file in the 04Lesson folder.

5 With the loaded graphic icon displayed, click in the upper left quadrant of the page to place the photograph.

Since the photographs extend to the edges of the page, each photograph was sized to allow for a bleed to overlap the edges of the page. For the sake of viewing the actual design of the cover, you will crop each photograph to

be aligned with the edges of the page. When the booklet is complete, one of the prepress tasks will be to pull the crop rectangles out again, to reestablish the bleeds.

Before you crop, you'll position the images.

6 In the Control palette, select the bottom right reference point in the Proxy icon, type **0** for both X and Y, and press Enter or Return to align the bottom right corner of the photograph with the zero point.

Precision will be important when cropping these images for two reasons. You will copy all the images on the cover and paste them onto the back cover. If cropped precisely to fit the page, they will be easier to position on the back cover. In addition, in the final printing of this booklet, the binding edges of the pages will abut each other, rather than bleed. If not cropped carefully, an image could overlap the adjacent page in the signature or not print all the way to the page fold. This is another example of the importance of talking to your service provider before you begin layout.

7 If necessary, reselect the photograph. Select the cropping tool (⌗), and position the tool over the top left graphic handle of the photograph, making sure the graphic handle shows through the center of the cropping tool. Hold down the mouse button until the tool changes to a double-headed arrow.

8 With the mouse button still held down, drag down and right to the top left corner of the page, and release the mouse button when W in the Control palette is 14p2, and H is 14p3.

PageMaker crops the view of the photograph.

Placing and cropping the three remaining graphics

As you place the three remaining photographs on the cover, crop each one to be aligned with the edges of the page.

1 Choose File > Place, and double-click the 04ArtB.tif file in the 04Lesson folder.

2 With the loaded graphic icon displayed, click in the upper right quadrant of the page to place the photograph.

3 In the Control palette, select the bottom left reference point in the Proxy icon, type **0** for both X and Y, and press Enter or Return.

4 Select the cropping tool (✄), and position the tool over the top right graphic handle of the photograph, and drag down and left to the top right corner of the page. Watch the values in the Control palette; W should be 14p2, and H should be 14p3.

5 Choose File > Place, and double-click the 04ArtC.tif file in the 04Lesson folder.

6 With the loaded graphic icon displayed, click in the lower left quadrant of the page to place the photograph.

7 In the Control palette, select the top right reference point in the Proxy icon, type **0** for both X and Y, and press Enter or Return.

You will use the cropping tool in the Control palette to crop the next two images.

8 Click the Cropping button (✄) in the Control palette. With the top right reference point still selected, type **14p2** for W, and **14p3** for H, and click the Apply button (▣).

9 Choose File > Place, and double-click the 04ArtD.tif file in the 04Lesson folder.

10 Position the loaded graphic icon in the lower right quadrant of the page and let it snap to the zero point. Then click to place the photograph.

11 In the Control palette, select the top left reference point in the Proxy icon, type **0** for both X and Y. Click the Cropping button, and type **14p2** for W, and **14p3** for H. Then click the Apply button.

12 Choose File > Save.

Creating a bordered frame for the title

Next to the rectangle, ellipse, and polygon tools in the toolbox, is a corresponding frame tool. Like standard PageMaker-drawn shapes, frames can have a stroke and fill. Unlike standard shapes, however, frames can also have content, either text or graphics. Frames make it easy for you to position objects and text within another shape and can serve as placeholders in templates or during the design phase of a publication.

You will create the title for this booklet in a bordered frame on the text layer.

1 In the Layers palette, select the Text layer. Then click the eye icon (👁) of the Art layer to temporarily hide the images.

2 Select the rectangle frame tool (⊠), and drag to draw a box of any dimension in the center of the page.

3 In the Control palette, select the center reference point in the Proxy icon. Type **0** for both X and Y (to center the frame on the page), type **9p7** for both W and H (to resize the frame), and press Enter or Return.

4 Click the Colors palette tab, make sure the Both button (⊠) is highlighted. Then select [Black] to apply the color black to the stroke and fill of the box.

5 Choose Element > Stroke > 6-pt triple line to create a triple-line border.

You now need to set the frame options. The frame options control the position of the content within the frame. You can center a text block vertically within a frame, or align its top or bottom with the top or bottom of the frame. You can also specify insets to offset text from the edges of the frame.

6 With the frame still selected, choose Element > Frame > Frame Options. Choose Center for Vertical Alignment, set the Top, Bottom, Left, and Right Insets to **0**, and click OK.

Note: *Vertical Alignment and Offsets are the only frame options that affect text. The other options apply to graphics in a frame.*

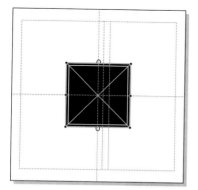

7 Choose File > Save.

Defining process colors

This booklet calls for two custom colors. Before you define these process colors, you'll remove any unused colors from the palette.

1 Choose Utilities > Define Colors, and click the Remove Unused button. When prompted, click Yes to All to remove all unused colors, then click OK when PageMaker lists the number of colors and inks removed. (Do not close the Define Colors dialog box.)

2 In the Define Colors dialog box, click New. Type **Sand** for Name, and choose Process for Type and CMYK for Model. Then enter the CMYK values shown below.

(You can press the Tab key to jump from one edit box to the next. (In Windows, press Tab twice.) After entering the Black value, press Tab again if you want to see the final color displayed in the color swatch.

3 Click OK, and then click New again.

4 Type **Dark Blue** for Name, and enter the CMYK values shown below.

5 Hold down either Shift (Windows) or Option (Macintosh) and click OK to close the dialog boxes.

6 Click the Maximize button in the top of the Colors palette to display the entire palette. (Click again if PageMaker minimizes the palette.)

PageMaker added the new colors Dark Blue and Sand to the palette.

7 Choose File > Save.

Creating the title

After creating the title, you will center it in the bordered box.

1 Select the text tool (**T**), and click inside the bordered frame to establish an insertion point. In the Character view of the Control palette, choose Birch for Font, type **24** for Size (⇕**T**), and click the Apply button (⊞).

2 In the Colors palette, select Sand to set the color for the text you are about to type.

3 Type the following text, breaking the lines as shown with Enter or Return:

> **Architectural**
> **Treasures**
> **of Italy**

4 Choose Edit > Select All. In the Control palette, type **.05** for Kerning (⇔). Click the Paragraph-view button (¶), and then click the Center-align button (≡) to center the text horizontally in the frame.

The text is now nicely centered horizontally in the frame, but vertically it is still a bit off-center. The frame option centers the entire block of text, including leading and Para-

graph Space After settings. You can either calculate a top offset to push the text down or change the leading method, which changes where the text sits in the leading slug. Of the three leading methods, the Top of Caps leading option provides the best spacing for centering text vertically in a frame.

5 With the text still selected, choose Type > Paragraph. Click Spacing, and select Top of Caps for Leading Method. Hold down Shift (Windows) or Option (Macintosh), and click OK to close the dialog boxes.

6 Choose File > Save.

Placing the subtitle in a frame

After creating another frame, you will place the subtitle within it.

1 Select the rectangle frame tool (⊠), and drag to draw a box of any dimension below the existing black frame.

2 In the Control palette, make sure the center reference point in the Proxy icon is selected. Type **0** for X, **11p8** for Y, **23p8** for

W, and **1p4** for H, and press Enter or Return to resize the box and center it horizontally on the page.

3 In the Colors palette, click the Stroke button (✐). Make sure [Black] is selected.

4 With the frame still selected, choose Element > Frame > Frame Options. Choose Center for Vertical Alignment, and set the Top, Bottom, Left, and Right Insets to **0**. Then click OK.

5 With the frame still selected, choose File > Place. Double-click 04TextA.doc in the 04Lesson folder.

The subtitle appears in the frame.

6 Select the text tool (**T**), triple-click the subtitle to select it, and choose Type > Paragraph.

7 Choose Center for Alignment. Click Spacing, and then select Top of Caps for Leading Method. Hold down Shift (Windows) or Option (Macintosh), and click OK to close the dialog boxes.

8 In the Control palette, click the Character-view button (T), and type **10** for Size (‡T), **10** for Leading (‡⸚), and **.06** for Kerning (⸚⸗). Click the Bold (**B**) and Italic (*I*) buttons.

To better set off the subtitle, you will change the frame to a solid black box and apply the paper color to the text. (As mentioned in the beginning of this lesson, clicking the Reverse button in the Control palette is the same as selecting the color [Paper] for text.)

9 With the text still selected, select [Paper] in the Colors palette to apply the paper color to the subtitle. (The text disappears until you change the frame to black.)

10 Select the pointer tool, select the subtitle frame, click the Fill button (✕) in the Colors palette, and select [Black].

11 Click the Layers palette tab, click to display the eye icon (👁) of the Art layer to redisplay the photographic images.

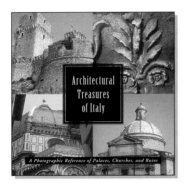

The front cover is completely assembled.

12 Choose File > Save.

Assembling the first double-page spread

In addition to placing the text and graphic elements, you will create rules above and below paragraphs, and create and apply styles.

Placing a graphic

After placing and positioning a graphic on the left page of the first double-page spread, you will apply a color to an illustration.

1 Click the page 2 icon to view the first double-page spread.

The zero point is still aligned with the center of the right page.

2 Double-click the hairline of the zero point (in the top left corner of the publication window) to return it to its default position at the top, intersecting edges of the facing pages.

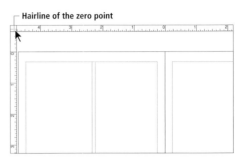

Hairline of the zero point

3 In the Layers palette, select the Art layer, choose File > Place and double-click 04ArtE.tif in the 04Lesson folder.

4 With the loaded graphic icon displayed, click the upper left quadrant of the left page (page 2) to place the illustration.

5 With the pointer tool selected, position the pointer on the illustration, hold down the mouse button, and quickly drag the illustration to display its bounding box. With the mouse button still held down, drag the bounding box until its top edge is aligned with the top margin guide, visually centering it between the left and right edges of the page.

6 Click the Colors palette tab to activate it. Select Sand to apply the color to the illustration.

Note: You can apply color to monochrome (1-bit) and grayscale bitmap images, but not color bitmap images.

7 Choose File > Save.

Creating a bordered frame for the table of contents

After creating the bordered frame for the table of contents, you will use the Control palette to size and position it, applying Dark Blue to the stroke and fill of the box. To see how easy it is to move elements to another layer, you will create the frame on the Art layer and move it to the Text layer.

1 Select the rectangle frame tool (⊠), and drag to draw a box of any dimension on the left page (page 2).

2 In the Control palette, make sure the center point of the Proxy icon is selected, type **-14p2** for X, **14p3** for Y, **12p6** for both W and H, and press Enter or Return to resize and center the box.

3 Choose Element > Stroke > 5-pt double line (heavy over light) to specify a border for the box.

4 In the Colors palette, make sure the Both button (⊠) is selected, and select Dark Blue to apply the color to the stroke and fill of the box.

5 Click the Layers tab to activate it.

Note that the frame appears on the Art layer, the layer that was the target layer when you created it. You can easily move an object from one layer to another using the Layers palette. When an object is selected, a small selection box appears in the palette. To move the object to another layer, you simply drag the selection box to the appropriate layer.

6 With the box still the only selected element on the page, drag the small selection box (next to the pencil icon in the palette) up to the Text layer.

PageMaker moves the box to the Text layer.

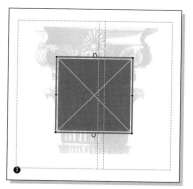

7 Choose File > Save.

Placing the table of contents

After placing the table of contents, you will format the text and then attach it to the frame.

1 Choose File > Place, and double-click 04TextB.doc in the 04Lesson folder.

2 With the loaded text icon displayed, drag below the blue box to define a text block that spans the width of the blue box (exact height is not important) to place the text.

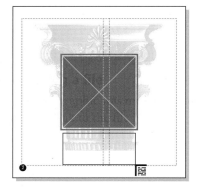

3 If the bottom windowshade handle contains a down arrow, drag the arrow down until the entire story is displayed.

4 Select the text tool (**T**), click an insertion point in the text, and choose Edit > Select All.

5 In the Control palette choose Birch for Font, type **15** for Size (‡T), **20** for Leading (‡), and **.1** for Kerning (‡), and click the Apply button (‡).

Depending upon how big you made the text block (or how far you dragged the bottom windowshade handle), some of the text may have disappeared from sight. Leave it as it is. The entire story is still selected even though it may not be displayed.

6 Choose Type > Paragraph. Choose Center for Alignment, and click the Spacing button. Then select Top of Caps for Leading Method. Hold down Shift (Windows) or Option (Macintosh) and click OK to close the dialog boxes.

7 Triple-click the first line of the table of contents to select it. In the Control palette, type **23** for Size, and click the All Caps button (C).

Don't worry if **WHAT'S INSIDE** seems too close to the second line. You'll be adding a rule between the two in the next procedure.

8 Choose Edit > Select All. In the Colors palette, select [Paper] to apply the paper color to the table of contents.

9 Select the pointer tool, and click the table of contents (which is no longer visible) to select it as a text block. Hold down Shift, and select the bordered box as well.

Sometimes the only way to locate paper-colored text is to select all items on the page. (With the pointer tool selected, choose Edit > Select All.) In this way, you can see exactly where the text block is located.

10 Choose Element > Frame > Attach Content.

PageMaker inserts the text into the frame. Using the frame options, you can center the text vertically in the frame.

11 Choose Element > Frame > Frame Options. Choose Center for Vertical Alignment, type **0** for Top, Bottom, Left, and Right indents, and click OK.

12 Choose File > Save.

Creating a rule below a paragraph

You will create the double-line rule that is positioned below the table of contents title. Even though a rule looks like a graphic object, it can be a paragraph attribute that is part of the text, moving whenever the text moves.

1 Select the text tool (**T**), and click **WHAT'S INSIDE** to establish an insertion point. Choose Type > Paragraph, type **0p8** for After, and then click the Rules button.

2 Select Rule Below Paragraph, choose the 5-point double line (heavy over light) for Stroke Style, choose Sand for Stroke Color, select the Width of Text option, and click the Options button.

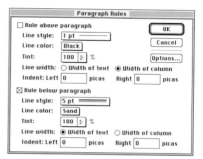

3 Type **1** for Bottom to override the default vertical position, hold down either Shift (Windows) or Option (Macintosh) to close the dialog boxes, and click OK.

Note: *The default (Auto) position of a rule below a paragraph places the bottom edge of the rule along the bottom of the slug of the last line of text. Depending upon the leading*

applied to the text, a large value for Picas Below Baseline can increase the size of the slug of the last line.

4 Choose File > Save.

Flowing text semiautomatically

Since the text is meant to be positioned in specific columns in the publication, you will flow the text semiautomatically, one column at a time. Flowing text semiautomatically is very much like flowing text manually, but the text icon is automatically reloaded after the text flows into the column. You may recall that the Autoflow option flows text automatically, column to column.

1 If necessary, magnify the view of the right page (page 3) so that you can see the entire page.

2 Choose File > Place, and double-click 04TextC.doc in the 04Lesson folder.

3 Position the loaded text icon in the top left corner of column 1, letting it snap to the margin guides. Hold down Shift (to specify semiautomatic flow), and click to place the text. Then release the Shift key.

Once the text has filled the column, the loaded text icon reappears automatically.

4 Click the page 4 icon to view the second double-page spread.

5 On the right page (page 5), position the loaded text icon in the top left corner of column 1, letting it snap to the margin guides. Hold down Shift (to specify semiautomatic flow), and click to place the text. Then release the Shift key.

6 Click the page 6 icon to switch to the final spread of the booklet.

7 Using the same technique, place the next portion of the story on page 7. Remember to let the loaded text icon snap to the margin guides.

Once placed, PageMaker again displays the loaded text icon, indicating there is more story to place. At this point, you don't need to place the remainder of the story. After you reformat the text in the next procedure, most of the text will flow back onto pages 3 and 5. Once there is room, the unplaced portion will automatically flow onto the page.

8 With the loaded text icon displayed, click the pointer tool to stop placing text. (The unplaced text remains part of the story.)

9 Choose File > Save.

Formatting the story

After using the Control palette to format the entire story you just placed, you will roughly align the text block in the left column on page 3.

1 Click the page 2 icon to view the first double-page spread.

2 Select the text tool (T), and click the text on page 3 to establish an insertion point. Choose Edit > Select All to select the entire story that spans multiple pages.

3 In the Control palette, type **8** for Size (↕T) and **13** for Leading (↕Ａ), and click the Apply button (▦).

You'll now zoom into column 1.

4 Hold down Ctrl (Windows) or Command (Macintosh) together with the spacebar (the pointer changes to the zoom tool), and drag the mouse diagonally across column 1 to enclose the top half of the text on page 3.

Notice how the text tool is still selected. This magnification shortcut lets you quickly zoom in to an area without changing tools.

5 With the text tool still selected, triple-click the first paragraph of the text to select it. (The paragraph spans most of the page.)

6 In the Control palette, type **.05** for Kerning (♨), then click the Bold (**B**) and Italic (*I*) buttons.

7 In the Control palette, click the Paragraph-view button (¶), and type **2** for First-line Indent (⇥≣), and click the Apply button.

8 Choose File > Save.

Wrapping text around a graphic

After placing a photograph, you will use the Text Wrap command to flow text around a rectangular graphic boundary that surrounds the photograph.

1 Click the pointer tool, and then choose View > Fit in Window. Click the Layers palette tab to activate it, and select the Art layer.

2 Choose File > Place, and double-click the 04ArtF.tif file in the 04Lesson folder.

3 With the loaded graphic icon displayed, click anywhere on page 3 to place the photograph. Then drag the photograph until it aligns to the bottom left corner of column 1.

The text overlaps the photograph. You will use the Text Wrap command to define how the text will wrap around the photograph.

4 With the photograph still selected, choose Element > Text Wrap. For Wrap Option, click the second icon (rectangular wrap). For Text Flow, make sure the third icon (wrap-all-sides) is selected. For Standoff in Picas, type **0** for Left, **p9** for Right, and **0** for both Top and Bottom. Then click OK.

The text stands 9 points from the right edge of the photograph.

5 With the pointer tool selected, click the text to select it as a text block, and drag the bottom windowshade handle down to display the last line of the paragraph.

6 Choose File > Save.

Placing a graphic

You will place and position another photograph in the upper portion of page 3.

1 Choose File > Place, and double-click the 04ArtG.tif file in the 04Lesson folder.

2 With the loaded graphic icon displayed, select the Art layer in the Layers palette, and click the upper portion of page 3 to place the photograph.

3 With the image still selected, drag the photograph until it snaps to the top left corner of column 2.

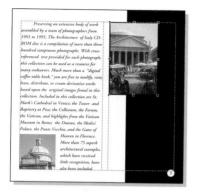

4 Choose File > Save.

Placing the caption

After placing and aligning the caption below the pantheon photograph, you will reduce the size of the caption text block.

1 Select the Text layer in the Layers palette.

2 Choose File > Place, and double-click 04TextD.doc in the 04Lesson folder.

3 Position the loaded text icon on page 3, column 2, underneath the photograph you just placed, and click to place the text.

4 Select the text tool (**T**), click the caption to establish an insertion point, and choose Edit > Select All.

5 In the Control palette, click the Character-view button (T), and type **10** for Size (T) and **13** for Leading ( ). Then click the Bold button (**B**).

You'll now zoom in to the area you are working, so you can align the caption with the adjacent text.

6 Hold down Ctrl (Windows) or Command (Macintosh) together with the spacebar, and drag the mouse diagonally across the bottom right quadrant of the page, stopping just above the page number. Be sure to include a small portion of the text in column 1.

7 From the horizontal ruler, drag to create a horizontal ruler guide at approximately 15p8, aligning it with the baseline of the text in column 1. From the vertical ruler, drag to create a vertical ruler guide at approximately 19p8.

You are ready to align the caption with the adjacent text.

💡 To toggle between the pointer tool and the currently selected tool, hold down Ctrl (Windows) or Command (Macintosh) and press spacebar.

8 Select the pointer tool, position the pointer over the caption and hold down the mouse button until the pointer changes to an arrowhead. Then drag the text block until the baseline of the first line of text is aligned with the horizontal ruler guide.

9 Choose View > Fit in Window.

You'll now reverse the text to the paper color and then move the text block onto the black box.

10 Select the text tool (**T**), click the caption to establish an insertion point, and choose Edit > Select All. In the Character-view of the Control palette, click the Reverse button (🖹).

11 Select the pointer tool, and then select the text block. Hold down Shift (to constrain the movement) and drag the text block to the right until it snaps to the 19p8 vertical ruler guide, maintaining its baseline alignment with the adjacent text.

You now need to resize the text block to fit in its new location.

12 With the text block still selected, in the Control palette, select the top left reference point in the Proxy icon. Then type **6p5** for W and **7p7** for H, and press Enter or Return.

13 Choose File > Save.

Creating a caption style

All captions in this publication will be formatted identically. You'll save time by creating a style that you can apply to each caption.

1 Select the text tool (**T**), and click the caption you just formatted to establish an insertion point. Then choose Type > Define Styles.

Notice that [Selection] is highlighted, and that the attributes of the caption are displayed under the style list. You'll create a new Caption style, replacing the default style of the same name.

2 Click New. Type **Caption** for Name, and click OK. When asked if you want to replace the existing style, click OK, and then click OK to close the dialog box.

PageMaker creates the new style using the attributes of the caption. The Styles palette displays the style Caption.

You will apply the style Caption to the caption. In this way, if you ever modify the Caption style, all captions will change uniformly.

3 With the insertion point still established in the caption, click Caption in the Styles palette.

You have completed assembling the first double-page spread.

4 Choose File > Save.

Assembling the second double-page spread

In addition to placing and formatting more text and graphic elements on the second double-page spread, you will create a rule above a paragraph. You will also use the Image Control command to modify an image.

Creating a rule aligned with a single-line paragraph

To frame each subhead visually, you will add a thick paragraph rule to the subheads. As in earlier steps in this lesson, you open a series of dialog boxes to set the stroke style and weight, color, horizontal width, and vertical positioning of the paragraph rules.

Remember: Rules are paragraph attributes and not independent graphic objects; they cannot be selected or edited with the pointer tool.

1 Click the page 4 icon to view the second double-page spread.

2 Magnify the view of the top portion of column 1 on page 5.

3 If necessary, select the text tool (**T**), and triple-click the subhead **Photographers** to select it.

4 In the Control palette, type **7** for Size (T) and **13** for Leading ( ). Choose Very Loose from the Tracking ( ) pop-up menu. Then click the Bold (**B**), Reverse ( ), and All Caps buttons ( ).

5 With the subhead still selected, choose Type > Paragraph, and type **2** for Left (to specify size of the indent). Make sure Left is selected for Alignment, and click the Rules button.

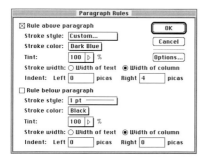

6 Select Rule Above Paragraph, and choose Custom for Stroke Style. In the Custom Stroke dialog box, choose the solid line, type **11** for Stroke Weight, leave Transparent Background selected, and click OK.

7 In the Paragraph Rules dialog box, choose Dark Blue for Stroke Color, and leave the Width of Column option selected. For Indent, type **4** for Right (to specify a 4-pica indentation).

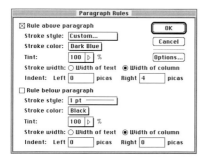

Note: The indent option indents the rule from the right or left edge of the column (for Width of Column) or text (for Width of Text).

8 Click the Options button. Type **p8** for Top (to specify where the top of the rule starts above the baseline), hold down Shift (Windows) or Option (Macintosh) and click OK to close all the dialog boxes.

9 Choose File > Save.

Creating and applying a subhead style

Since one more subhead must be formatted, you will save time by creating a style using the subhead you have already formatted.

1 With the subhead still selected, choose Type > Define Styles, and click New.

2 Type **Subhead** for Name, hold down Shift (Windows) or Option (Macintosh), and click OK.

3 With the subhead still selected, click Subhead in the Styles palette.

You will apply the Subhead style to another subhead. To center the subhead within the rule, you will change the indent of the second subhead.

4 Scroll to the bottom half of the page. With the text tool selected, click in the next subhead, **System Requirements**, to establish an insertion point. In the Styles palette, click Subhead.

5 With the insertion point still established in the second subhead, choose Type > Paragraph, and type **1** for Left, and click OK.

You will roll up the windowshade handle of this text block to push the system requirements subhead and paragraph to page 7 (where the remainder of the story is placed).

6 Select the pointer tool, click the text in column 1 to select it as a text block. Drag the bottom windowshade up just above the subhead **System Requirements**.

7 Choose File > Save.

Placing and cropping a graphic

After placing a photograph on the left page of the second double-page spread, you'll crop the edges of the photograph to align it with the edges of the page.

1 Choose View > Fit in Window. In the Layers palette, select the Art layer.

2 Choose File > Place and double-click 04ArtH.tif in the 04Lesson folder.

3 When prompted to include a copy of the graphic in the publication, click No.

4 With the loaded graphic icon displayed, click the upper portion of the left page (page 4).

Using the control palette, you'll align the right edge of the photograph precisely with the inside edge of the page, letting its other edges overlap the outside edges of the page.

5 In the Control palette Proxy icon, select the top right reference point. Type **0** for X, and **–0p9** for Y. Press Enter or Return.

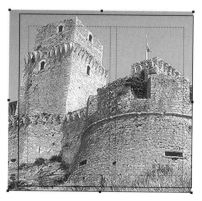

As with all images in this project that extend to the edge of the page, this photograph was sized to allow for a bleed. Once again, you'll crop the photograph to the page edges.

6 Select the cropping tool (☐), position the tool over the top left graphic handle of the photograph, and drag down and right to the corner of the page.

7 With the cropping tool still selected, position the cursor over the bottom-center graphics handle, and drag up to the bottom edge of the page.

8 Choose File > Save.

Placing a graphic

You will place a photograph in the lower right corner of page 5. You'll align it to a ruler guide just above the page-number and the right margin.

1 Magnify the view of the lower half portion of page 5.

2 From the horizontal ruler, drag to create a horizontal ruler guide at approximately 25p6.

3 Choose File > Place, and double-click 04ArtI.tif in the 04Lesson folder.

4 With the loaded graphic icon displayed, click anywhere in the lower right corner of the right page to place the photograph.

5 Once placed, drag the photograph until its bottom edge snaps to the 25p6 horizontal ruler guide and the right margin guide.

6 Choose File > Save.

Placing and modifying an image

The Image Control command makes it possible to alter the appearance of line art or bitmap or grayscale images, adjusting the lightness or darkness of an entire image and adjusting the screen pattern (where you specify whether the image is composed of dots or lines).

You will place a grayscale image and use the Image Control command to reverse the light and dark areas within the image.

Note: You cannot use the Image Control command to alter a color image. Also, images adjusted with the Image Control command must be printed to a PostScript printing device.

1 Choose View > Fit in Window.

2 Choose File > Place, and double-click 04ArtJ.tif in the 04Lesson folder.

3 With the loaded graphic icon displayed, click in the upper right corner of the right page (in the black box) to place the illustration.

4 With the illustration still selected, in the Control palette make sure the top left reference point in the Proxy icon is selected. Type **20p4** for X and **p7** for Y, and press Enter or Return to position the illustration.

5 With the illustration still selected, choose Element > Image > Image Control.

Refer to the *Adobe PageMaker 7.0 User Guide* for more information about the Image Control command.

6 Depending upon your system, do one of the following:

• Windows: Set the Contrast option to **-50**, and click OK.

• Macintosh: Click the Reverse Grey Levels button (), and click OK.

The black portions of the image reverse to white, and vice versa.

Note:: Unlike text, you cannot reverse an imported bitmap image by applying the paper color to it. PageMaker applies a color to only the black and gray portions of the image. The white would remain white.

7 Choose File > Save.

Placing the captions

After placing the captions that accompany the illustration and photograph on the right page, you will apply the style Caption and position the captions above the photograph.

1 From the vertical ruler, drag to create a vertical ruler guide at approximately 19p8.

2 Magnify the view of the portion of the black box between the two images, then click the Text layer in the Layers palette.

3 Choose File > Place, and double-click 04TextE.doc in the 04Lesson folder.

4 With the loaded text icon displayed, drag to define a text block that extends from the 19p8 vertical ruler guide to the right margin guide on the right page (exact height is not important), taking note of its approximate position to be able to select it with the text tool.

Since the placed text is colored black, it cannot be viewed on the black rectangle.

5 Select the text tool (**T**), click in the area where you just placed the captions to establish an insertion point, choose Edit > Select All, and select Caption in the Style palette.

(Windows only) If the captions remain invisible, press Ctrl together with the Shift and F12 keys to redraw the screen.

6 From the horizontal ruler, drag to create a horizontal ruler guide at approximately 12p5, aligning it with the baseline of the text in column 1. (You may need to scroll the page.)

7 Select the pointer tool, and click the caption text to select the text block. Use the arrow keys or Control palette nudge buttons to move the text block until the baseline of the first line of the caption is aligned with the 12p5 horizontal ruler guide.

8 With the captions still selected as a text block, drag the bottom windowshade handle down to display the entire story.

You need to separate the two captions. You'll edit the Caption style to include space after each paragraph.

9 Hold down Control (Windows) or Command (Macintosh), and click the Caption style. Click the Para button, and type **p26** for After. Then hold down Shift (Windows) or Option (Macintosh), and click OK to close the dialog boxes.

PageMaker inserts 26 points between the captions. Because 26 points is twice the leading value, the captions remain aligned with the adjacent text.

The second double-page spread is complete.

10 Choose View > Fit in Window.

11 Choose File > Save.

Assembling the last spread

The design of the last spread closely follows the design of the previous spread.

Placing the large graphic on page 6

As with page 4, you'll place a full-page version of one of the photographs from the cover onto page 6. Rather than repeat the steps of placing, positioning, and cropping the image, you can copy and paste the image

from page 4, and then replace it with the new image. PageMaker will replace the image, using the existing cropping rectangle.

1 With the pointer tool selected, click the image on page 4 to select it. Choose Edit > Copy.

You'll now paste it on page 6 using the *power paste* option, which pastes a copy in the exact same position on the page.

2 Click the page 6 icon. Hold down Alt (Windows) or Option (Macintosh), and choose Edit > Paste.

3 With the pasted image still selected, choose File > Place. Click 04ArtK.tif in the 04Lesson folder (do not double-click it). Select Replacing Entire Graphic, and make sure Retain Cropping Data is selected, then click Open (Windows) or OK (Macintosh).

PageMaker replaces the image. In addition to cropping the image using the existing cropping rectangle, PageMaker also scales the image, if necessary, to fit within the bounding box of the original image.

4 Choose File > Save.

Finishing the last spread

After placing and positioning a photograph on page 7, you'll move the address and copyright information to the bottom of the page and reformat it.

1 From the horizontal ruler, drag to create a horizontal ruler guide at approximately 25p6.

2 Choose File > Place and double-click the 04ArtL.tif file in the 04Lesson folder.

3 With the loaded graphic icon displayed, make sure the Art layer is still selected, and click in the lower portion of page 7 to place the photograph. Then drag the photograph until its bottom right corner snaps to the intersection of the 25p6 ruler guide and the right margin guide.

You'll now zoom in to the area you'll be working on.

4 Hold down Ctrl (Windows) or Command (Macintosh) together with the spacebar, and drag across the top two-thirds of column 1, page 7 (as shown below), enclosing the entire text block and a small portion of the image in column 2.

Before you move the address and copyright information to the bottom of the page, you'll first change the text to a smaller point size and reduce the leading.

5 Select the text tool (**T**), position the tool over the sentence that begins "For more information," and triple-click to select the entire paragraph. Hold down Shift, and click the last line (containing the words "All rights reserved.").

PageMaker extends the selection to the end of the text block.

6 In the control palette, type **7** for Size (↕**T**) and **9** for Leading (⊥ₐ), and click the Apply button (▤).

7 Select the pointer tool, click the text to select it as a text block. Drag the bottom windowshade handle up, just below the last line of the paragraph listing the system requirements.

8 Click the down arrow in the bottom windowshade handle. The pointer changes to the loaded text icon. Position the icon in the lower portion of column 1, and click. (You'll reposition the text block once it is placed.)

9 Select the hand tool (✋). Position the tool in the middle of the page and drag the page up to display the bottom half of the page.

10 Select the pointer tool. Drag the text block to align the baseline of the last line of text with the 25p6 ruler guide.

You have finished this spread.

11 Double-click the hand tool to switch to the fit-in-window view.

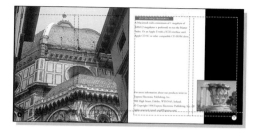

12 Choose File > Save.

Assembling the back cover

The back cover uses the same four images as found on the front cover. As with the front cover, you will deselect the display of the master-page elements.

1 Click the page 8 icon to switch to the back cover. Then, choose View > Display Master Items to deselect the option.

PageMaker turns off the display of the master page elements.

You are now ready to copy the four images from the cover.

2 Click the page 1 icon.

3 In the Layers palette, click the lock column (next to the eye icon) in the Text layer to lock the layer. The Lock icon appears. Click the Art layer to activate it.

4 Select the pointer tool, and choose Edit > Select All. Then, choose Edit > Copy.

5 Click the page 8 icon. Then Choose Edit > Paste.

Because the images were on a right page and the back cover is a left page, PageMaker pastes the images on the pasteboard to the right of page 8 (where a right page would be).

You'll now use the control palette to position the images on the page. The top right corner of the page is the zero point and therefore is the easiest point to use for alignment.

6 With the images still selected, click the top right reference point in the Proxy icon. Type **0** for both X and Y, and click Enter or Return.

PageMaker positions the images on the page.

You have finished assembling the booklet.

7 Choose View > Hide Guides to hide the guides.

8 Choose File > Save to save the 04Work.pmd publication.

If you have determined that your service provider will perform all the prepress tasks (including resetting the bleeds), you are ready to deliver the 04Work.pmd file to your service provider. Be sure to include all image files that are linked to the publication.

9 If you would like to Print the Jewelcase booklet, choose File > Print. Select the printer you want to print to (Windows) and select the appropriate PPD. Click Print. You can also Export Adobe PDF, as described in Creating an Adobe PDF version of the flyer on page 41.

Building a booklet

The Build Booklet plug-in lets you create a copy of your current publication in which pages are arranged for printing multipage spreads or signatures. This publishing technique is known as *page imposition*. For this project, two pages are printed on each sheet of paper. When the paper is folded, the book pages are in the correct order. In your booklet, the first and last pages will be printed on one page, the second page on the same sheet as the second-to-last page, and so on.

Previewing the pages

Before building the booklet, you want to make sure that your text and layout are finished. Major changes may change the pagination and require that you rebuild your booklet.

To help you understand the results of using Build Booklet, you'll also open a finished version of the booklet with the pages already rearranged by Build Booklet.

1 Browse through your publication, making sure that everything is in order.

PageMaker's page sorting option lets you view thumbnails of your publication pages so you can see the entire publication at once.

2 Choose Layout > Sort Pages. On the Macintosh, click the Options button, select Show Detailed Thumbnails, and click OK.

Resize the window if necessary to see all the pages at once.

3 Click Cancel when you have finished viewing the pages.

4 Choose File > Open, and double-click 04FnlBkt.pmd in the 04Lesson folder.

5 Choose Layout > Sort Pages. Resize the window if necessary to see all the pages at once. To increase the size of the thumbnails, click the Build Booklet zoom tool.

The eight pages of the booklet have been distributed between four larger pages. Page 1 of the booklet contains the original page 1 and page 8. Booklet page 2 contains the original pages 2 and 7; booklet page 3 contains original pages 3 and 6; and booklet page 4 contains original pages 4 and 5.

6 Click Cancel when you have finished viewing the pages.

7 Choose File > Close to close 04FnlBkt.pmd and return to your publication. If prompted to save before closing, click No.

Using Build Booklet

You are now ready to use Build Booklet.

1 With 04Work.pmd open, choose Utilities > Plug-ins > Build Booklet.

2 Choose 2-up Saddle Stitch for Layout.

This option is for standard booklet printing, where double-sided pages are folded once and fastened along the fold.

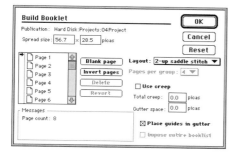

After you choose a layout, PageMaker calculates the spread size for you.

The Build Booklet plug-in gives you several additional options for arranging your booklet. You can adjust the spread size, delete extra pages, insert blank pages, rearrange pages, and adjust for creep. For more information, refer to the *Adobe PageMaker 7.0 User Guide*.

3 Leave the Place Guides in Gutter option selected. Click OK to create the booklet.

4 When prompted, choose to save your original document.

The Build Booklet plug-in saves and closes the current document, and then opens a new, untitled version that has the expanded spread size and new page sequence.

5 Save the new file as 04Booklt.pmd in the 04Lesson folder.

Page 1 of the booklet is a 56p7 by 28p6 page that contains the original page 1 and page 8.

Notice that the left edge of page 1 and the right edge of page 8 abut each other and will not need to bleed. Because this is a saddle-stitch booklet, the binding edge of each page always abuts another page in the printed signature. Therefore any cropping you applied to images on the binding edge will be left in place during the prepress preparations.

Continue to page through your document.

6 When you have finished browsing through the booklet, close all open files and quit the Adobe PageMaker application.

Printing the booklet

In addition to trapping and resetting the bleeds, the prepress tasks will include specifying a custom page size and including printer's marks and page information. For more information on these prepress tasks, refer to the *Adobe PageMaker 7.0 User Guide*.

Designed to be printed on a commercial printing press, this publication requires a total of four process color (CMYK) film separations. Knowing your printer plans to print this publication using a line screen frequency of 150 lpi, your service provider will create the four film separations on a image-setter at a resolution of 2400 dpi. Once the film separations are prepared, you can deliver them to your printer.

Review questions

1 What is meant by the term bleed?

2 What are some advantages to using layers?

3 How do you adjust the position of text within a frame?

4 How do you make text flow around a graphic?

Answers

1 Printed areas that extend beyond the trim marks of the page.

2 Layers let you do the following:

• Work with objects without accidentally moving or modifying objects on other layers

• Treat similar objects together without grouping

• Hide or display objects

• Lock a layer to prevent modification of its objects

• Quickly change the stacking order of objects

3 Choose Element > Frame > Frame Options. Select options and click OK.

4 Select the graphic, and choose Element > Text Wrap. For Wrap Option, click the second (rectangular wrap) icon. For Text Flow,

PageMaker selects the third (wrap-all-sides) icon. Type the degree of offset you want and click OK. For irregular wraps, you can click on the text-wrap border to add new handles, and drag edges or handles to modify the area that keeps text away.

Lesson 5

Cycling guidebook

In this eight-page guidebook to the Tour de France, one of the world's great cycling events, you get a chance to go beyond the basics of using PageMaker. As you assemble and change this dramatic and playful piece, you will learn the power of PageMaker's automatic layout adjustment options, see how multiple master pages and paragraph styles can streamline the production of a publication, and become adept at manipulating text blocks and frames.

To create this guidebook, you begin by opening an Adobe PageMaker publication that has been partially completed. First you will finish the cover, then resize the page and margins to see how PageMaker can automatically adjust the layout for you. Next, you will edit the other master pages to match the Document Master. Then you will revise the paragraph styles and refine the layout on several spreads.

This project covers:

• Creating a polygon frame

• Placing text or graphics within frames

• Converting an existing rectangle into a frame

• Editing styles

• Basing one style on an existing style

• Using the Bullets and Numbers plug-in

• Using the Drop Cap plug-in

• Using the adjust layout options when changing page size, margins, and master pages

• Editing and applying master pages

At the end of this lesson, you'll have an eight-page, six-color booklet.

It should take you about 2 hours to complete this project.

Before you begin

1 Before launching PageMaker, return all settings to their defaults by deleting the PageMaker 7.0 preferences file. See "Restoring default settings" in Lesson 1.

Note: Windows users need to unlock the lesson files before using them. For information, see Copying the Classroom in a Book files on page 4.

2 In addition to the commonly used fonts listed in the Getting Started chapter, make sure that the following fonts are installed: AGaramond, AGaramond Bold, Myriad Bold, Myriad Roman, and Zapf Dingbats.

Windows only: Because of the way Windows handles fonts, you must apply bold to Myriad Roman to use Myriad Bold.

For this lesson, you need the French hyphenation and spelling dictionary.

3 If you did not install the French dictionary when you installed PageMaker, drag the Français folder from the 05Lesson folder into either PageMaker 7.0\rsrc\linguist\prx (Windows) or Adobe PageMaker 7.0:RSRC: Linguist:Proximity (Macintosh).

4 Start PageMaker, and then open the 05Final.pmd file in the 05Lesson folder.

This publication is an eight-page booklet containing photographs, maps, and text. The text was entered and formatted in a word-processing application, and then placed into the Adobe PageMaker document.

5 If the publication window does not fill the screen, click the Maximize button in the title bar to expand the window.

6 Leave this file open so you can use it as a visual reference during the lesson. Click the page icons in the bottom left corner to examine each spread in the document. Zoom in where you want to take a closer look.

Setting up the document

Start by opening a document that has been partially completed for you.

1 Choose File > Open, and then open 05Begin.pmt in the 05Lesson folder.

Since the focus of this project is automatic layout adjustment and working with paragraph styles, much of the placing and positioning of text and graphic elements has been done for you. Some colors, styles, and master pages have already been defined in the Colors, Styles, and Master Pages palettes as well.

This booklet starts out as an eight-page document, 6 inches by 9 inches in size. Once you finish the cover, you will change its page size and margins to see how PageMaker can automatically adjust a publication for you.

2 If the publication window does not fill the screen, click the Maximize button in the title bar to expand the window.

3 Choose File > Preferences > General. Choose Picas for both Measurements In and Vertical Ruler. In order to speed up screen redraw, keep Standard selected for Graphics display. Leave all other settings at their default values as well. Click OK.

The three palettes you'll use most often in creating this booklet are the Styles, Colors and Master Pages palettes. You can combine the three, and leave more room to view your page.

4 Choose Window > Show Master Pages. Drag the Master Pages tab to the Colors and Styles palette, and then click the Close box of the Layers palette.

5 Choose File > Save As, type **05Work.pmd** for the name, and save the publication in the 05Lesson folder.

Finishing the cover

The cover of the booklet is complete except for a photographic image, which you'll place in a polygon frame.

Creating the polygon frame

You'll first create the polygon frame on the cover and set the frame options.

1 If necessary, click the page 1 icon in the bottom left corner to go to the cover page.

2 Drag the Control palette over the pasteboard just right of the page so you can view the entire page. You need to see only the X and Y values of the Control palette to draw the polygon frame. Minimize and move the palettes as well if they are blocking your view of the page.

3 Choose View > Show Guides.

The prepositioned guides and the Control palette will help you position the points of the polygon.

4 Select the polygon frame tool (⊗). Starting at the center of the wheel, position the tool at each location shown in the illustration and click to create the points of the polygon. Keep in mind the following tips:

• Create the polygon in a clockwise direction.

• Let the tool snap to the guides.

• Click only once for each point. (If you double-click before you complete the polygon, PageMaker closes the polygon, but does not draw a stroke between the start and end points. If you double-click over the starting point, PageMaker closes the polygon, and begins another polygon at the same point.)

• Use the Control palette to determine the tool location.

• Hold down shift as you create the horizontal or vertical edges of the polygon, that is, as you move between B and C, C and D, and D and E.

• Press Backspace or Delete to erase the last point you clicked.

- To close the polygon, position the tool over the center of the wheel (the pointer changes to a square), and click.

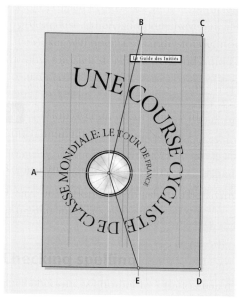

A. Start and end here: x=15p, y=36p
B. x=22p, y=0p C. x=36p, y=0p D. x=36p, y=54p
E. x=22p, y=54p

It is important that the polygon touch the edges of the page. If it doesn't, PageMaker may not resize it correctly. You can reposition the points of a polygon after you have drawn it.

5 If you need to reposition some points of the polygon, double-click the polygon to display its points. Drag the points to the correct locations. (Remember to pause before you drag so PageMaker will display the mouse position in the Control palette.)

6 With the frame still selected, choose Element > Frame > Frame Options.

The frame options control the position of the content within the frame, as well as reconciling the difference in size between the frame and the content. You can choose whether PageMaker should clip the content to fit the frame, resize the frame to fit the content, or scale the content to fit the frame.

For this cover, you'll clip the content (a photograph) to match the frame. By clipping (rather than scaling) the photograph, the image maintains its original dimensions, even when you increase the page size later.

7 Click Open or OK to accept the default setting.

8 Choose File > Save to save the publication.

Placing the image in the frame

You'll place the photographic image directly into the frame and then apply a color to it. Once you've placed a graphic inside a frame, you cannot rotate, skew, or flip it independent of its frame. However, depending upon the type of image, you can apply a color, manipulate the image using image control or Photoshop effects, or pan the image within the frame.

1 Select the pointer tool and select the frame.

2 Choose File > Place and select 05ArtA.tif (in the 05Lesson folder). Click Open (Windows) or OK (Macintosh) to accept the default place options.

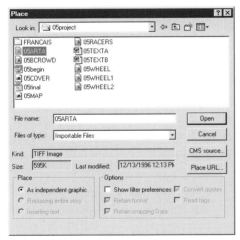

Default option inserts content into selected frame

PageMaker inserts the photograph into the frame, clipping the portion that doesn't fit within its boundaries.

Just like any other PageMaker drawn object, a frame can have both a stroke and fill. Because the photograph fills the entire frame, the fill of this frame is not visible. However, if the image was small, you could apply a fill as well. For this project, you'll remove the stroke from the frame.

3 With the frame still selected, click the Colors tab to display the Colors palette. Then, click the Stroke button (✎) in the Colors palette and select None.

You may notice a gray outline around the polygon frame. Unlike a regular polygon, a polygon frame displays a non-printing gray outline, even when it has no stroke, to help you distinguish between the two types.

You will apply a green spot color to the image. It is important to note that if you select only the frame and apply a color, you change the color of its stroke or fill or both (depending upon which button is selected in the Colors palette). If you select the content and apply a color, you apply the color to the image.

4 To select the content, hold down Ctrl (Windows) or Command (Macintosh) and click the image until four special handles appear as shown below. If you click on top of other objects, you may have to click several times to select the frame content.

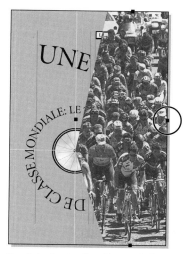

Special selection handles mark frame content

5 With the content still selected, select Pantone 802 2x CVC in the Colors palette.

Note: *You can apply color to 1-bit (monochrome) and grayscale bitmap images, but not color bitmap images.*

The polygon is covering other objects on the page and needs to move back in the stacking order. It should be behind all the objects except the orange background. Rather than use the Send Backward command repeatedly to send it back object by object in the stacking order, you'll send it all the way to the back, and then bring it up one level.

6 With the pointer tool selected, select the frame (currently the content is selected, not the frame). Choose Element > Arrange > Send to Back. (The polygon disappears behind the orange background.) Choose Element > Arrange > Bring Forward.

The cover is complete.

7 Choose File > Save to save the publication.

Changing the page size and margins

You'll now change the page size and margins of the Document Master and watch PageMaker adjust the layout automatically.

When you change the page settings of a publication, PageMaker can move and scale text and graphics automatically, based on their relationships to the page edges, margins, and guides.

1 Choose File > Preferences > Layout Adjustment and select "OK to Resize Groups and Imported Graphics." Leave all other settings at their default values. Click OK.

2 Choose File > Document Setup. Set the page dimensions to **36** by **57** picas. Select Adjust Layout. For Margins, type **2p6** for Inside, Outside, and Top, and type **2p10** for Bottom. Then click OK.

PageMaker changes the page size and margins. It adjusts the column width, and because the yellow frame spanned the column, it stretches it to the new width. The polygon frame and the orange background, which are aligned precisely to the edges of the page, also stretch to match the page size. However, the image within the polygon frame does not change size because the

frame option "Clip content to fit frame" maintains the original size of the content, regardless of how you change the frame.

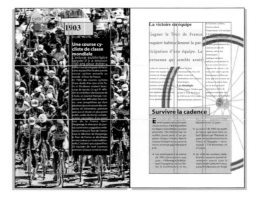

Before 　 *After*

3 Choose File > Save to save the publication.

4 Click the page 2 icon to switch to the next spread.

Notice that PageMaker changed the page size throughout the document, but did not change the margins on this spread. When you change margins using the Document Setup dialog box, PageMaker changes the margins of only the Document Master (master page) and any pages that have the

Document Master applied to them. To change the margins of pages that have other master pages applied to them, you must modify each master page individually.

5 Click the Master Pages palette tab to display the Master Pages palette.

Notice that the 2-Col / 3-Col master is selected for pages 2 and 3.

So that you can see the power of the Adjust Layout option, you will first change the margins without selecting Adjust Layout.

6 Choose Master Page Options from the Master Page palette menu. Change the Inside, Outside, and Top margins to **2p6** and change the Bottom margin to **2p10**. Click OK.

You can copy a value in an edit box, and paste it in another edit box. First select the value, hold down Ctrl (Windows) or Command (Macintosh) and press **C**. Move the cursor to the next edit box by pressing tab. Then hold down Ctrl (Windows) or Command (Macintosh) and press **V**.

PageMaker changes the margins and column guides, but leaves any existing text or graphics untouched.

After margin change without Adjust Layout

7 Choose Edit > Undo Change Master.

The spread returns to the previous margin settings. Now change the margins again using the Adjust Layout option.

8 Choose Master Page Options from the Master Page palette menu. Once again, change the Inside, Outside, and Top margins to **2p6** and change the Bottom margin to **2p10**. Select Adjust Layout, and click OK.

PageMaker changes the margins and column guides, adjusting the text and graphics
that were aligned to the guides to the new
layout.

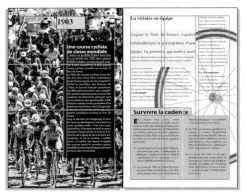

After margin change with Adjust Layout

The sidebar on page 2 was originally
touching the yellow frame containing
1903. Because the sidebar was not aligned
to any horizontal guides, PageMaker did
not move it as it did the yellow frame.

9 Select the pointer tool, hold down Shift
(to constrain the movement), and then drag
the black frame on page 2 up until its top
edge touches the bottom edge of the yellow
frame.

This guidebook includes one more master
page, 3-Col / 3-Col. You need to change the
margins on this master as well.

10 Double-click 3-Col / 3-Col in the Master
Pages palette.

Note: *This shortcut opens the Master Page
Options dialog box but does not apply the
master page to the currently displayed pages.*

11 Type **2p6** for Inside, Outside, and Top margins and **2p10** for Bottom margin. Because no page currently uses this master page, you do not need to select the Adjust Layout option. Click OK.

12 Choose File > Save to save the publication.

Working with styles

Before you fix the layout on page 3, you'll first work with the paragraph styles.

As you learned in Lesson 3, a style is a set of formatting attributes that you can name and apply to paragraphs. Even in this guidebook, which does not have a rigidly consistent style, styles make formatting the text much easier. Styles are especially useful when you repeat formatting characteristics in several places or are still experimenting with the layout of a publication.

You'll change several styles in this guidebook.

Editing the Body Text style

The first style change you'll make is to the Body Text style. You'll change its alignment and dictionary settings.

Body text is the style applied to the body of the story **La victoire en équipe**.

1 With pages 2 and 3 still displayed, select the zoom tool ( ) and click the upper middle portion of page 3. Click again if necessary so that you can clearly see the text in all three columns.

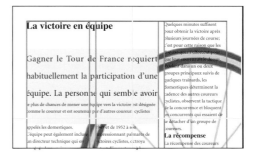

2 Click the Styles palette tab to display the Styles palette (or choose Window > Show Styles palette).

3 Select the text tool (**T**), and in the middle of column 2, click an insertion point in the paragraph below the yellow box.

Body Text is highlighted in the Styles palette. Notice that the paragraphs in this story have no hyphenation and are left-justified with a ragged right edge.

4 Double-click Body Text in the Styles palette. Click the Para button, choose Justify for Alignment and Français for Dictionary menu. Press Shift (Windows) or Option (Macintosh) and click OK to accept your changes and close the dialog boxes.

Notice that the body of the article changes to full justification and several words are now hyphenated. Now that the spelling and hyphenation dictionary matches the language of the text, PageMaker can use it to hyphenate words when necessary.

5 Choose File > Save to save the publication.

Basing styles on other styles

Styles in PageMaker can be based on other styles. For example, the Subhead 1 style is based on the Headline style, and Subhead 2 is based on Subhead 1. The subheads contain all the characteristics of the Headline style, except the point size and leading are smaller, and they use a different leading method. Basing one style on another saves time when creating and editing styles. If you change the font of the Headline style, the font of each style that is based on the Headline style changes as well.

Next you'll examine the current styles, then change the font and color of the Headline style and see how the Subhead 1 and Subhead 2 styles also change. You'll use several different techniques to edit the styles.

1 Select Type > Define Styles. Select the Subhead 1 style, and then click Edit to display the Style Options dialog box.

Notice that the Subhead 1 style is based on the Headline style.

2 Click Cancel, and then double-click the Headline style. The Headline style is based on No Style because it is the top style in the hierarchy.

Note: The Next Style pop-up menu lets you specify the style to apply to the next paragraph you create when you press Enter or Return. This feature works only on text that is typed directly into PageMaker and does not change existing text in the publication.

Next, you'll look at three examples of paragraphs using Headline, Subhead 1, and Subhead 2.

3 Hold down Shift (Windows) or Option (Macintosh) and click Cancel to close the dialog boxes.

4 Hold down Alt (Windows) or Option (Macintosh) and double-click the zoom tool (🔍) in the tool palette to return to the Fit in Window view.

5 Select the text tool (**T**), click an insertion point in **1903** at the top of page 2. Notice that Headline is highlighted in the Styles palette and that the Control palette shows the selected font is AGaramond. Now click an insertion point in the head **La victoire en équipe** at the top of page 3. Notice that Subhead 1 is the selected style and that the font is still set to AGaramond. Finally, click the small subhead **La stratégie** a little farther down column 1. (Zoom in if necessary.) This paragraph uses the Subhead 2 style and AGaramond is still the selected font.

You are now ready to redefine the Headline style.

6 Hold down Ctrl (Windows) or Command (Macintosh) and click Headline in the Styles palette.

Note: *This shortcut to the Style Options dialog box does not apply the style to the paragraph containing the cursor (or to selected paragraphs if any are selected). However, when you double-click a style in the palette (as you did when you edited the Body Text style), PageMaker applies the style and then displays the Style Options dialog box. You can also open the Style Options dialog box from the Styles palette menu or by choosing Type > Define Styles.*

7 Click the Char button. Change the font to Myriad Roman, choose Purple for Color, and select Bold for Type Style. Click OK.

Note: *Because of the way fonts are defined, when you apply bold to Myriad Roman, PageMaker actually uses Myriad Bold. On the Macintosh, you can get the same result if you select Myriad Bold directly.*

8 Click the Para button. Select Center for Alignment and Français for Dictionary. Hold down Shift (Windows) or Option (Macintosh), and then click OK to close the dialog boxes.

The font changes in all text tagged with the Headline, Subhead 1, or Subhead 2 style. This is an excellent way of ensuring that elements in a document remain consistent.

9 Click an insertion point in the Subhead 1 (**La victoire en équipe**) and then in the Subhead 2 (**La stratégie**), that you checked before, and notice that they have all changed to purple Myriad.

Now you fine-tune the Subhead 1 and Subhead 2 styles.

10 Choose Type > Define Styles. Then double-click the Subhead 1 style.

11 Click the Char button, type **26** for Size and **26** for Leading, and then click OK.

12 Click the Para button. Choose Left for Alignment. Click OK twice to return to the Define Styles dialog box.

You'll now change the point size of Subhead 2. To keep the text aligned in adjacent columns, you'll change the leading for Subhead 2 to the same value as used in the Body Text style.

13 Double-click the Subhead 2 style. Click the Char button, and type **13** for both Size and Leading. Then click OK.

So the Subhead 2 stands out more from the body text, you'll add space before each subhead. You'll set the space to the same value as the leading, again to maintain alignment between columns.

14 Click the Para button and type **p13** for Before. Press Shift (Windows) or Option (Macintosh) and click OK to close dialog boxes.

Note: Although 12 points make a pica, you can enter higher values entirely in points (preceded by p, such as p13 or 0p13) and let PageMaker convert the number into picas and points for you.

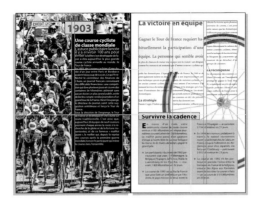

15 Save 05Work.pmd.

Creating a style based on another style

Now you'll create a second body text style that incorporates an indent. You'll base it on the Body Text style. While you'll apply Body Text Indent to only one paragraph in this story, you'll need both these styles for text you place later in this lesson.

1 Zoom in to the middle of column 2 on page 3.

2 With the text tool selected, click an insertion point in the paragraph that starts "Quelques minutes…."

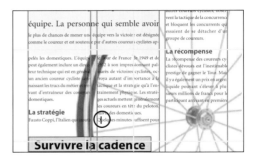

3 Click the New button (⬚) in the Styles palette.

The Style Options dialog box appears with Body Text selected for Based On.

4 Type **Body Text Indent** for Name.

5 Click the Para button, and then type **1p2** for First line indent. Press Shift (Windows) or Option (Macintosh) and click OK to close the dialog boxes.

PageMaker creates the new style but does not change the paragraph containing the cursor.

6 Click the new Body Text Indent style in the Styles palette to apply it to the paragraph.

7 Save 05Work.pmd.

Finishing the first spread

With the new page size, margins, and style definitions, the **La victoire en équipe** story no longer fits the three columns. You'll need to adjust the yellow box and each of the text blocks.

To make it easier to work, you'll first magnify the top half of page 3.

1 Adjust the view of the page if necessary so you can see all three columns in the top half of the page.

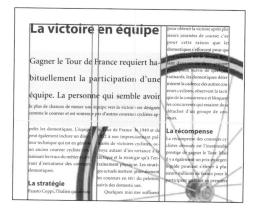

2 Select the pointer tool, and then select the yellow box. Depending upon where you click, you may need to hold down Ctrl (Windows) or Command (Macintosh) and click again to select the box and not the text block.

3 Drag the box until its top edge rests on the baseline of the headline **La victoire en équipe**.

4 With the pointer tool still selected, click on a character in the text on top of the yellow box to select the text block. Drag the text block up so that the top of its bounding box rests on the baseline of the headline **La victoire en équipe**.

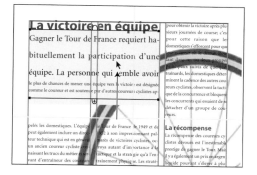

5 Drag the bottom windowshade handle up so that only three lines of text are displayed.

Instead of pulling down a ruler guide, you'll keep the text block selected and use its bounding box as a guide.

6 Hold down Shift and select the yellow box. Release the Shift key, and then drag the bottom center handle of the box up flush with the bottom edge of the text block. (The Y location in the Control palette should be approximately 11p11.)

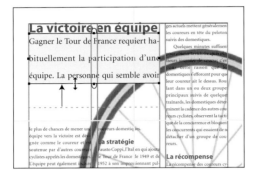

Now you will move the two smaller text blocks up. To help you align these text blocks with the text in column 3, you'll first reposition a ruler guide.

7 Position the pointer tool in the margin or between columns 1 and 2, over the ruler guide that currently sits at the top of the small text blocks in columns 1 and 2. Drag the guide until it's flush with the first baseline below the yellow box in column 3 (as shown below; a Y location of approximately 12p11 in the Control palette). Zoom in if necessary.

8 Select the text block in column 1, and then hold down Shift and select the text block in column 2. Drag both text blocks up until the baseline of the first line of text in each aligns with the newly moved ruler guide.

9 Drag the bottom windowshade handle of the text block in column 1 down until the subhead **La stratégie** and three more lines of text move to column 1 (approximately 29p8 for Y in the Control palette).

Remember: If you pause before you begin dragging, the Control palette displays the mouse position as you drag.

10 Drag a new ruler guide from the horizontal ruler so that it is flush with the bottom edge of the text block in column 1.

11 Drag the bottom windowshade handle of the text block in column 2 down until it is aligned with the new ruler guide.

12 Select the text block in column 3 and drag its bottom windowshade handle down until it's aligned with the new ruler guide.

13 Hold down Alt (Windows) or Option (Macintosh) and double-click the zoom tool (🔍) to return to the Fit in Window view.

14 Save 05Work.pmd. Then click the page 4 icon.

Laying out the next spread

Now you will complete the layout for the spread on pages 4 and 5. As you work, pan the page as necessary and use the zoom tool to magnify the area you are editing.

Setting text wrap

Before you place the text for this spread, you'll first apply text wrap to the graphic. As you learned in previous lessons, text wrap forces text to move around or jump over a graphic, rather than flow on top of it.

PageMaker provides a default rectangular text wrap boundary, but you can customize the boundary by adding and moving points as needed to create the shape you want.

1 Select the pointer tool, and then click the map to select it.

2 Choose Element > Text Wrap. For Wrap Option, select the second icon (rectangular wrap). For Text Flow, make sure the third icon (wrap all sides) is selected. Then for Standoff in Picas, type **0** for Left, Right, Top, and Bottom, and then click OK.

PageMaker displays the text wrap boundary (the dotted line with the diamond-shaped handles).

You'll now customize this text wrap boundary. Be careful in the next step to drag the boundary, not click it. (Clicking a text wrap boundary inserts a new handle, which you'll do in step 4.)

3 With the map still selected, hold down Shift (to constrain the movement) and drag the top text wrap boundary straight down until it is flush with the top of the **A** of **Après.**

4 Click on the top wrap boundary at the margin guide of page 5 to create a new text wrap handle. Create another new handle to the left of the first (its location is not important).

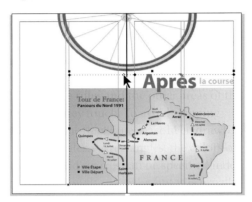

The top boundary now consists of three segments.

5 Drag the left segment of the top wrap boundary down to the top edge of the map. (Be careful to keep the handles aligned with the column guides.)

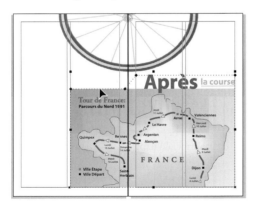

6 Hold down Shift and drag the newest handle to the right, below the other handle you created.

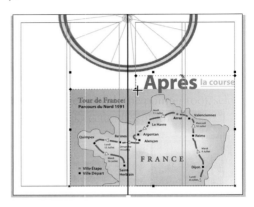

7 Save 05Work.pmd.

Flowing the story

You'll now place the text for this spread. As with the other text used in this project, the text was prepared in Microsoft Word. The text has been formatted with styles whose names are the same as style names in the PageMaker publication. When you place text with a style name that matches an existing PageMaker style, PageMaker applies the PageMaker version of the style to the text.

1 Choose File > Place, select 05TextA.doc in the 05Lesson folder, make sure the Retain Format option is selected, and click Open or OK.

When a style name doesn't match an existing PageMaker style, the Retain Format option retains the style definition used in the word-processing program.

2 Choose Layout > Autoflow to turn on the Autoflow option.

3 Position the loaded text icon at the top of column 1 on page 4 (the icon should snap to the margins) and click.

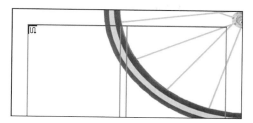

The text flows from column to column across the spread, wrapping around the graphic boundary.

When you autoflow text, PageMaker flows each text block the full length of the column. Even if a graphic with text wrap applied forces the text to wrap, the text block definition spans the full length and width of the column. PageMaker remembers these boundaries. If you resize or move a graphic, the text reflows into any remaining space in the column.

To see for yourself how the text reflows, you'll temporarily move the map. You'll then return it to its current location. Be careful when you drag the map that you keep the pointer in the middle of the map. You don't want to resize it or reshape the text wrap boundary.

4 With the pointer tool selected, position the pointer in the middle of the map and drag the map half-way up the page. Watch the text reflow. Then drag it to the top of the page.

With each move, PageMaker reflows the text to fill the columns. You'll next return it to the bottom right corner.

5 With the map still selected, select the bottom right corner reference point in the Control palette Proxy icon. Change X to **33p6** and Y to **54p2**. Press Enter or Return.

Remember: Unless otherwise stated, the reference point in the Control palette Proxy icon should be a square point, not an arrow.

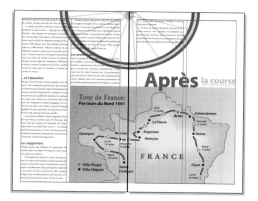

6 Save 05Work.pmd.

Creating the headline

The article you just placed requires a headline within a yellow frame.

1 Zoom in to the top third of page 4.

2 Drag a guide from the horizontal ruler down to the baseline of the fourth line of text in columns 1 and 2.

3 Select the rectangle frame tool (⊠). Position the tool on page 4 at the top left corner of column 1 (allow the tool to snap to the guides). Drag across both columns until the tool snaps to the right edge of column 2 and to the ruler guide you just placed.

You'll use the Control palette to adjust the height of the frame so it extends above the margin.

4 With the bottom left corner reference point in the Proxy icon selected in the Control palette, adjust the values so W is **31p** and H is **5p**. Press the Apply button.

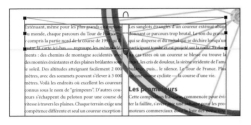

5 Choose Element > Fill and Stroke. In the fill portion of the Fill and Stroke dialog box, choose Solid for Fill and Pantone 810 2X CVC for Color. In the stroke portion of the dialog box, choose 4pt solid line for Stroke and Black for Color, and then click OK.

6 With the frame still selected, choose Element > Frame > Frame Options. Choose Center for Vertical Alignment, and type **0** for Top, Bottom, Left, and Right Insets, and click OK.

Just as you did with the map, you'll define a text wrap boundary for the frame to force the text to jump below the frame.

7 Choose Element > Text Wrap. For Wrap Option, select the second icon (rectangular wrap). For Text Flow, make sure the third icon (wrap all sides) is selected. Then, for Standoff in Picas, type **0** for Left, Right, Top, and Bottom, and click OK.

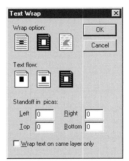

8 Select the text tool (**T**), click an insertion point in the frame. Click the Paragraph button in the Control palette and choose Headline for Style to set the style before typing the text.

9 Type **L'échappée**. To enter an accented e (é), type one of the following key sequences:

• Windows: Make sure the Num Lock key is down. Then, while holding down Alt, type **0233** on the numeric keypad. (No text appears until you release the Alt key.)

• Macintosh: While holding down Option, type **e** (nothing appears on the screen), and then type **e** again.

PageMaker includes a file in the Utilities folder called Character Set that lists the numeric code for most special characters.

10 Double-click the hand tool (🖑) to return to the Fit in Window view.

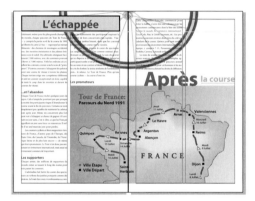

11 Save 05Work.pmd.

Changing to the 3-Col master page

The two-column layout is not working well for this spread. The text does not fill the columns. You will now change it to a three-column layout. Because the graphics have text wrap applied and the text is autoflowed into the columns, PageMaker easily adjusts the layout for you when you apply the three-column master page.

1 If the Master Pages palette is not currently displayed, choose Window > Show Master Pages or click the Master Pages palette tab.

Notice that the Document Master is selected for pages 4 and 5.

2 Choose Adjust Layout from the Master Page palette menu to turn this option on.

When Adjust Layout is on, PageMaker automatically adjusts the layout of a page when you apply a new master to it. (This option also changes the default state of the Adjust Layout option in the Master Page options dialog box.)

3 Select 3-Col / 3-Col in the Master Pages palette.

PageMaker applies the new master page and reflows the text automatically.

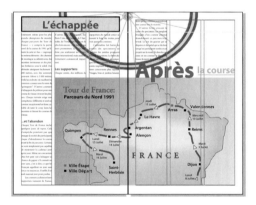

Because you had turned on "OK to Resize Groups and Imported Graphics" in the Layout Adjustment Preferences dialog box (at the beginning of the lesson), PageMaker has resized the map and framed headline. When resizing, PageMaker maintained the map's alignment with the left edge of column 2 (page 4) and the right margin guide (page 5), and kept the headline aligned with the left and right margin guides of page 4.

The larger size map has helped fill the layout, but the headline frame needs to be smaller.

You'll resize the headline frame so that it spans two, instead of three, columns.

4 Select the pointer tool, and then select the headline frame.

Because the text wrap boundary precisely overlaps the bounding box on the top and sides of the frame, you must hold down the Ctrl or Command key to resize the frame, otherwise you'll resize only the text wrap boundary.

5 Hold down Control (Windows) or Command (Macintosh), and drag the middle handle on the right edge of the frame until it snaps to the right edge of column 2.

The text wrap boundary resizes with the frame, and the text adjusts to fill column 3.

6 With the pointer tool selected, select the text block in column 1 on page 4. Drag the bottom windowshade handle just below the bottom margin guide to pull one more line of text into the column. (The windowshade handle will tend to snap to the margin guide. Drag it just below the snap point.)

7 If the text in column 1 no longer aligns with the text in column 2, pull the top windowshade handle back to the top of the column.

8 If the bottom windowshade slips up again, repeat steps 6 and 7 until the text runs to the bottom of the column and aligns with the text in column 2.

You now need to finish flowing the text on page 5.

9 Select the text block in column 1 on page 5.

Notice that the bottom windowshade handle contains a down arrow, indicating that there is more text in the story that hasn't been placed.

10 Click the bottom windowshade handle. Position the loaded text icon in column 2 on page 5, snapping it to the top left corner of the column. Click to flow the text.

PageMaker flows the remainder of the story into columns 2 and 3.

You have finished this spread.

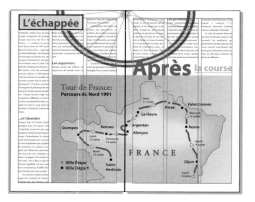

11 Save 05Work.pmd, and then turn to page 6.

Finishing pages 6 and 7

Page 6 contains all the art for the spread. You only need to finish the sidebars.

Converting the rectangles to frames

Before you place the sidebar text, you first need to convert the rectangles to frames, set the frame options, and thread them together. You'll use frames for this portion of the layout because it makes positioning the text so easy. The frame options control the placement of the text in the frames. You center the headline automatically, and offset the body text below the headline.

Before you begin, you'll take a look at the final version to see what the completed sidebar looks like.

1 Choose Window > 05Final.pmd (to switch to the final version of the guidebook), click the page 6 icon, and then select the yellow frame with the pointer tool.

The windowshade handle at the bottom of the yellow frame contains a plus sign, indicating that the text continues in another frame.

2 Choose Window > 05Work.pmd.

You are now ready to convert the frames.

3 With the pointer tool selected, select the yellow rectangle, hold down Shift, and select the green rectangle. (Release Shift.)

4 Choose Element > Frame > Change to Frame.

You next need to thread the two frames together so when you place the sidebar text it flows from the yellow frame to the green frame.

5 Click the bottom windowshade in the yellow frame (the pointer changes to the thread icon (▶§)), and then click anywhere in the green frame to thread the frames together.

Notice that a plus sign appears in the bottom windowshade handle of the yellow frame and in the top windowshade handle of the green frame.

6 Hold down Shift and click the green frame to deselect it.

7 With the yellow frame still selected, choose Element > Frame > Frame Options. Choose Center for Vertical Alignment, type **0** for Top, Left, Bottom, and Right, and click OK.

8 Choose File > Place, select the 05TextB.doc file, make sure both Within Frame's Thread and Retain Format are selected, and click Open (Windows) or OK (Macintosh).

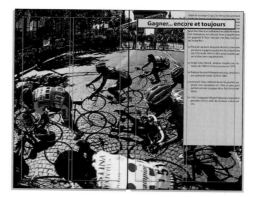

The text flows from the yellow frame to the green frame, but the yellow frame obscures some of the text. You will use the frame options to reposition the text within the green frame. You need the text in the green frame offset from the top of the frame so the text starts below the headline. The body text also needs to be offset from the edges of the green frame.

9 Use the pointer tool to select the green frame and choose Element > Frame > Frame Options. Then, choose Top for Vertical Alignment, type **6p11** for Top, **1p6** for Left, **0** for Bottom, and **2p6** for Right. Click OK.

10 Save 05Work.pmd.

Removing an unused style

You'll now remove Normal from the Styles palette. (Normal is a style imported with Word documents.) While removing unused styles is not necessary, it ensures that you won't apply them by accident and keeps your Style palette more compact.

1 If necessary, click the Styles tab in the palette group to view the Styles palette.

2 Drag Normal in the Styles palette to the trash icon at the bottom of the palette.

3 When prompted to delete the style, click OK (Windows) or Delete (Macintosh).

Adding special bullets to the list

The sidebar text that you just placed on page 7 has several paragraphs that need stars inserted as was done on page 3. You use the Bullets and Numbering plug-in to create these.

Adobe PageMaker comes with a variety of plug-ins that help you to perform complex procedures easily, or to perform special tasks. You can also acquire additional plug-ins created by independent developers. If you have access to the Internet, see Adobe's Web page at http://www.adobe.com.

1 Zoom in on the text you just placed onto page 7.

2 Select the text tool (**T**), and click an insertion point in the second paragraph (it begins **Le français Jacques Anquetil**).

3 Choose Utilities > Plug-ins > Bullets and Numbering.

Bullets and numbering

Bullet style:

Edit...

Range:
- For next: 3 paragraphs
- All those with style: Body Text
- Every paragraph in story
- Only selected paragraphs

OK | Cancel | Bullets | Numbers | Remove

The Bullets and Numbering plug-in inserts consecutive numbers (autonumbering) or a bullet character of your choice, along with a tab, at the beginning of each designated paragraph. You can specify that they should be added to selected paragraphs, to paragraphs that have a specific style, to a specific number of paragraphs based on the location of your cursor, or to every paragraph in the story. In this example, you begin by editing the bullet style.

4 Select the All Those with Style option, and choose Hanging Indent for the paragraph style.

5 Click the Edit button.

6 Choose Zapf Dingbats for Font, choose **10** for Size, and choose any star character.

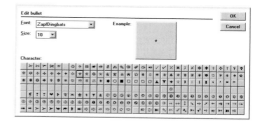

Note: To see a character more clearly, temporarily set the size to something large, like 36 points, and click the character. It displays in the sample box at the chosen size. When you have identified the character you want, return the size to 10 points.

7 Click OK, and then click OK again to exit the Bullets and Numbering dialog box.

PageMaker adds the character that you chose and a tab to each paragraph in the story that has the Hanging indent style.

✪ Le français Jacques Anquetil devint la première personne à gagner quatre fois la compétition (en 1957 et de 1961 à 1963), pour ensuite capter le titre une cinquième fois.

✪ Le belge Eddy Merck amassa ensuite cinq victoires, de 1969 à 1972 et encore

Inserting a drop cap

As a design element for this page, you will increase the size of the initial character of the main paragraph, creating a drop cap.

1 With the text tool selected, click an insertion point in the first paragraph of the body text in the sidebar. Choose Utilities > Plug-ins > Drop Cap.

2 Click OK to accept the default drop cap size of three lines.

You have completed the layout of this guidebook.

3 Save 05Work.pmd.

4 Close all open files, and quit PageMaker.

Review questions

1 How do you close an irregular polygon so that the start and end points are joined?

2 How do you select a graphic inside a frame without merely selecting the frame?

3 What objects are most likely to be adjusted correctly when using PageMaker's automatic layout adjustment?

4 How do you apply a special bullet style to a series of paragraphs?

Answers

1 When drawing the polygon, position the cursor over the starting point (the pointer changes to a square), and click once.

2 Hold down Ctrl (Windows) or Command (Macintosh) and click in the frame.

3 PageMaker will be most successful adjusting objects that are aligned with page edges, margins, and ruler guides.

4 Select some text in all the paragraphs to which you want to apply special bullets. Choose Utilities > Plug-ins > Bullets and Numbering. Select a bullet style or click Edit to select a different bullet. Select other options as desired and click OK.

Lesson 6
Adventure newsletter

This project is a newsletter published by a consortium of companies that provide travel-related services. Although it is short enough to be called a newsletter, the variety and complexity of its layout are comparable to a magazine. This project focuses on creating professional-level typography and layout. Many page elements are stored in a library, so you can streamline importing and concentrate on mastering professional layout skills.

To maintain the professional appearance of this highly designed publication, you will create a leading grid to ensure that the pieces align in an ordered way so that the complex page retains a unified and harmonious overall appearance. You will also employ a number of PageMaker's typographic controls and use the story editor for tasks such as spell-checking and replacing certain characters.

In this project you learn how to:

• Use semiautomatic text flow.

• Apply Expert Kerning.

• Create a page that has different column layouts on different parts of the page.

• Use paragraph settings to control column breaks.

• Use the Add Cont'd Line plug-in.

• Use the story editor to find and replace characters.

• Perform a spell check.

• Use PageMaker's image-control features.

• Force-justify a line.

• Control hyphenation and widows.

This project should take you about 2 hours to complete.

Before you begin

1 Before launching PageMaker, return all settings to their defaults. See "Restoring default settings" in Lesson 1.

Note: Windows users need to unlock the lesson files before using them. For information, see Copying the Classroom in a Book files on page 4.

2 Make sure that the AGaramond, AGaramond Semibold, Birch, and Myriad Roman and Myriad Condensed families of fonts are installed.

Windows only: Because of the way Windows handles fonts, AGaramond Semibold appears in the ATM Fonts list as AGaramond, Bold (notice the comma). However, neither AGaramond Semibold nor AGaramond, Bold appear in font menus in Windows applications. You must apply bold to AGaramond to use AGaramond Semibold. Similarly, you must apply bold to Myriad Condensed to use Myriad Condensed Bold (Myriad CN Bold on Mac OS).

3 Start Adobe PageMaker 7.0. Open the 06Final.pmd file in 06Lesson to see how the completed newsletter will look.

4 If the publication window does not fill the screen, click the Maximize button in the right corner of the title bar to expand the window.

Starting the publication

The newsletter uses an unusual tall and narrow shape to reinforce the exotic nature of its stories. You will begin building the publication by setting up the page size.

1 Choose File > New to open the Document Setup dialog box.

2 Enter **9** by **16** inches for Dimensions, and select Tall orientation. Make sure that the Double-sided and Facing Pages options are selected. Enter **2** for Number of Pages, and

type **.75** inches for all four margins. Choose 2400 dpi for Target Output Resolution and, in Windows only, choose AGFA-ProSet9800 for Compose to Printer. Click OK.

Note: If you do not have the required printer, you can still create the project as directed and then print it on your own printer by selecting your printer and its PPD (if it is a PostScript printer) in the Print dialog box when it is time to print. You can also use the Export Adobe PDF command to create an Adobe PDF version of the project rather than a printed copy, as described in Creating an Adobe PDF version of the flyer on page 41.

The newsletter layout was designed using picas as a unit of measure. Now that you have set up the page size, you can switch the unit of measure to picas.

3 Choose File > Preferences > General. Choose Picas for Measurements In and also for Vertical Ruler. Click OK.

4 Choose File > Save, and go to the 06Lesson folder. Enter **06Work.pmd** as the publication name, and then click Save.

Setting up the master pages

The majority of pages in this newsletter have three columns, so you begin by specifying a three-column layout on the master pages. While you're on the master pages, you also create the title header that appears at the top of the inside pages.

Setting up columns

When you set columns on a master page, they appear on all publication pages that use that master page.

1 Click the master page icon (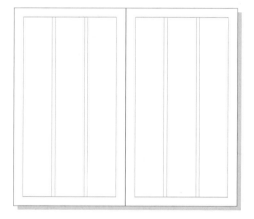) at the bottom of the document window to display the left and right master pages.

PageMaker shows you both master pages because you chose Facing Pages in the Document Setup dialog box.

2 Choose Layout > Column Guides and specify three columns with 1 pica 6 points (1p6) of space between columns. Click OK.

Your settings apply to both right and left document pages because the Set Left and Right Pages Separately option was not selected when you specified options in the Document Setup dialog box.

Creating the running head

The title of the newsletter appears at the top of every page. You can easily make this happen by setting up the title as a running head

on the master pages. Because the publication uses double-sided facing pages, you'll put the running head on both the left and right master pages. First you will zoom in to the specific area where you want to work.

1 Select the zoom tool (🔍) and drag to draw a marquee starting near the top of the left master page and extending across the full width of the page. Make it only a couple of inches high.

2 Drag a guide from the horizontal ruler down to 3p1. Select the text tool (T) and drag a text column across the entire width of the page above the columns. Type in the words **Adventure—Travel,** putting an em dash (with no spaces) between the two words.

Note: To type an em dash hold down Alt+Shift as you type a hyphen (Windows), or hold down Option+Shift as you type a hyphen (Macintosh).

3 With the text tool still selected, select the text. In the Control palette, make sure the Character view button (T) is selected. Choose Myriad CN Bold for the font, and 10 point for the size. (In Windows, you must apply bold to Myriad Condensed to use Myriad CN Bold.) Click the All Caps button (C) to make the text uppercase. Click the Paragraph-view icon (¶), and apply a left indent (⭾≡) of 18 picas and a right indent (≡⭾) of 18 picas.

Character view

Paragraph view

Next, you want to add letterspacing.

4 With the text still selected, click the Force Justify Alignment button (≡) in the Control palette.

ADVENTURE —TRAVEL

PageMaker adds equal amounts of space between each character to make the text fill the measure. The degree of space is limited by the right and left indents you set.

Note: PageMaker justifies a line by increasing space between words before increasing the space between letters. If a regular word space was used on either side of the em dash, there may be too much space between words and not enough between letters. If you want additional space around the em dash while maintaining more balanced spacing, you can use nonbreaking spaces instead, by typing Ctrl+Alt+spacebar (Windows) or Option+spacebar (Macintosh).

5 Select the pointer tool and size and position the text block so it extends the full width of the page. Position the bottom of the windowshade on the guide at 3p1.

The bottom of the windowshade snaps easily to the guide because you have Snap to Guides turned on.

So far so good: you've created a page header for the left pages. Now you need to duplicate it on the right master page.

6 With the pointer tool, select the header text block and copy it. Use the scroll bars or the hand tool (🖑) to pan to the right master page. Zoom in on the top, just as you did for the left master page, and paste. Then use the pointer tool to drag the text block so that it sits against the left side of the page (filling the page width) and so that the bottom of the windowshade snaps to the 3p1 guide.

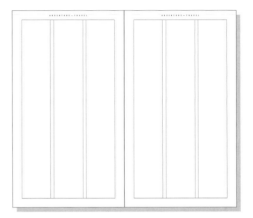

You've completed the master pages.

7 Save 06Work.pmd.

Beginning page 1

You don't want the header to appear on page 1, the title page.

1 Click the page icon 1.

2 Choose View > Display Master Items to deselect it.

The header that you created on the master page is no longer visible on page 1. It will still be visible on all pages that have Display Master Items enabled.

Adding guides

Next, you'll create a series of guides to help you position material on the page.

1 Drag a ruler guide down from the horizontal ruler. Watch the Control palette as you drag, so that you can accurately position the ruler guide so that Y reads 25p6.

When you create guides, you can monitor the guide position on the Control palette or on the ruler opposite the one from which you dragged the guide.

2 Drag to create three more ruler guides from the horizontal ruler. Position the additional horizontal guides at 49, 53p3, and 58p8 picas.

Note: If the Control palette isn't displaying the ruler increment you want, the current magnification may be causing ruler increments to round off to the nearest pixel. If you zoom in on the page and the Control palette, the rulers will display finer increments.

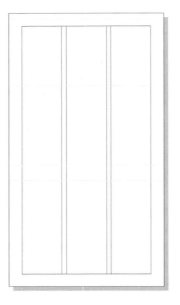

You created these guides on page 1 because it is the only page that uses this layout. If you wanted to create the same set of guides on all pages, you would have created them on the master pages.

3 Now is a good time to save your work. Remember to save often, even though this book reminds you only once in a while.

If you're creating a visible grid of regularly-spaced guides, you can also use the Grid Manager plug-in. Choose Utilities > Plug-ins > Grid Manager.

Placing art on page 1

For this project, we have provided all of the art that you need, including the drop caps. Some—but not all—of the elements have been saved in a library. Several of the elements in the library were created in PageMaker itself and do not exist as separate files. The largest graphics are not included in the library, in order to conserve disk space.

1 On page 1, choose Window > Plug-in Palettes > Show Library. In the Library palette, choose Open Library from the palette menu. Navigate to the 06Lesson folder, and double-click 06Lib.pml. You should see one or two thumbnails, each with a title underneath. If you don't see both images and titles, choose Display Both from the palette menu. The masthead items at the top of page 1 were created in PageMaker and added to the library as AT Logo-Heading.

Note: Items stored in the Library palette don't snap to guides or the grid as you drag them from the Library palette to the layout, nor do they display a preview until you release the mouse. Therefore, throughout this lesson you will move Library palette items onto the layout, let go, and then drag them precisely to their final positions.

2 If necessary, scroll the Library palette until you see ATLogo-Heading. Drag AT Logo-Heading out of the Library palette, but don't let go yet. As you drag, the loaded graphic icon indicates where the top left corner of the graphic will be when you release the mouse button. Position the top left of the loaded graphic icon near the top left corner of the page margin, and then release the mouse button.

3 Press and hold the mouse button on the masthead until you see the preview image for the masthead, then drag it into its final position so that the left edge snaps to the left page margin and the top of the **Volume 23** text characters are aligned with the top page margin, as shown below.

The next element is the large duotone photograph intended for the top half of page 1.

4 Drag LeapDuo from the Library palette to the layout, position the loaded graphic icon along the left page margin and under the masthead, and then release the mouse button. Then drag the photograph so that the left side snaps to the left margin and the top snaps to the guide at 25p6 picas (you can check the Control palette for the location of the top edge as you drag, if you make sure any of the top reference points are selected in the Proxy icon).

Placing the text

The 06TextA.doc file contains the text of several articles for the current issue, including the bungee-jumping story. You can save time by using the most appropriate text-flow method. If you use the fully automatic text-flow option (the Autoflow command), the text will fill all three columns immediately. You don't want that, because the right column is reserved for another story. Manual flow would work, but you'd have to reload the cursor after each column. PageMaker's semiautomatic flow is the perfect way to place this story, because you can choose which columns to fill and the text cursor stays loaded.

1 Begin by displaying the page at Actual Size if it isn't already, and use the scroll bars or hand tool (🖑) to pan so that the two left columns below the large photograph are visible.

2 Choose File > Place, open the 06Lesson folder, and double-click 06TextA.doc.

PageMaker imports the text and gives you the automatic text-flow icon or the manual text-flow icon, depending on whether Autoflow is enabled in the Layout menu. Autoflow is turned off by default, so you probably see the manual text-flow icon.

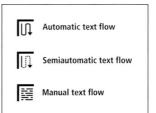

3 Hold down Shift to change to the semiautomatic text-flow icon.

4 Continue to hold down Shift and click inside the left column, starting several picas below the photograph. You'll position the text more precisely later.

The text fills the column and stops. Your cursor is still a loaded text icon, ready to place more text.

5 Holding down Shift, click inside the second column at the same position to fill the second column.

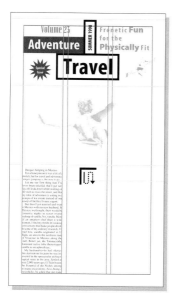

There's more to the story, but you'll place that later.

6 Click the pointer tool in the toolbox to deselect the loaded text icon.

Note: When you click with a loaded text icon to place text, the text fills the width of the column if the icon is inside the column when you click. If you click outside the column margin, PageMaker spreads the text the full width of the page margins. If that happens, drag the bottom windowshade handle up to roll the column completely up, and click the red triangle to reload the text icon. Then place it again, being careful to position the pointer within the column.

Formatting the Bungee article

Other lessons in this book teach you how to format paragraphs and create paragraph styles, so for this project, you will simply use paragraph styles to quickly format different parts of the publication.

Importing styles

Whenever the styles you want to use exist in another publication, save time by importing them instead of creating them from scratch.

1 Choose Type > Define Styles, and click Import in the Define Styles dialog box.

2 Navigate to the 06Lesson folder if you're not there already, and double-click to open 06Styles.pmd.

When you're asked if you want to copy over existing styles, click OK. Click OK again to close the Define Styles dialog box.

Your document now contains a complete and up-to-date set of paragraph styles that you will use to format the newsletter text.

Adding heads, graphics, and styles

The next step is to apply paragraph styles to all the paragraphs of the bungee-jumping story. You first apply the Body Text style to all of the text. After that, all you have to do is apply headline styles where needed.

1 Select the text tool (**T**) and click an insertion point anywhere in the article you just placed. Now choose Edit > Select All, and apply the Body Text style.

Note: *You can use the Styles palette or the Control palette to do this, or you can choose Type > Style > Body Text.*

Because you chose the Select All command, the Body Text paragraph style is now applied to the entire file that you just imported, not just the portion that's visible.

Now you will lay out the headline of this story in a way that keeps it threaded to the rest of the story.

2 Select the pointer tool, and then click the top windowshade handle of the first column. The loaded text cursor appears so that you can create a new first text block for this story, threaded to the rest of the story.

3 Drag the loaded text cursor to create a new text block across the top of the two columns under the photograph.

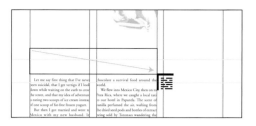

4 Drag the top windowshade handles of the two columns of body text so that each snaps to the 58p8 guide. Then click the headline you just pasted, and make sure that the text block fills the two-column width completely.

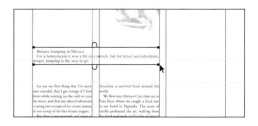

5 Select the text tool, click in the first head (the one that says **Bungee Jumping in Mexico**) and apply the Head 1 paragraph style.

Tracking and kerning

Compare the current headline with 06Final.pmd, and notice that in the final version, the headline fits on one line and there is not so much space between the characters.

Default letter spacing for headline

After kerning

Typographers would say that the headline in 06Final.pmd has a *firmer texture*. The perception of type texture affects the design of the page. Texture is affected by the visual arrangement of the shapes of and spaces between type characters. Your goal is to create a texture that is even and feels pleasant to look at—neither crowded nor loose. There are two ways to control typographic texture: tracking and kerning.

Tracking adjusts the space between characters evenly, adding or removing space between each pair of characters. As type gets larger, characters should be closer together for proper texture. Type that is smaller than 14 points rarely needs tightening and sometimes requires a looser texture, whereas most type larger than 30 points needs tightening. Tracking automatically adjusts letter spacing as you change the type size. The amount of tracking applied to a certain size depends on font- and size-specific tracking tables which you can edit if you are typographically experienced. If you don't have a proper tracking table for a font, the result may not be optimal.

The second technique for controlling texture in type is called *kerning*. Kerning is an adjustment of letter space between individual pairs of characters. If you select a range of text and then apply kerning, this is known as *range kerning*, which is similar to tracking. However, unlike tracking, applying a kerning value does not automatically compensate for different type sizes. For example, if you select a paragraph containing several sizes of type, the kerning value you enter is applied whether or not it is appropriate for all the sizes of type you selected.

Display type, or type larger than approximately 36 points, is more of a challenge to kern manually. To help you, PageMaker provides the Expert Kerning feature. Expert Kerning examines each selected character shape to determine optimal letter spacing, which in display type is quite likely to be different between each pair of characters.

Expert Kerning is intended to be applied only to several words of larger type sizes, typically 36 points or over. The level of precision at which Expert Kerning calculates kerning is not visible at smaller sizes. In the next step, you use PageMaker's Expert Kerning feature to reduce space selectively between characters of a headline.

1 Select the text tool (**T**), select the entire **Bungee Jumping** headline, and then choose Type > Expert Kerning. Set Kern Strength to 1.20, and set the Design Class to Display. Click OK.

PageMaker's Expert Kerning reduces the space between each pair of characters. The headline should now fit on one line and match the one in 06Final.pmd.

2 Locate the paragraph that begins **For a honeymoon…** and apply the Head 2 paragraph style.

Note: If any part of the **For a honeymoon…** *paragraph moves down to the main story, select the pointer tool, select the headline text block and pull down its bottom windowshade until that second paragraph is completely visible under the headline again.*

3 Drag the **Bungee Jumping** headline so that the first baseline rests on the 53p3 guide. This may not happen easily if the bottom of the text block snaps to the next guide down. You can move the headline baseline close to the 53p3 guide, and then press the vertical arrow keys to nudge the headline into position. Make sure that the left side of the block is flush with the left margin and that it fills the two-column width completely.

Adding a graphical drop cap

The decorative drop cap for the bungee-jumping article has been provided for you in the library. It was created in PageMaker and is a combination of the letter **L**, a rectangle, and a text wrap.

1 Select the text tool (**T**) and delete the **L** from the phrase "Let me say…" at the beginning of the body text for the article.

2 If necessary, scroll the Library palette so that you can see the LCap drop cap.

3 Select the pointer tool, drag LCap out of the library, position it near the beginning of the bungee-jumping article, and release the mouse button. Now fine-tune its position by lining up the bottom of the drop cap graphic with the baseline of the fifth line of the first paragraph of the article, and then release the mouse button.

Because the piece already has a wrap applied to it, the surrounding text positions itself nicely around the drop cap.

4 Select the text tool, click three times in the first paragraph of body text to select the entire paragraph, and then switch to the paragraph view of the Control palette. Change the first line indent (⁺≣) from 1 pica to 0.

The drop cap procedures in this lesson are useful for adding a graphical drop cap, but if you simply want to convert the first letter of a paragraph into a drop cap, you would select the first letter and choose Utilities > Plug-ins > Drop Cap.

Fixing a widow

The last line of the first paragraph ends with a very short line—a widow. A widow is generally considered to be typographically undesirable, so there's an easy way to fix it.

1 Display the Character view of the Control palette.

2 With the first paragraph still selected, click the Decrease Kerning button in the Control palette once or twice until the single word moves up one line.

Decrease kerning

Make sure that the bottom of the text block in each of the two columns is even with the bottom page margin.

Placing the circle graphic

Now it's time to place the circular graphic that goes between the two columns of the bungee-jumping article. It's called Circle Photo in the Library palette. This graphic has text wrap already applied to it. It's also a *mask*, which allows the photograph to be cropped using a circle drawn in PageMaker. The circle and the photo it masks are grouped to make them easier to position.

1 If necessary, scroll the Library palette to locate Circle Photo. Drag Circle Photo from the library onto the pasteboard or a white area of the page.

This time you will use the Control palette to position the graphic precisely.

2 In the Control palette, select the top left corner of the Proxy icon, type 15p for X, type 69p9 for Y, and then click the Apply button or press Return or Enter.

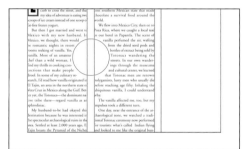

3 Save 06Work.pmd.

You may want to check 06Final.pmd again to see if your work matches it.

Adding the continuation line

The bungee-jumping article continues on a later page, so you will add a continuation line where it ends on page 1 to tell the reader where the article continues, or jumps. To do this, you must first place the rest of the article. The file containing this article is large

because it contains other articles as well, so you are going to flow the remainder of the 06TextA.doc file into the document so you can see what you're working with.

1 With the pointer tool still selected, select the text block in the second column, and load the text icon by clicking the bottom windowshade handle.

2 Go to the second page, and hold down Ctrl (Windows) or Command (Macintosh) to toggle from manual flow to automatic text flow. Click in the top of the left column to place the text.

3 PageMaker flows all the unplaced text into the publication.

4 Return to the first page, and select the text block in the second column by clicking it with the pointer tool.

5 Choose Utilities > Plug-ins > Add Cont'd Line. In the dialog box that appears, select Bottom of Textblock and click OK.

By choosing Bottom of Textblock, you tell PageMaker that you want the jump line to say "Continued on page…" If you choose Top of Textblock, PageMaker adds a line at the top that says "Continued from page…" PageMaker knows where you placed the next text block of the article, and it inserts a line of text that contains the correct page number. It also creates a paragraph style called Cont. On, which has the default formatting for the continuation line. You can edit this style exactly as you would edit any other paragraph style.

6 If necessary, choose Window > Show Styles to display the Styles palette. To change the look of the continuation line, display the Edit Style dialog box by holding down Ctrl (Windows) or Command (Macintosh) as you click the Cont. On style in the Styles palette.

7 Click Char, and choose AGaramond for Font, and choose both Bold and Italic for Type Style. Choose 9 for size and 14 for leading. Click OK, and then click Para. To remove the ruling lines from the style definition, click Rules, and then deselect Rule Above Paragraph and Rule Below Paragraph. Hold down Shift (Windows) or Option (Macintosh) as you click OK, to close all dialog boxes.

Note: Because of the way fonts are defined, when you apply bold to AGaramond, PageMaker actually uses AGaramond Semibold. On the Macintosh, you can get the same result if you select AGaramond Semibold directly.

The final step is to position the continuation line more precisely. It's in a separate text block, so all you have to do is drag it.

8 With the pointer tool still selected, select the text block containing the jump line. Drag it up until its baseline sits on the bottom margin.

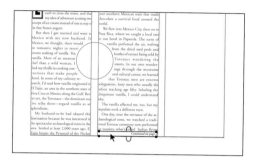

Adding the Editor's Note

The Editor's Note is a *sidebar* and rests on top of a screened blue rectangle that forms one of the major design elements on the front page. The rectangle serves as a focal point and visually unifies the top and bottom of the page.

Creating the blue background

Take another look at 06Final.pmd and note the blue background on the right side of page 1.

1 Return to 06Work.pmd on page 1, and select the rectangle tool (□). Drag a tall narrow rectangle on the pasteboard to the right of page 1. The size and position are not important. You will adjust them soon.

2 With the rectangle still selected, be sure the top left reference point of the Proxy icon in the Control palette is selected. In the Control palette type **19p6** for W, and **77p6** for H, and then press Enter or Return.

3 If necessary, choose Window > Show Colors to display the Colors palette. With the rectangle still selected, click the Both button (⊠), click PANTONE Blue 072 CV and then choose 20% for Tint.

The rectangle is now a lighter version of the blue color you selected. Tinting a color is also known as *screening back* when you apply a halftone screen to lighten it.

4 Zoom out and use the scroll bars or hand tool (🖑) to pan the page so that you can see the bottom right corner of the page. Select the pointer tool and drag the rectangle so that its bottom right corner lines up with the bottom right corner of page 1.

5 With the rectangle still selected, choose Element > Arrange > Send to Back so that the blue background is behind the photograph and the title art is at the top of the page.

6 Choose Element > Lock Position. This locks the rectangle so that it will not accidentally be moved as you work on the page.

7 Save 06Work.pmd.

Placing and formatting the text

In the next steps, you will place and format the text for the Editor's Note. Take a look at the Editor's Note in 06Final.pmd to see where you're headed. Notice that the title is white type against a dark blue box.

1 Choose File > Place and double-click 06TextB.doc. Click the loaded text icon in the right column about a pica below the big photograph.

2 Select the text tool (**T**), click in the Editor's Note, and choose Edit > Select All. Apply the Sidebar Text paragraph style.

3 Select the pointer tool and select the text block. In the Control palette, select the top left reference point of the Proxy icon, type **35p6** for X and **50p4** for Y, and then press Enter or Return.

In the next steps, you will apply a paragraph style to the header, create a dark blue rectangle, place it behind the header, and group the rectangle and text block together.

4 Zoom in on the top of the Editor's Note article. Select the rectangle tool (▢) and draw a rectangle over the "Editor's Note" title; draw it as wide as the column. Select the pointer tool, select the rectangle, and in the Control palette, type **14** picas (the width of the column) for W, and **2p4** for H. Press Enter or Return.

5 With the rectangle still selected, display the Colors palette, click the Both button (⊠), and apply PANTONE Blue 072 CV.

6 Choose Element > Arrange > Send Backward. If necessary, repeat this step until the dark blue rectangle is behind the text.

7 Select the text tool and click in the title of the sidebar ("Editor's Note"), and apply the SideHead paragraph style. The title is now easier to read over the dark rectangle because Reverse is applied to the type as part of the paragraph style definition. If you don't see distinct characters, the text may be greeking—zoom in to see it better.

8 Select the pointer tool and select the blue rectangle. If you accidentally select the text block which is now in front of the rectangle, hold down Ctrl (Windows) or Command (Macintosh) and click again to select through the text block.

9 Use the Up and Down arrow keys on the keyboard or the vertical nudge buttons on the Control palette to move the blue rectangle in small increments until it is centered vertically behind the Editor's Note text.

Using the nudge technique works especially well for this kind of precise positioning.

At this point, the dark blue rectangle and the text block should both be as wide as the column. The dark blue rectangle should stay with the reversed headline text, so you'll group them to keep them together.

10 With the rectangle still selected, hold down Shift as you click on the text block to add it to the selection, and choose Element > Group.

11 Select the text tool and click an insertion point in the first text paragraph of the Editor's Note. Display the Paragraph view of the Control palette, and change the first line indent from 1 pica to 0.

The last paragraph of the Editor's Note may end with a widow—a word or fragment of a word that looks awkward alone on a line. If you see one, you can correct it by applying range kerning, as you did to the first paragraph in the **Bungee Jumping** article.

12 Save 06Work.pmd.

Finishing the Bungee article

Next, you will go to page 2 and position the remainder of the bungee-jumping article.

1 Click the page 2 icon and zoom in on the top of the page. Make sure that the top of each of the two text blocks aligns exactly with the top margin.

Now you will add guides to make it easier to size the story for this layout. You may refer to 06Final.pmd to review how this story fits into the rest of the page.

2 Pan down and, if necessary, zoom out so that you can see the bottom half of the two columns.

3 Drag a ruler guide out from the horizontal ruler and position it at 57p. Drag to create two more horizontal ruler guides and position them at 61p8 and 70p4.

4 With the pointer tool still selected, select the left text block and drag the bottom handle up until the bottom is on the 61p8 guide (the second one from the bottom). Then select the second column and drag its bottom windowshade handle up to the guide at 57p.

5 Click the windowshade handle at the bottom of the text block in the second column to load the text icon, and flow the remaining text into the third column. If the top of the text block does not already touch the top margin, drag the top windowshade up until it snaps to the margin.

Formatting the Kayaking article

Next, you will apply formatting to the **Kayaking with Crocs** article, which begins near the bottom of the second column in 06Final.pmd.

1 Zoom in on the middle of the second column, and apply the Head 1 style to the words **Kayaking with Crocs**.

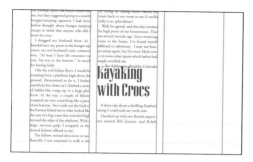

2 Select the same words with the text tool so that you can apply Expert Kerning just as you did for the headline of the bungee-jumping article.

3 Choose Type > Expert Kerning. Set Kern Strength to 1.20, and set the Design Class to Display. Click OK.

Now you will use the Column Break option to move the headline to the top of the third column.

4 Click anywhere in the Kayaking with Crocs headline, and choose Type > Paragraph. In the Options section, select Column Break Before, and click OK.

The head promptly moves to the top of the next column because you added the column break option to it.

5 With the text tool still selected, click an insertion point in the paragraph which begins **A short tale**, and apply the Head 2 style.

6 Select the pointer tool. Drag the Kayaking Photo out of the Library palette, position it close to the top of the third column, and then release the mouse button. Drag the photograph again to fine-tune its position, snapping it to the left column guide of the third column and the top page margin.

The photo already has a wrap applied to it, so it pushes the text down and out of the way. Since Snap to Guides is on, the picture snaps easily into the column when you move it close to the column guides.

7 With the pointer tool still selected, drag the bottom windowshade of the Kayaking article down to reveal the entire story.

8 Save 06Work.pmd.

Positioning the pull quote

The pull quote for this page includes a photograph. By putting the pull quote and the photograph inside a frame, you'll be able to set text wrap once for the entire pull quote, and still be able to edit the text and photo.

1 Select the rectangle-frame tool (⊠) from the toolbox. Draw a frame on the pasteboard, and leave it selected.

2 Choose Element > Text Wrap. For Wrap Option, select the second icon (rectangular wrap). Type **0p9** for all Standoff Values, and then click OK.

3 With the frame still selected, display the Colors palette, click the Fill button (✕), and then select PANTONE Blue 072 CV. Choose Element > Stroke > 6 pt.

4 Be sure the top left reference point of the Control palette Proxy icon is selected. Type −**39p9.5** for X, **24p5.5** for Y, **10p2** for W, **14p3** for H, and then press Enter or Return.

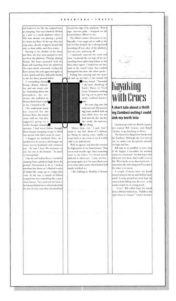

5 With the frame still selected, choose File > Place. Select the file 06TextC.doc in the 06Lesson folder, make sure the Within Frame option is selected, the Show Filter Preferences option is deselected, the Retain Format option is selected, and then click Open (Windows) or OK (Macintosh). The text is placed within the frame.

The text may be difficult to read because it is black on a dark blue background. You will apply a style that will make it easy to read.

6 Select the text tool (T), click an insertion point in the pull quote text, and choose Edit > Select All. Display the Styles palette and click the Pull Quote style.

Now you will add a duotone image to the pull quote. First you will add a paragraph return so that the image will be in its own paragraph.

7 With the text tool still selected, click at the beginning of the text you just placed and press Enter or Return. Then press the Left Arrow key to move the insertion point back to the top of the text block.

8 Choose File > Place, select the 06Art1.eps file from the 06Lesson folder, make sure the As Inline Graphic option is selected, and then click Open or OK.

The text and photograph don't appear properly aligned right now, but you will fix that in the following steps.

9 Select the pointer tool, select the frame (do not select any of the frame contents), and choose Element > Frame > Frame Options. Type **0** for each Frame Inset, and then click OK.

Not enough of the top of the photograph is visible, so you'll add leading to the line that contains it.

10 Select the text tool and triple-click the photograph in the pull quote to select the paragraph containing the photograph. In the Character view of the Control palette, type **38** points for leading ( ), and then press Enter or Return.

11 Click the text tool within the first line after the photo, and in the paragraph view of the Control palette, type **1** pica for space before the paragraph ( ), and then press Return or Enter.

Laying out the Tibetan Treks sidebar

To finish page 2, you will place the prepared title graphic for the Tibetan Treks sidebar and then place a graphic at the bottom of the page. You will then modify the graphic in several ways: you will enlarge it, color it blue, and alter it with PageMaker's Image Controls. Finally, you will change the layout to two columns, place the sidebar text, and add the drop cap.

Placing the sidebar title

You will fill out the bottom of page 2 by adding another sidebar. In this section you add the title of the sidebar, which is stored as a graphic in the Library palette.

1 Take another look at 06Final.pmd to see what this part of the page looks like.

2 Select the pointer tool. Locate Side Head in the Library palette and drag it onto the page, positioning the loaded graphic icon approximately at the top left of the empty area at the bottom of the page, and then release the mouse button. Drag the graphic to fine-tune its positioning, so that the left

edge snaps to the left margin and the top edge aligns with the guide at 57, and then release the mouse button.

Placing the background graphic

The sidebar text will appear on top of a background photograph, so you will add the photograph next.

1 Select the pointer tool. Locate Tibetan Treks in the Library palette, drag it to the empty area at the bottom of the page, and release the mouse button. Drag the photo again to fine-tune its position, so that the left and right edges are against the left and right edges of the page, and the top edge aligns with the bottom of the blue rectangle containing the text **Tibetan Treks**. The photograph may hang below the page edge slightly.

2 Select the sidebar title graphic that you just dragged from the library, and choose Element > Arrange > Bring to Front so that it is in front of the enlarged background photograph.

3 Select the Tibetan Treks photo. Display the Colors palette and apply PANTONE Blue 072 CV.

Applying special effects to a photo

For the type to be readable over the photo, the photo should be lighter. You will use the Image Control feature to screen back the photo and create special effects.

Macintosh:

With the photo selected, choose Element > Image > Image Control. Experiment by clicking different buttons above the graph and with clicking the Lightness and Contrast controls.

The buttons produce an immediate effect, but for the other controls, you have to click Apply. On a Macintosh, you can adjust each bar in the graph individually, or drag across the graph to shape the bars together. Click Apply to see the effect.

When you're done exploring, use the pointer to draw a line across the graph. The line should begin at the middle of the left side and go to the top right corner of the graph. Click Apply, and then click OK.

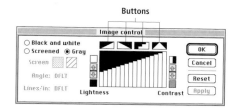

Windows:

With the photo selected, choose Element > Image > Image Control.

Set the Lightness to 90% and the Contrast to 24%. Click OK.

Placing the text in two columns

Now you've prepared the background graphic for the Tibetan Treks article. The next step is to place the text. This article is laid out in two columns rather than three, so you will change the column guides.

1 Choose Layout > Column Guides. This time, enter **2** for the number of columns. Keep **1p6** as the Space Between Columns, and click OK.

Notice that changing the number of columns does not affect text that is already placed on the page.

2 Choose File > Place, and double-click 06TextD.doc in the 06Lesson folder. As you position the loaded text icon, turn on semi-automatic text flow again by holding down

Shift as you click in the top of each column below the head **Beckoning the Intrepid**. If you still have a loaded text icon after flowing the second column, click the pointer tool to cancel placing text. You will make adjustments later that will make all the text fit.

3 Select the text tool (**T**), click in the new story, and choose Edit > Select All. Display the Styles palette, and apply the Sidebar Text paragraph style.

4 If the top of either column does not already touch the guide at 70p4, select the pointer tool and drag the top windowshade of each text block as necessary.

5 If the bottom of the left column does not already touch the bottom margin, select the pointer tool (if necessary) and drag its windowshade so that it snaps to the bottom margin.

6 Select the text tool, and click an insertion point in the first paragraph of the text you just placed. In the paragraph view of the Control palette, change the first line indent from 1 pica to **0**. Press Enter or Return.

7 Select the pointer tool. Locate TCap in the Library palette and drag it approximately to the beginning of the story. Drag the drop

cap again to fine-tune it, so that the left edge is against the left margin and the bottom edge aligns with the fifth baseline of the story, and then let go of the mouse button.

8 Delete the first letter of the story—the **T**—since it is now redundant with the drop cap.

The library you opened for this project will stay open until you close it. You won't be using this particular library any further in this project or for any other projects in this book, so you will close it now. Simply closing the palette window won't close the library file itself, so you will use a palette menu command to close the library file.

9 In the Library palette, choose Close Library from the palette menu. Then close the Library palette.

For the next step, you want to select all of the Tibet article except the first paragraph. This can be difficult to do precisely, but there is a quick way.

10 Select the text tool. Triple-click the second paragraph in the article, and then hold down Shift as you click the last paragraph in the article.

The selection technique in step 10 also works for whole words. Just start dragging by double-clicking a word at either end of the desired range.

11 In the character view of the Control palette, change the track from Normal to Tight.

12 Save 06Work.pmd.

Using the story editor

PageMaker's story editor is a text-only view where you can edit text quickly and easily because PageMaker does not have to display graphics or sophisticated formatting, and stories are all together in one place instead of being spread out over various pages.

Some tasks can be performed only in story editor view, such as finding, changing, and checking the spelling of text.

By setting some preferences, you can control the appearance of text in the story editor.

1 Choose File > Preferences > General, and then click More.

You can also display the Preferences dialog box by double-clicking the pointer tool.

2 In the story editor section of the More Preferences dialog box, choose a Font and Size that you'd like to use in the story editor. For this project, choose 12-point Helvetica.

These settings are provided to make it easier to read and edit text in the story editor, and they do not affect the text on the layout.

3 Make sure Display Style Names is selected. This shows the style name of each paragraph in a column to the left of the text. When you're working in story editor, this option quickly identifies the paragraph style applied to each paragraph.

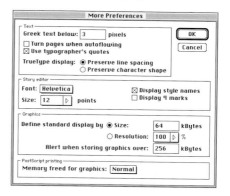

4 Hold down Shift (Windows) or Option (Macintosh) as you click OK to close both Preferences dialog boxes.

Finding and changing text

If you carefully examine the text you imported for the various articles, you will find that there is an unusual character—ó— in places where there should be em dashes. Similar characters may appear when text is moved between applications or computer platforms. PageMaker's Find and Change feature makes it easy to fix these instances. To use find and change, you must work in story editor view.

1 Go to page 1. To display the story editor, select the text tool (**T**) and click an insertion point in the first paragraph of the body text in the bungee-jumping article. Don't click next to the drop cap (**L**), because the drop cap is a graphic separate from the story.

2 Choose Edit > Edit Story.

The story editor opens to the position in the story where you clicked an insertion point.

💡 You can also open the story editor by triple-clicking on the story with the pointer tool.

3 In story editor, examine the last sentence in the fourth paragraph. There are two instances of the **ó** character in the sentence **óthe dominant native tribe thereó**. Select one and copy it.

> the curb to cross the street, and that my idea of adventure is eating two scoops of ice cream instead of one scoop of fat-free frozen yogurt.
>
> But then I got married and went to Mexico with my new husband. In Mexico, we thought, there would be romantic nights in resort rooms reeking of vanilla. Yes, vanilla. More of an amateur chef than a wild woman, I find my thrills in cooking concoctions that make people drool. In some of my culinary research, I'd read how vanilla originated in El Tajin, an area in the northern state of Veracruz in Mexico along the Gulf. Better yet, the Totonacs the dominant native tribe thereóregard vanilla as an aphrodisiac.
>
> My husband-to-be had okayed this destination because he was interested in the spectacular archaeological ruins in the area. Settled at least 2,000 years ago, El Tajin boasts the Pyramid of the Niches among its many excavations. Also, being a chocoholic, he asked that our route include a few days in Tabasco, the adjacent southern Mexican state that made chocolate a survival food around the world.

4 Choose Utilities > Change. Paste the copied character into Find What.

*Note: You can also type the character directly into Find What. In Windows, hold down Alt and type **0243** on the numeric keypad. On a Macintosh, hold down Option as you type **e** and then let go of Option and type **o**.*

5 Type an em dash in Change To by typing ^_ (Windows) or pressing the keyboard shortcut Option+Shift+- (Macintosh). Leave Match Case and Whole Word deselected, leave Current Publication selected for Search Document, and select All Stories for Search Story.

The case (uppercase or lowercase) doesn't matter, and the character you're looking for is not a whole word, because in this publication it is always typed without a space next to it.

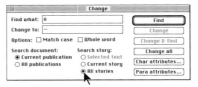

You can click Change All to change all instances of the character to an em dash. However, Change All should be used with great caution to avoid unintended results. For instance, if the character is present as a legitimate character in a word, Change All will replace it anyway. It's far safer to check each occurrence as it is found.

6 Click Find. Look at the found character highlighted in the story window. It's one you want to change, click Change & Find.

PageMaker makes the change and automatically searches for the next occurrence of the character.

7 Change each occurrence of the character to an em dash. There should be seven in all. PageMaker will open a separate story editor window for each story where it finds an occurrence.

To skip over an occurrence without changing it, click Find Next.

8 Close the Change dialog box.

9 Save 06Work.pmd. (You should be saving at regular intervals.)

Checking spelling

Spell checking is another task that you can perform only in story editor view. You should still be in story editor, but because PageMaker creates a separate window for each story, you are in the window for the "Tibetan Treks" story.

You want to begin checking spelling in the bungee jumping story. If you have not closed the window for that story, you can quickly return to it by choosing it from the Window menu. The story is listed in a menu under the name of the publication that contains it. PageMaker identifies each story window in the menu by the first few characters in the story.

1 Choose Window > 06Work.pmd > Bungee Jumping in M, and click an insertion point at the beginning of the story. Choose Utilities > Spelling. Select Alternate

Spellings, deselect Show Duplicates, leave Current Publication selected, select All Stories, and then click Start.

The Alternate Spellings option makes PageMaker suggest alternate spellings for questionable words. Normally, you'd also select Show Duplicates, but in this text the writer uses phrases like **thump, thump, thump.** Finally, selecting the All Stories option lets you check all editable text in the publication using a single spell-checking session.

PageMaker looks for both misspelled words and unexpected capitalization, such as a sentence beginning with a lowercase letter.

The first word that the spell checker questions is **bungee.** You want to add it to the dictionary so that PageMaker will recognize it in the future.

2 Click Add.

PageMaker presents the word with suggested hyphenation, indicated by tilde characters (~), and proposes to add it as all lowercase (not a proper noun).

3 Make sure As All Lowercase selected, and click OK. Click Continue.

If the word must always have the capital letters that you've typed in the Word option, you would select Exactly as Typed. If the word should be lowercase except at the beginning of a sentence, you would select As All Lowercase. PageMaker will capitalize it as necessary; for example, at the beginning of a sentence.

The next questioned word is **amatuer**. This word is wrong, but the correct spelling appears in the list of possible replacements.

4 Select **amateur** in the replacement list to make it appear in Change To, and then click Replace. At the word **Tajin**, click Ignore.

PageMaker continues the spelling check without adding **Tajin** to the dictionary. The next word is **Veracruz**. You want to use a different form of the name.

5 Type **Vera Cruz** for Change To and click Replace.

The change appears in the text. **Cruz** is not in the dictionary either, but you don't want to add it to the dictionary, so click Ignore to continue spell checking.

Note: Sometimes when you type in a change and click Replace, PageMaker continues the search without waiting for you to click Ignore or Add. That means that PageMaker found the substitution in its dictionary.

This project contains many proper and place names that should be ignored. Others, like **hippo**, are odd or rare and don't need to be added to the dictionary. Click Ignore for all of the following words:

Totonacs	chocoholic
Tabasco	Poza
Rica	Papantla
Totonac	

6 When you get to **ubquitous**, choose the correct spelling, **ubiquitous**, from the list, and click Replace. When you reach the word **dented**, click Add to add the word to the dictionary, because it is spelled correctly.

PageMaker displays the Add to User Dictionary dialog box, which shows how it would hyphenate the word. You don't want it to hyphenate before the **ed**, so remove the three tildes from the word.

7 Be sure that As All Lowercase is selected, and click OK.

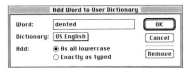

You use the tilde characters to specify which hyphenation points have priority. Typing a single tilde in a word indicates the most desirable hyphenation points. Typing two tildes indicates acceptable but not ideal hyphenation points, and typing three tildes indicates the least preferable hyphenation points. When you don't want the word to be hyphenated at all, remove all tildes from it.

8 Click Continue. Click Ignore for the following words:

Tawanda   Kathy

Bev   Eddington

When you get to **kayaking**, click Add and change the hyphenation to **kayak~ing**. Click OK and then click Continue.

9 Click Ignore for the following words:

Crocs   Zambesi

10 When you get to **expatriats**, choose **expatriates** from the list, make sure it appears as shown, and click Replace.

11 Click Ignore for the following words:

Zeman   Ralph

Christie   hippo

Croc   betcha

Jon   Benson

12 When the spell checker questions **whitewater**, click Add and change the hyphenation to **white~water**. Be sure As All Lowercase is selected and click OK.

13 Click Continue, then click Ignore for **Yangtze**. Replace **reluctently** with **reluctantly** from the list, and then click Ignore for the following words:

who've   say…happy

Britta   Munstead

The next word that the spell checker questions is the h at the beginning of the Tibetan Treks sidebar story. The word begins with a lowercase letter because you removed the capital T and replaced it with a drop cap. Under these circumstances the word is OK but should not be added to the dictionary.

14 Click Ignore, and then click Ignore for the following words:

Khumbu   Himalaya

Everest   Sagarmatha

14-day   Med

simpatico

The next word that the spell checker questions is the T in the drop cap at the beginning of the Tibetan Treks sidebar story. Under these circumstances the word is OK but should not be added to the dictionary.

15 Click Ignore. When the spell checking is complete, click the top left corner (Macintosh) or top right corner (Windows) to close it.

Closing story editor

There is one story editor window open for each of the three stories in the project that were opened by the spelling checker. You can close all of them at once.

1 Hold down Shift (Windows) or Option (Macintosh) as you choose Story > Close All Stories.

Congratulations! You have completed this project. If you have a printer available, you may print your completed version of the publication.

2 Close all open files, and close PageMaker.

Review questions

1 How do you suppress master page items on just one page?

2 What is a quick method to space text evenly across a column?

3 How do you reuse styles among publications?

4 What are the differences between tracking, kerning, range kerning, and the Expert Kerning command?

5 How do you add a continuation line to a story that jumps to another page?

Answers

1 Choose View > Display Master Items to turn off the display of master page items for the current page.

2 Select the text tool, click in the paragraph, click the Paragraph-view button in the Control palette, and click the Force Justify Alignment button.

3 To use the styles of one publication in another, open the publication to which you will add styles. Choose Type > Define Styles, and click Import. Locate and double-click the publication that has the styles you want to copy. Click OK to confirm copying over existing styles. Click OK to close the Define Styles dialog box.

4 *Kerning* refers to adjustments of letter space between individual pairs of characters. *Range kerning* refers to selecting three or more consecutive characters and applying kerning to them. *Tracking* is similar to range

kerning, but it also compensates for the size of the text to which the track is applied. The Expert Kerning command calculates optimal kerning for individual letter pairs in the selected text but makes adjustments that are only noticeable at larger type sizes (usually over 36 points).

5 With a story completely placed, select a text block with the pointer tool and choose Utilities > Plug-ins > Add Cont'd Line. Select whether the continued line should appear at the bottom or top of the selected text block and click OK.

Lesson 7

Recreational catalog

You complete the annual "Best Of" catalog for Utah Gear, a fictional company specializing in recreational equipment. Type, colors, and graphics are designed both to draw customers to the products and to print successfully on press. Adobe Systems extends its thanks to Recreational Equipment Inc., which supplied all text and props for this project. Some product information has been modified slightly for these training materials.

In this project you will complete a catalog that will be printed by a commercial printer. You work with a variety of imported graphics, including scanned photographs, and Kodak Photo CD® images, as well as colors, links, inline graphics, and various file formats. You also learn how to set up color separations to print to an imagesetter, and explore issues that affect color reproduction.

In this project you learn how to do the following:

• Insert inline graphics.

• Create custom rules.

• Edit a spot color.

• Work with color in the context of commercial color printing.

• Manage linked graphics.

• Import a Kodak Photo CD image.

• Prepare files for a prepress service provider.

This project should take you about 2 hours to complete.

Before you begin

As before, you delete the existing PageMaker preferences or configuration file to return all settings to their defaults and make sure that the fonts for this project are installed. Then you open and inspect a final version of the document that you create in this project.

Note: *Windows users need to unlock the lesson files before using them. For information, see "Copying the Classroom in a Book files" on page 4.*

1 Before launching PageMaker, return all settings to their defaults. See "Restoring default settings" in Lesson 1.

2 Make sure that the fonts are installed on your system: AGaramond, AGaramond Italic, AGaramond Semibold, AGaramond Semibold Italic, Myriad Bold, and Myriad Roman.

Windows only: *Because of the way Windows handles fonts, AGaramond Semibold appears in the ATM Fonts list as AGaramond, Bold (notice the comma) and AGaramond Semibold Italic appears in the ATM Fonts list as AGaramond, Bold Italic (notice the position of the comma). However, none of these font names appears in font menus in Windows applications. You must apply bold to AGaramond to use AGaramond Semibold; you must apply bold and italic to AGaramond to use AGaramond Semibold Italic; and you must apply italic to AGaramond to use AGaramond Italic. You must apply bold to Myriad Roman to use Myriad Bold.*

3 Start the Adobe PageMaker application, then open the 07Final.pmd file in the 07Lesson folder. If the publication window does not already fill the screen, click the Maximize button.

4 To see a self-running "slide show" presentation of the catalog, hold down the Shift key and choose Layout > Go to Page. When you use the slide show features, PageMaker automatically hides the palettes, and each page in the publication displays in sequence.

5 Click the mouse button to stop turning the pages.

6 Leave the final file open so you can use it as a visual reference as you work through the project.

This publication contains the first five pages of the catalog, including the cover, contents page, and several partially completed pages where you will add product photographs.

The document master consists of a simple three-column grid with a one-half-inch gutter. The partially empty pages have the major graphic elements already in place. The template has text styles defined in the Styles palette, and custom colors defined in the Colors palette.

You will now open and save the copy of the publication in which you will work.

1 Open the 07Begin.pmt file in the 07Lesson folder.

Next you will make sure that a certain printer description file (PPD) is installed. You will choose it later in the lesson.

2 Choose File > Print and make sure Agfa 9800 appears in the PPD pop-up menu, and then click Cancel. If it is not present, you must install it from the Classroom in a Book CD, as described in "Installing PPDs (Windows only)" on page 3.

Note: If you do not have the required printer, you can still create the project as directed and then print it on your own printer by selecting your printer and its PPD (if it is a PostScript printer) in the Print dialog box when it is time to print. You can also use the Export Adobe PDF command to create an Adobe PDF version of the project as described later in this lesson.

3 Save the untitled document in the 07Lesson folder as 07Work.pmd. If the publication window does not already fill the screen, click the Maximize button.

Placing a Kodak Photo CD image

You start working on the catalog by placing a Kodak Photo CD photograph on the cover. A Photo CD stores an image in several standard resolutions for popular uses, such as computer display or reproduction on a printing press. PageMaker chooses a high-resolution version by default, but you can specify a new size and resolution as you import the image into PageMaker. You can apply your changes to the original Kodak Photo CD file, or you can save the settings with the image in CIE Lab TIFF format. The CIE Lab color model contains device-independent color information that can reproduce color accurately on a PostScript Level 2 or later printer.

1 On page 1, the cover of the catalog, choose File > Place, open the 07Lesson folder, and double-click 07Img14.PCD. (In Windows, if the file doesn't appear in the list, choose All Files for Files of Type.)

Note: If necessary, Choose File > Preferences > General. In the Preferences dialog box, click CMS Setup. For Color Management, choose On. Click OK.

Because you selected a Kodak Photo CD image, PageMaker displays the Kodak Photo CD Import Filter dialog box, which contains a preview of the selected image. Photo CD images are scanned directly from slide or negative film, so they always appear in landscape (wide) orientation before you import them.

2 Select Save to CIELAB TIFF File.

Selecting this option will save a TIFF version of the image with your settings on your hard disk, letting you use the image the same way as other imported graphics. If you don't select this option, the original Photo CD must be in the CD-ROM drive for the image to stay linked with the publication.

3 In the Image Enhancement section, select Medium for Sharpen Output, and then select Auto-Color Balance. Click OK when a warning message appears.

Note: Auto-Color Balance is useful only when the lightest point in a picture should be pure white. Otherwise, Auto-Color Balance may introduce an unwanted color cast.

Although the default resolution would be adequate for a commercially printed publication, a file at that resolution would be unnecessarily large for this lesson, so you'll specify a lower resolution.

4 For Size, select Constrain Proportions, and make sure Units is set to Inches for Width and Height.

5 Enter **7** for the width. Set the Image Resolution to 100 pixels per inch.

For real-world production, a general guide-line is to specify a resolution of twice the screen ruling—lines per inch (lpi)—that will be used to print the image. For this project, a resolution of 100 is sufficient and uses less disk space and memory.

6 Click OK.

Because you selected the Save to CIELAB TIFF file option, a dialog box appears where you can name the file.

7 Name the file 07Photo.tif in the 07Lesson folder, and click Save. When a window appears asking if you want to include the graphic inside the publication, click No. This creates a link to the external file instead of copying the file into the publication.

Note (Macintosh only): *If PageMaker displays an alert telling you that there is not enough memory to place the image, increase the memory size for PageMaker. For more information, see the documentation that came with your Macintosh.*

PageMaker creates the new TIFF file and displays the loaded graphic icon. As you move the icon, the horizontal and vertical rulers display indicator lines to show the position of the top left corner of the graphic. You can also check the position using the X and Y values in the Control palette. On the rulers and in the Control palette, negative values are to the left of or below the zero point of the rulers.

8 To place the TIFF image, position the loaded icon so that X is -1p6 (left of the page) and Y is -4p6 (above the top of the page).

9 Click to place the image.

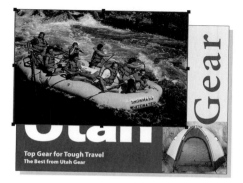

10 While the image is still selected, choose Element > Arrange > Send to Back.

If the image draws too slowly on your screen, you can speed redraw by reducing the amount of detail PageMaker displays for placed images. This does not change the resolution at which images will print.

11 Choose File > Preferences > General. Select Standard for Graphics Display, and then click OK.

When positioning elements precisely over images or when checking the publication closely before printing, remember to select High Resolution for Graphics Display.

12 Save 07Work.pmd.

If high-resolution graphics display is off, you can temporarily view graphics at high resolution without turning it on in the Preferences dialog box. Hold down Ctrl+Shift (Windows) or Control (Macintosh) as you redraw the screen (for example, when changing the view).

Cropping an image

The part of the image that hangs out over the edge is called a *bleed* and is necessary for printing images that come all the way to the edge of the paper. To evaluate the composition of the page, however, you will want to crop the bleed temporarily. Before you print separations, you'll pull the bleed back out again.

Note: If this publication was really going to press, elements currently touching the page edges would extend past them so that they can bleed properly. For simplicity of viewing, bleeding elements have been cropped to the edge in this publication.

1 If needed, select the image you just placed.

2 To crop the bleed, select the cropping tool (⌗) from the toolbox. Position it over the upper left corner handle of the image, and drag inward until the edges of the image are even with the edges of the page. Remember that you can use the rulers or the Control Palette to help you position elements on the page; the top left corner of this page is 0,0 on the rulers.

3 Save 07Work.pmd.

Working with color

Many print jobs are printed using either spot or process color printing methods. *Spot color* uses a separate ink to print each color in the publication, which can allow accurate color reproduction. However, spot color cannot easily reproduce the thousands of colors in a photograph, because it would require too many separate inks. *Process color* reproduces a wide range of colors using just four standard inks, by combining the inks in varying proportions on a page. When you want to reproduce photographs or other art with many colors, process color is more economically feasible than spot color, but not all colors can be reproduced accurately.

Printing overlapping colors on press

Most color printing inks are partially transparent, so printing one ink on top of another usually alters the color of both inks. For spot colors, PageMaker attempts to avoid this effect by using the standard printing industry practice of *knocking out*, or removing, inks where they print below the topmost ink, keeping the color pure.

In the following example, the spot ink of the shape knocks out the background ink. On the black separation, the shape appears as negative space in a black background.

If the spot ink were to *overprint* the black, the two inks would mix and the result would be darkened by the black. To produce the results you expect, PageMaker creates knockouts by default when you specify color, though you can choose to overprint.

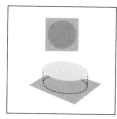
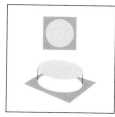

Shape overprints   *Shape knocks out*

Note: *In general, process inks do not knock each other out because they reproduce a color by being combined. However, process inks can be knocked out by a spot color.*

Misregistration and trapping

When you prepare a publication for commercial printing, you must take printing requirements into account in advance of printing. Failure to do so often results in unexpected costs and delays. As you work through this publication, you will specify and adjust colors with press requirements in mind.

When you print separations, you create a separate set of paper or film images for each ink used in the publication. A commercial printer uses these separations to create the plates used to print the job—one plate for

each ink. This publication will use five inks—cyan, magenta, yellow, black, and PANTONE 5405 CVC.

When a file is printed by a commercial printer using printing plates, the paper passes between rollers for each ink used in the publication. Each time the paper passes a roller, there is the possibility of misalignment or *misregistration*, if the paper is stretched or compressed by the printing press. Misregistration can cause thin gaps of white (often called *light leaks*) or color shifts between adjacent objects on the page.

Registration   *Misregistration*

To compensate for this misregistration, you can use a technique called *trapping*, which overlaps adjoining color areas slightly, preventing gaps between colors.

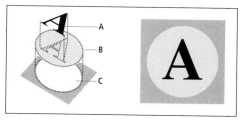

A. *Character overprinted* **B.** *Circle trapped by spreading its edges* **C.** *Circle knocked out of underlying object*

The trapping process has many variables. Light objects on dark backgrounds are trapped differently from dark objects on light backgrounds. There are special considerations for text, black objects, and imported files. The amount of trap varies, depending on the paper, print quality, and printing press.

Trapping can be daunting for even the most experienced designer. It is essential that you work closely with your printer or prepress service provider to avoid costly complications when you print.

Trapping cannot make a publication completely perfect—the way trapping affects the edges of type and graphics can actually make them look less polished. When you use trapping, your goal is to minimize the negative effects of misregistration while keeping the detrimental effects of trapping under control. In some cases it is actually better not to trap. Your commercial printer can help you decide.

This full-color catalog is currently designed to be printed using the four process ink plates: cyan, magenta, yellow, and black. Discussions with the commercial printer revealed several potential problems with the current design. For example, on pages 3 through 5, product price text is currently specified as a red process color, which is likely to lose legibility if misregistered.

To solve this problem, the printer has recommended converting one of the process colors to a spot ink. This will create a fifth plate which will use a dark blue-green spot color from the PANTONE color library. In this project you will replace the current blue process color with a PANTONE spot color.

For this catalog publication, you will set up the Colors palette by deleting unused colors and then redefining the blue process color as a PANTONE spot color.

Redefining a color

In the next steps, you redefine the blue process color as the PANTONE 5405 spot color. You can edit colors from either the Define Colors command or the Colors palette menu. For this project, you'll use the Colors palette menu.

1 In the Colors palette, double-click the color Blue.

2 Select Spot for Type, then choose PANTONE® Coated for Libraries.

The pop-up menu contains a selection of electronic color swatch books that are included with PageMaker 7.0. Most of the choices are electronic versions of standard swatch books traditionally used by commercial printers.

3 Enter **5405** to select PANTONE 5405 CVC.

4 Click OK to close the Color Picker. Select Overprint.

You selected Overprint because the PAN-TONE 5405 spot color will often be printed on top of process colors. If PANTONE 5405 is set to knock out the colors underneath it, normal misregistration may introduce undesirable registration gaps between the PANTONE 5405 ink and the underlying process inks when the catalog is printed on press. If you are not sure whether a color should be set to overprint, consult your printer or prepress service provider.

5 Click OK to close the Color Options dialog box.

The icon to the far right of the color name (■) indicates that the color you just added is a spot color.

In the publication, all objects that used the original process color now use the PANTONE 5405 spot color.

6 Save 07Work.pmd.

Using a process version of a spot color

On page 1, the solid rectangle behind the Utah text currently uses the PANTONE® spot color. However, there is too much potential for the spot plate to cause a visible break in the type where it straddles the photograph and the rectangle. It's been decided that it would be slightly better to use the process color equivalent of the PANTONE spot color. For example, the common process inks used by the photo and the rectangle

will make it unnecessary to trap their common edge. You will find the process equivalent of PANTONE 5405 and apply it.

A possible effect of spot ink misregistration

1 In the Colors palette, select PANTONE 5405 CVC. Choose New Color from the Colors palette menu.

2 In the Color Options dialog box, choose PANTONE® ProSim from the Libraries pop-up menu. Make sure **PANTONE 5405 CVP** is selected by default. Click OK.

Note: The PANTONE® ProSim library is specifically designed to provide approximations of PANTONE spot inks. However, the process equivalent may not be exact in all cases.

3 Choose Process for Type, make sure CMYK is chosen for Model, and click OK.

4 Save 07Work.pmd.

Applying a color

Now you will apply the new process color to the rectangle.

1 With the pointer tool, select the solid rectangle under the word Utah.

2 In the Colors palette, click the Fill button and then click PANTONE 5405 CVP.

Creating rich black rules

Pages 2 through 5 use wide black rules that abut photographs and areas of solid color. Misregistration on press may cause gaps between the rules and the other areas of the page that they touch. To avoid trapping problems, the thick rules have been drawn as thin rectangles. As rectangles, the colors of their fills and strokes can be specified independently.

Also, process black is designed to be partially transparent so that it mixes well with other process inks. However, this makes process black appear "thin" or weak when it covers an area wider than a narrow rule. Therefore, you will fill the rectangles with a deeper black color called a *rich black*, which includes cyan to make it look more solid.

Process black rules
set to overprint

Rich black rules

1 In the Colors palette, choose New Color from the Colors palette menu.

2 Type **Rich Black** for the name.

3 Select Process for Type, and make sure CMYK is selected for Model. Type 10 for Cyan, 0 for Magenta, 0 for Yellow, and 100 for Black. Click OK.

4 Go to page 2. With the pointer tool, select the two black rectangles on the page.

5 Choose Element > Fill and Stroke. In the Fill section, choose Rich Black for Color. In the Stroke section, make sure [Black] is selected for Color, select Overprint, and click OK.

The stroke is a custom width of .3 points to manually trap the edge of the rectangle. Now apply the rich black color to the same objects on the other pages.

6 Go to page 3. Repeat steps 4 and 5 for page 3. Go to pages 4 and 5 and repeat steps 4 and 5 for those pages as well.

Making an overprinting version of a color

Now finish making changes to page 2. By default, PageMaker overprints black type smaller than 24 points, but the S drop cap is 78 points. You will trap it by overprinting. An Overprint option is not available for selected text, but you can create and apply a version of the default black that overprints.

1 Choose Edit > Deselect All to make sure no objects are selected. In the Colors palette, select New Color from the Colors palette menu. Type **Black Overprint** for Name, choose Tint for Type, choose Black for Base Color, and select Overprint. Make sure **100** is the Tint %, and click OK.

In this case it is possible to duplicate the color and overprint it but, with a spot color, that would generate an unwanted additional color separation. The black ink functions as both a spot and process ink, so using a 100% tint ensures that Black Overprint objects print on the same default black separation.

2 Go to page 2. Select the text tool (**T**), select the S drop cap by highlighting the top of the S in the first line of the paragraph, and in the Colors palette, select Black Overprint.

Note: If you highlight the middle or bottom of the S, you will only be selecting a tab space that exists to make room for the S drop cap.

3 Save 07Work.pmd.

Working with inline graphics

The introductory paragraph on page 2 of the catalog will contain several inline graphics that break up the monotony of the large text block. *Inline graphics* are images that are inserted into a text block so that they stay with the text as it is moved or edited. In the following steps, you will learn how to add inline graphics.

Placing an inline graphic

When you want to add an inline graphic that isn't in the publication yet, you can import it directly into the story.

1 Zoom in so that the text in the bottom left corner of page 2 fills the publication window. Select the text tool (**T**), and click an insertion point right after the comma after the word **tents** in the second line.

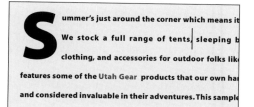

2 Choose File > Place and select 07TentIc.tif in the 07Lesson folder.

Because you have an insertion point, the As Inline Graphic option is selected. This is what you want, so leave the option selected.

3 Click Open (Windows) or OK
(Macintosh).

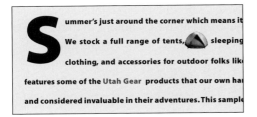

PageMaker places the image at the insertion
point. The graphic is now attached to the
text. If you move or edit the text, the inline
graphic will follow along with the text. The
spacing may not look right, but you will fix
it later.

4 With the text tool still selected, click an
insertion point after the comma after the
word **hiking** in the seventh line. Choose
File > Place once more and double-click
07Boot.tif.

When the graphic is already in the
publication, you can make it an inline
graphic using the Clipboard. Select the
graphic with the pointer tool, choose
Edit > Copy (or Edit > Cut), click an
insertion point in the text with the text
tool, and then choose Edit > Paste.

Adding fixed spaces

You now want to add some space around
each inline graphic. You placed each graphic
immediately after a phrase, so each one currently has a word space after it, but not
before it. One option is to make sure that a
regular space character exists before and
after the graphic, but if you try this, you may
find that there is not enough space around
the graphic. High-end publishing programs
like PageMaker can vary the width of a regular space character in the course of maintaining the letter spacing, word spacing, and
hyphenation settings specified for the publication. When you want to specify an exact
amount of space between characters, you
can use *fixed* spaces, which cannot be made
wider or narrower. Two commonly used
fixed spaces are the *em* and *en* spaces. An em
space is generally equal to the point size of
the font, and an en space is usually 3/4 the
point size of the font. On this page, you want
to have an en space before and after each
inline graphic.

1 With the text tool selected, click to the left
of the first inline graphic, and type
Ctrl+Shift+N (Windows) or
Command+Shift+N (Macintosh) to insert
an en space. Click to the right of the graphic,
delete the existing space character, and type
another en space.

2 Add an en space before and after each of the other inline graphics as needed, being sure to remove or replace any existing word space that follows each one.

3 Save 07Work.pmd.

Attaching rules to text

In addition to attaching graphic images to text, you can attach lines or rules to text to create a variety of effects. Take a look at page 2 of the final file. The table of contents is in front of a striped background. The orange stripes are not graphic elements, but rules, defined as part of the paragraph styles applied to the table of contents text.

To format the table of contents, you will first place the contents text. Then you define a paragraph style that positions wide rules behind alternate lines of text.

1 Pan the window so that you can see all of the empty space in the lower right corner of the page.

2 Select the pointer tool, and then choose File > Place. Select 07TextA.doc in the 07Lesson folder, be sure that As New Story is selected, and deselect Retain Format. Then click Open (Windows) or OK (Macintosh).

You make sure As New Story is selected because you want this story to be separate from any other story in the publication, unlike the inline graphics you just placed, which you intended to be part of the story on the left side of the page.

3 Position the loaded text icon so that the X value in the Control palette is approximately 34p and the Y value is approximately 15p. Place the text on the lower right quarter of page 2 by dragging between the black vertical line and the right edge of the page, then down about 2 inches, as shown below.

4 Select the text tool (**T**), and select all of the newly placed text. In character view in the Control palette, set the font to Myriad Bold (Mac OS) and Myriad Roman (Windows), the font size (**↕T**) to **17** points, and the leading (↕⥮) to **36** points. In Windows, click the Bold button (**B**) to apply boldface.

Click the Paragraph-view button (⊞) in the Control palette. Enter 1p6 for the left indent (→≡), and click the Apply button (⊞).

5 If necessary, choose Window > Show Colors to display the Colors palette, and with the text still selected, apply the color PANTONE 5405 CVC.

6 Double-click the word **Introduction**. Notice that the selection highlight extends above and below the word. The highlight indicates the height of the leading slug, which is 36 points, as you entered in the Control palette.

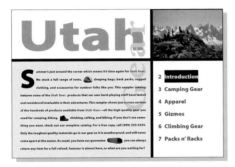

7 Choose Type > Paragraph, and then click Rules.

8 Select Rule Above Paragraph. Choose Custom for Stroke Style and enter **36** points (the size of the leading slug) for Stroke Weight. Click OK.

9 Select Orange for Stroke Color, make sure Tint is set to 100%, and make sure Width of Column is selected.

In the next step you will set the vertical placement of the rule. Rules can be positioned relative to either the top or the bottom of the leading slug. The thickness (Stroke Weight) of the rule always starts at the top of the rule and grows downward.

10 Click Options. Type **2** for Top. To close all dialog boxes, hold down Shift (Windows), or Option (Macintosh) as you click OK.

An orange 36-point rule is now attached to the text. The rule starts 2 picas above the baseline and hangs down, allowing the text to appear in the middle of the rule. Now you will define a style based on the text that you just formatted.

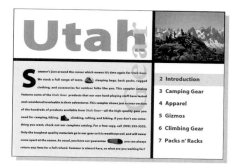

One advantage to using paragraph rules is that you can quickly make all rules bleed just by extending the right side of the text block past the edge of the page.

Creating a style based on formatted text

Because you want to apply the rule to several lines of text, it will be more efficient to define a style that includes the rule attributes so you can apply a rule with just one click. You will define a style by example, using text already formatted the way you want it.

1 Make sure the word **Introduction** is still selected. In the Styles palette, press Ctrl (Windows) or Command (Macintosh) as you click [No Style].

2 Name the new style **TOC Rule**. For Based On, make sure No Style is selected. For Next Style, choose Same Style. Click OK.

When entering text, you can automatically apply rules to alternating paragraphs as you type by taking advantage of the Next Style option. Define a style named No Rule without the rule attributes. In TOC Style, specify No Rule as the Next Style. In No Rule, specify TOC Rule as the Next Style.

3 Use the Styles palette to apply the TOC Rule style to every other line, creating a set of stripes.

4 Select the pointer tool, click the text block, and make sure that the bottom of the text block windowshade is dragged all the way down to the bottom margin of the page. Select the text tool (**T**) and click in the empty line below Packs n' Racks, and apply the TOC Rule style to this blank paragraph. (If necessary, click an insertion point at the end of the Packs n' Racks line and press Enter or Return to create a new line.)

5 Select the pointer tool, select the table of contents text block and examine it. If necessary, adjust the position of the text block so that it exactly fills the width between the heavy vertical line and the edge of the page. Position the text block so that the last orange rule touches the bottom of the page.

6 With the text block still selected, choose Element > Arrange > Send to Back.

7 Save 07Work.pmd.

Editing the color of a style

On pages 3 through 5, product prices currently appear in serif type colored in process red. However, on most printing presses, combining serifs, process color type, and process color backgrounds causes legibility problems whenever misregistration occurs on press, and the type is too small to trap as a process color. The type will hold together much more nicely if it is printed using a spot color. You will edit the style used for prices, replacing the red process color with the PANTONE 5405 spot color you created earlier.

1 Go to page 3, select the text tool (**T**), and select any of the red prices in the text. In the Colors palette, you see that the applied color is Red.

2 Click the Styles palette tab. In the Styles palette, you see that prices in this catalog use the Price style.

3 Double-click the Price style. Click Char, and choose PANTONE 5405 CVC for Color. To close all dialog boxes, hold down Shift (Windows) or Option (Macintosh) as you click OK.

All of the price text in the publication updates to use the spot color, and the price text will overprint.

4 Save 07Work.pmd.

Making a version of a color that knocks out

At the top of page 4, you find a white heading inside a long shape with round ends. The fill is currently PANTONE 5405, which is set to overprint. However, on the colored background, this heading will print better if its fill knocks out. You will create and apply a version of the color that knocks out.

1 Choose Edit > Deselect All to make sure no objects are selected. In the Colors palette, select New Color from the Colors palette menu. Type **Spot Knockout** for Name, choose Tint for Type, choose PANTONE 5405 CVC for Base Color, and select Overprint. Make sure **100** is the Tint %. Click OK.

2 Go to page 3. With the pointer tool, select the heading graphic and, in the Colors palette, select Spot Knockout.

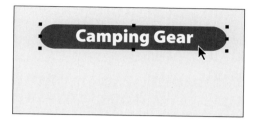

If you select the text block by mistake, hold down Ctrl (Windows) or Command (Macintosh) as you click with the pointer tool to bypass the text and select the shape under it.

3 Save 07Work.pmd.

About graphic file formats

In the next set of topics you will place more graphics into the catalog. PageMaker supports many graphic file formats. The two graphic file formats most often used for high-end color work are EPS (Encapsulated PostScript) and TIFF.

TIFF is the best file format for scanned images or digital paintings because it preserves image quality and reproduces color accurately. TIFF files are bitmap images that consist of a grid of pixels with a specific resolution (in pixels per inch). TIFF and other bitmap formats are created by scanners and by image-editing and painting programs such as Adobe Photoshop. Although you can change the size and orientation of a TIFF or other bitmap image in PageMaker, the image will display and print faster if you save it at its final size and orientation from your image-editing application.

Most EPS graphics are vector-based files created in drawing programs such as Adobe Illustrator. This kind of EPS file always prints at full resolution and quality even if you resize or rotate it. The high-quality printing of EPS graphics is made possible using methods which can't be displayed on screen on most systems, so an EPS file must include a preview image to display. These low-resolution preview images may not be viewable on all platforms. If a readable preview image does not exist, PageMaker can generate one automatically.

An EPS file can contain a mix of bitmap images and vector graphics, such as an Adobe Illustrator file that includes a TIFF image, or Photoshop EPS file that contains a clipping path. When any kind of file contains a bitmap graphic, you will get best results if you prepare a bitmap image at its optimum size and orientation for your publication before you import it.

Other popular graphics formats, such as GIF and JPEG, are less capable of handling the color information required for high-quality commercial printing.

Using clipping paths for transparent backgrounds

Many images in this publication are photographs that were scanned and then saved from Adobe Photoshop as TIFF files. Notice that most of the product images are obviously not rectangular, but if you select them, their handles indicate that they are actually rectangular images with transparent backgrounds. This is because each image includes a *clipping path* that was applied in Photoshop. A clipping path masks out a portion of an image, usually a background. Without a clipping path, a TIFF image would appear on a colored area with an undesirable white rectangular background.

Using Adobe Photoshop 3.0 or later, you can include a clipping path with an image saved as an EPS or TIFF file. On Windows 95, a clipping path displays more accurately if it is saved with a file in the TIFF format.

Placing and linking a graphic

When you place a graphic, PageMaker creates a screen-resolution preview image so that you can position, resize, rotate, and crop the graphic quickly. The changes you make to the low-resolution preview are applied to the full-resolution original when you print the publication.

PageMaker also creates a link that associates the graphic inside the publication with its original version on disk, so that you can track updates to the original. PageMaker creates links for text files as well, but text files are always included in the publication so that you can edit the text.

When placing a graphic, you have the option of copying the graphic completely into the publication, or including only a screen-resolution preview of it. As a rule, it's better to leave a large graphic outside the publication, particularly if you use the large graphic more than once. Copying entire graphics into a publication means you duplicate them each time you place them, consuming disk space unnecessarily. When you place just a screen preview of a graphic and its link, PageMaker can still print it at high resolution by following the link to the original graphics file.

In the following steps, you place several graphic images and explore linking options. As you place the following images, refer to 07Final.pmd or to the illustrations in this chapter as a guide.

1 Choose Edit > Deselect All, and go to page 3. Choose File > Place, and double-click 07Tent1.tif to place it as an independent graphic. If a dialog box appears asking you if you want to include a complete copy of the graphic in the publication, click No.

2 Click the loaded graphic icon under the Camping Gear heading. Click the top left reference point of the Proxy icon in the Control palette, and drag or nudge the tent graphic, or type values in the Control palette, so that the X value is approximately 33 and the Y value is approximately 4p5. There is extra space to the left of the graphic because you will be placing another graphic next to it later.

Managing links

As you work on a PageMaker file, you may occasionally move, rename, or update a file you have placed. When this happens, the link to that file is no longer current.

You can use the Links dialog box to see the status of all the linked files in a document and to update the links.

Setting link option defaults

When you placed the tent image, Page-Maker interrupted the place procedure to ask whether you wanted to import the full-resolution version or not. This can become tedious if you will be importing many images. If you always want PageMaker to import just the link to the original and create a screen-resolution preview for the layout, you can change the link option defaults.

1 Choose Edit > Deselect All to be sure no graphic is selected.

If a graphic is selected, the next step will set the option for only that one graphic, rather than set a new default.

2 Choose Element > Link Options. In the Graphics section, deselect the option for Store Copy in Publication, then click OK.

The Link Options: Defaults dialog box controls how placed objects are stored and updated. The Store Copy in Publication option to store a file outside the publication is only available for graphics. Text files are always copied into a publication so that you can edit the text in PageMaker.

Now all placed images will automatically remain outside the PageMaker document. If you are taking your file to a service provider, you need to bring all the linked graphic files with you. Without them, the file will be printed using the screen-resolution preview images, which do not include enough information for high-quality printing.

When you take your publication to a service provider, you can use the Save for Service Provider plug-in (included with PageMaker 7.0) to automate the process of gathering all the files your publication needs to print properly, such as fonts and linked graphics. For more information, see "Verifying and packaging a publication for commercial printing" on page 235.

3 Choose File > Place and double-click 07Tent2.tif in the 07Lesson folder. The file-size alert doesn't appear because you changed the link option default. Click to place the image to the left of and below the first tent. In the Control palette, fine-tune the position of the tent by clicking the top

left reference point in the Proxy icon and making sure that 24 picas is entered for X and 12 is entered for Y.

4 Save 07Work.pmd.

Viewing the status of publication links

The Links Manager dialog box is specifically designed to help you monitor link status and resolve linking problems.

1 Switch to the 07Final.pmd publication, and choose File > Links Manager.

The Links Manager dialog box displays a list of imported text and graphic files in your publication, along with file format information and page locations. When files are not up to date, a symbol appears to the left of the filename. If no symbol appears next to the document name, the document is up to date. As you select each item, a message below the list indicates its current status.

2 Click OK.

Simulating link status changes

In the following steps, you will move one graphic file and simulate updating another file by replacing it with a copy that has a newer date. Then you will look at the Links Manager dialog box to see the results.

1 Do one of the following:

Macintosh Go to the Application menu in the top right corner of your screen and choose Finder. Open the 07Lesson folder, and display the Save folder and the Links folder in separate windows. This makes it easier to move files around.

Windows Choose Start > Programs > Windows Explorer. Navigate to the 07Lesson folder.

2 Drag 07Tent2.tif from 07Lesson into the Links folder.

You have moved the file, so the file location recorded in PageMaker is no longer true.

In the following simulation, the file does not change location, but you replace it with a more recent version, to simulate a file that is updated.

3 Drag 07Pants.tif from the 07Lesson folder into the Save folder. Then drag the copy of 07Pants.tif from the Links folder to the 07Lesson folder. Be sure to begin by dragging the copy in the 07Lesson folder, not the one in the Links folder.

By moving 07Pants.tif into the Save folder instead of in the Recycle Bin (Windows) or Trash (Macintosh), you can easily return the project to its original state when you have finished.

Because the copy you moved into 07Lesson has a more recent date than the one that you moved from 07Lesson, you have simulated updating the 07Pants.tif file in another application, such as Adobe Photoshop.

4 Return to 07Final.pmd in Adobe PageMaker and choose File > Links Manager.

Notice that there is a diamond symbol (Macintosh) or an x (Windows) next to 07Pants.tif. The diamond or *x* indicates that the file is stored outside the publication and that the external copy has been modified. This is because you replaced the file with a file with a different modification date. In a production setting, this would happen if you updated the image and then saved it.

There is also a question mark next to 07Tent2.tif. This indicates that the file is no longer being stored at the location recorded when the file was placed. In a production setting, this would happen if the original image was moved or renamed.

To the far right of both files is an upside-down question mark. This lets you know that the file won't print in high resolution, either because the graphic is no longer stored where the link says it is, or it has been updated and no longer matches the low-resolution preview you currently see in the publication.

There are many other symbols that can appear in this Links Manager dialog box. If you aren't sure what symbols mean, select an item and read the Status area at the bottom of the dialog box, or see the *Adobe PageMaker 7.0 User Guide.*

If you tried to print the publication now, the graphics with broken links would not print properly. To resolve this, you'll update the links.

Relinking a file

The tent graphic was moved, so you need to create a link to the file in its new location.

1 In the Links Manager dialog box, select 07Tent2.tif.

A message appears at the bottom of the dialog box, indicating that the file is missing; moving the file broke the link.

2 To create a link to the file in its new location, click Info. Then open the Links folder, select 07Tent2.tif, and click Open (Windows) or Link (Macintosh).

PageMaker updates the link to the new location of the file. The question mark disappears from the item in the link list.

Updating a link

The pants graphic still has the same name and location, but you have simulated editing the file in another application. If the graphic were stored outside PageMaker, you wouldn't have to do anything; PageMaker would automatically read the current version of the file. This graphic is stored inside the publication, however, so you need to tell PageMaker to update its internal copy of the file so that it is storing the latest version.

1 In the Links Manager dialog box, select 07Pants.tif.

2 Click Update to update the link to the file and the preview image in the publication. Click OK.

You simulated file linking changes by moving files around and checking links from the 07Final.pmd publication. Now you'll put the files back in their original places so that you can continue to work from 07Work.pmd.

3 In Explorer (Windows) or the Finder (Macintosh), drag 07Pants.tif from the Lesson folder to the Links folder, then drag the other copy of 07Pants.tif from the Save folder to the Lessons folder.

4 Drag 07Tent2.tif from the Links folder to the 07Lesson folder.

Preparing for commercial printing

In this section, you will prepare the publication and its associated files for the stage of publishing known as prepress. At the beginning of the prepress stage, publication pages are completely designed and laid out, but are not yet prepared for the combination of imagesetter, press, paper, and inks that will be used.

The success of your print job depends on communication with your commercial printer.

Specifying a PPD

PageMaker creates separations based on the characteristics of the selected printer, so in a real-world situation, you would select and install a PPD (PostScript Printer Description) that is appropriate for the printer on which the separations will be output. The PPD that you choose determines the default settings in the Print dialog box. You can install additional PPDs at any time. Separations from this publication will be printed on an Agfa 9800 imagesetter, so that is the PPD you will choose.

For PPDs to be available, the publication must be composed for the printer (Windows) or a PostScript printer must be selected in the Chooser (Macintosh).

1 In 07Work.pmd, choose File > Print.

2 Choose the Agfa 9800 PPD from the PPD pop-up menu.

3 To save your change without printing, hold down Shift as you click Done.

You must choose a PPD that is appropriate for the imagesetter you will use. The printer for that PPD does not have to be attached to your system.

Turning on color management

At the beginning of this project, you placed a Photo CD image into the catalog. Before you can separate it and the other Photo CD images in the catalog, you must check that the color-management system is turned on so that the CIE Lab colors can be converted accurately to the CMYK color model in which the images will be printed.

1 In 07Work.pmd, choose File > Preferences > General, and click CMS Setup.

2 If needed, choose On for Color Management, click the Kodak ICC icon on the left, and choose Kodak ICC from the New Items Use pop-up menu.

Note: For color management to provide optimal viewing and printing results, you must set the Kodak ICC settings to match the RGB source, monitor, and proof printer you use for the project. For more information about color management, see Chapter 8 in the Adobe PageMaker 7.0 User Guide.

3 Click OK to close the Color Management System preferences dialog box, and then click OK.

Specifying automatic trapping values

You can specify trapping values for objects created in PageMaker. Always consult with your commercial printer to determine the correct values for your project. Trapping values depend directly upon many factors, such as kind of paper and inks being used and the kind of press. In the following steps, you set trapping values for the catalog.

1 Choose File > Preferences > Trapping.

2 Click to select Enable Trapping for Publication.

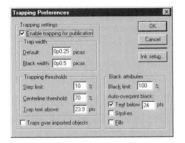

3 In the Trap Width area, leave the Default set to 0p0.25 (¼ point).

This is a common trapping value. The Default option specifies the trap (amount of overlap) for all colors except black. PageMaker applies traps based on a set of internal rules. Usually, lighter colors will expand or spread into adjacent darker colors. Trapping isn't visible on the screen, nor accurately represented by color composite proofs.

4 Leave Black Width set to 0p0.5 (½ point).

The Black Width option specifies trap for colors next to or under black. Usually, black width is 1.5 to 2 times the default trap. Again, get this number from your printer or prepress service provider.

5 Leave the three Trapping Thresholds options set to their default values.

The Step Limit sets the threshold at which a trap will be applied. The higher the number, the more extreme the color difference needs to be before PageMaker applies an automatic trap.

Centerline trapping, where a trap grows outward from the center of an edge, is used when colors have similar *neutral densities*, meaning neither color is much darker or lighter than the other. The Centerline Threshold value determines when PageMaker uses centerline trapping placement. Higher numbers use centerline trapping only for very similar colors. Lower numbers use it for a greater relative range of colors.

PageMaker traps only text above the point size indicated in the Trap Text Above option. Smaller point sizes typically overprint if specified to do so in the Black Attributes options.

6 Select Traps Over Imported Objects.

This option enables one or more objects drawn in PageMaker to trap to one another when an imported graphic is between them in the stacking order.

7 Leave Black Limit set to 100%.

The 100% value for Black Limit tells PageMaker that only colors containing 100% black should be counted as black. The Black Limit option is useful when compensating for extreme *dot gain*, in which the porous surface of the paper causes the halftone ink dots to spread. This most often occurs when printing on newsprint or other low-grade paper stock.

8 In Black Attributes, select the Strokes and Fills options.

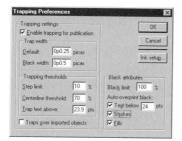

This causes the lines and fills of objects that you draw with the PageMaker tools to overprint if they are black. Black objects are usually overprinted.

9 Click Ink Setup.

The Ink Setup button lets you change the neutral density of specific inks. The default values are based on industry standards. A commercial printer would use a densitometer to measure a particular ink's density percentage, and then change the number in this dialog box to reflect the findings. Changing this number will change the way PageMaker traps colors.

10 Click Cancel.

Again, for more information on any of these options, see the *Adobe PageMaker 7.0 User Guide*.

11 Click OK, and save 07Work.pmd.

Trapping Options affect only elements created in Adobe PageMaker—strokes, fills, rules, and text. You cannot specify traps within imported photographs or illustrations. Any trapping for imported files must be applied within the application that created the image.

Your commercial printer may be taking advantage of other trapping methods that work with PageMaker, such as the fast in-RIP trapping available through PostScript® 3™ imagesetters, or a specialized and comprehensive trapping program such as Luminous TrapWise. If your printer is using another trapping solution, you should not use PageMaker's trapping options. Talk with your printer or prepress service provider to determine who will be responsible for applying traps to your publication.

Verifying and packaging a publication for commercial printing

The success of a remote print job (a job where you must transport the publication files to another location) depends on the presence of elements used in the file, such as fonts, colors, imported graphics, and the tracking values file. Many of these elements are stored outside the publication in various folders or even across a network. You must provide those external elements along with the publication, but tracking them down can be time-consuming. To automate this task, PageMaker includes the Save for Service Provider plug-in. This plug-in can determine whether all necessary elements are present, gather the files in one place, and create a detailed report of verification results and publication information. This plug-in is a valuable tool even if you print the final separations at your own location.

1 Choose Utilities > Plug-ins > Save for Service Provider.

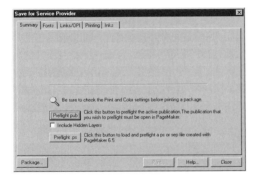

2 Make sure the Summary tab is selected, and click Preflight Pub. If an alert appears telling you that the publication has not been saved, click Continue or Yes to save the publication.

Preflight, a term used by many prepress service providers, means avoiding costly mistakes by verifying that all required elements are present for high-resolution output. The term is taken from the preflight checklists used by airplane pilots.

Some service providers prefer to receive PostScript files from clients, so the Preflight PS button lets you check PostScript files that have already been created by PageMaker.

3 When PageMaker has completed checking the publication, click each of the report tabs.

If there are any problems that would prevent a successful print job, PageMaker will indicate them here. If there aren't any missing fonts or files, you are ready to package the publication and all its elements.

4 Click Package at the bottom of the window. If prompted, click Continue or Yes. In the Save As dialog box, specify the Package folder in the 07Lesson folder.

When you are preparing a removable cartridge drive to bring to a prepress service provider, the most reliable way is to create the package in a folder on a hard disk first, and then copy the contents of the folder to the cartridge.

Note: You cannot specify a filename here, as you usually can in a Save As dialog box, because PageMaker is saving all the publication files under their original names.

5 In the Include section, select Copy Fonts. This ensures that your prepress service provider will have the fonts you used in the publication.

6 Click Notes, and type your name, contact information, and output information. At the bottom, you can type additional instructions or notes for the printer. Click OK.

The next set of options let you open the report automatically in PageMaker, check the links one last time, and specify the report format.

7 Select Auto Open Package Report, Update Links in Source Pub Before Packaging, and make sure Formatted (.pmd) is selected for the Report Type.

Note: For the next step, you will need approximately 12MB of free disk space.

8 Click Save. Processing may take a few minutes. When PageMaker finishes processing, click Close. You can examine the report. When you finish, close Report.pmd. (In Windows, the Report may be saved with a .p65 extension.)

9 Open the folder Package and take a look at the package you just created. (In Windows, the report is saved in the same directory as the Package folder.)

The folder Package now contains all the files required for prepress output.

 If you want to gather all the necessary files for remote printing (such as at a prepress service provider) but you don't need the level of detail provided by the Save for Service Provider plug-in, you can use Files Required for Remote Printing option in the Save As dialog box.

Printing color separations

Before you create color separations, you must tell PageMaker which colors to print, and select other options such as crop marks and registration marks. If you are taking the publication to a prepress service provider,

you will not normally be performing the following tasks. If you are a prepress service provider, this topic is recommended.

1 Choose File > Print, and make sure the Agfa 9800 PPD is selected in the PPD pop-up menu.

2 Click Paper. Select Letter for Size, and then select Printer's Marks and Page Information.

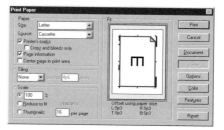

These options place crop marks, registration marks, density control bars, and color control bars on the output. All of these help your commercial printer and prepress service provider align separations and check color accuracy. The Printer's Marks option adds ¾-inch to the size of the paper that is required. The Page Information option prints the filename, page number, current date, and color separation name in the lower left corner of each separation.

3 Examine the Fit section of the dialog box.

It shows the relationship between the page size of your document and the paper size you selected. Use this dialog box to check whether crop marks, registration marks, and other page information such as color and density, will fit on the paper. These items are all printed outside of the document page, so the physical paper must be larger than the document size to allow for these. If the publication and selected marks are too large for the printable area of the paper, the values appear in red in the Fit area.

4 Click Color, and then select Separations.

If the imagesetter is a PostScript Level 2 device, you may be able to print faster by selecting the Perform on Printer option; ask your prepress service provider if you are not familiar with the equipment.

The Ink column lists the names of each spot and process color ink needed to print the colors in your publication. These inks are the spot and process colors that have been defined in the Colors palette or imported with your placed EPS files.

5 Scroll through the list to examine the inks that are available. Notice that the four process inks have a check mark next to them, indicating that they will be output as separations.

Notice that the PANTONE spot color is currently not set up to be printed. You will turn on this ink.

6 Select PANTONE 5405 CVC in the list, and select Print This Ink.

At this point in a real-world scenario, you would click Print to output the five sets of pages—one set for each ink that you have specified to print.

7 If you have a printer attached to your system, and you'd like to see the separations, choose a PPD appropriate for your local printer, specify settings, and click Print. If you are not going to print, but you want to save the settings you made, hold down Shift as you click Done. If you want to close without printing or saving print settings, click Cancel.

If you are proofing separations to a desktop printer, the page size plus printer marks may be larger than the paper in your desktop printer. You can scale the page to your paper size by clicking Options in the Print dialog box and then selecting Reduce to Fit for Size.

8 Save 07Work.pmd.

Creating separations using Adobe PDF

You can use the Export Adobe PDF command and a custom-defined printer style to create Adobe PDF separations in much the same way as you created paper separations on a color printer in the previous section. (All the components you need to create an Adobe PDF file are included on your PageMaker application CD.)

You first define a printer style in PageMaker for creating separations. Then you use this newly defined printer style with the Export Adobe PDF command to create Adobe PDF versions of the color separations.

Creating and saving a printer style is a useful way of saving printer settings that you use often, and it ensures consistent output in subsequent print jobs. Any printer style you create can be selected from the Printer Style pop-up menu.

1 Choose File > Printer Styles > Define.

Note: In Mac OS, you must first select a Post-Script driver in the Chooser.

2 In the Define Printer Styles dialog box, click New. Name the printer style **PDF Separations**, and click OK to close the Define Printer Styles dialog box.

The new style, PDF Separations, is now listed in the Define Printer Styles dialog box.

3 With the name PDF Separations highlighted, click Edit.

You will now set the PostScript printer and its PPD, depending on the platform you are working on, and set color options and paper size.

• Windows: In the Print Document dialog box, for Printer, choose Acrobat Distiller from the pop-up menu. For PPD, choose the Acrobat Distiller PPD installed with PageMaker.

• Mac OS: In the Print Paper dialog box, verify that Acrobat Distiller is selected for PPD.

If you have an odd-sized paper, you must define it in this dialog box.

4 Click Paper. For Paper Size, select Custom. Click OK.

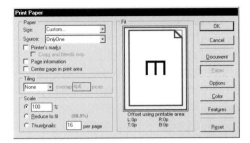

If you want to add registration marks, select the Printer's Marks option. If you do this, however, you must use a larger page size to accommodate these marks or you can select the Reduce to Fit option for Scale.

Now you are ready to make sure that all the colors in the job are output as separations.

5 Click Color. In the Print Color dialog box, select Separations. Scroll through the list of inks that are available. Notice that the four process inks have a check mark next to them, indicating that they will be output as separations.

Notice that the PANTONE spot color is currently not set up to be printed. You will turn on this ink as you did in the previous section.

6 Select PANTONE 5405 CVC in the list, and select Print This Ink.

7 Click OK and OK again to close the dialog boxes.

Now you are ready to create the PDF versions of the separations.

8 Save the PageMaker file. Choose File > Export > Adobe PDF.

9 In the PDF Options dialog box, for Printer Style, choose PDF Separations, the printer style you just defined. For Distiller Settings Job Name, choose Press. Notice that the PDF Style box is now empty.

10 Click Save Style, and name the style PDF **Separations**. Click Save. By saving the PDF Style, it is available for reuse at any time with any other PageMaker file.

11Click Export. Close any alert boxes that may appear. In the Export as PDF dialog box, save the file in the 07Lesson folder.

Note: On Mac OS, a window opens showing the progress of Distiller. The setting displayed in this window may not match those you selected in the PDF Options dialog box. Your PDF files will be created using the correct settings you specified, however.

12PDF versions of the color separations are created and displayed automatically in Acrobat or Acrobat Reader. This may take a few minutes. Page through the file to see how the plates for the different inks will look. Close the PDF file and Acrobat or Acrobat Reader when you are finished, and then exit PageMaker without saving any changes to the open file.

You've completed this lesson. Congratulations!

Review questions

1 How is an inline graphic different from an independent graphic?

2 What is a quick way to draw rules behind many lines of text?

3 How do you import a graphic with a shape other than a rectangle?

4 What is the difference between spot and process color?

5 What is the difference between knocking out and overprinting?

Answers

1 An inline graphic is inserted into the flow of text so that it moves whenever the surrounding text moves. An independent graphic is not connected to any other objects on the page (unless you use the Group command).

2 Create one or more styles in which a paragraph has a rule as part of its formatting. To format a paragraph with a rule, click in the paragraph, choose Type > Paragraph, and then click Rules. Select the desired settings and click OK for each dialog box. Then apply this style to as many paragraphs as need rules behind them.

3 You must create a clipping path for the graphic in an application like Adobe Photoshop. The clipping path can be any (even irregular) shape. After you place the graphic in PageMaker, the area outside the clipping path does not print.

4 *Spot color* uses a separate ink to print each color in the publication. *Process color* reproduces a wide range of colors by combining varying proportions of four standard inks (cyan, magenta, yellow, and black) on the page.

5 With overprinting, a second ink is applied on top of the first ink on the page. With knocking out, the first ink is not applied to the area (called the knockout) where the second ink will appear.

Lesson 8

Sailing publication

In this project, you'll learn how to manage a document divided into several chapter files. First you'll assemble three chapters into a book. Then you'll learn several ways to create index entries. You will generate and format an index and a table of contents for all the publication files that make up the book.

This project is a multichapter book about sailing. You are provided with three chapters that have already been completed. To the existing chapters you will add index markers, create an index and a table of contents in separate publications, and integrate all of the publications into a completed book.

In this project you learn how to do the following:

- Create a book list.

- Insert index markers.

- Create and format an index.

- Create a table of contents.

This project should take you about 2 hours to complete.

Before you begin

Before beginning to assemble the publication for this lesson, you will use the Preferences dialog box to establish application defaults, and then you will open the final version of the publication you will create.

Note: *Windows users need to unlock the lesson files before using them. For information, see Copying the Classroom in a Book files on page 4.*

1 Before starting PageMaker, return all settings to their defaults by deleting the PageMaker 7.0 preferences file. See "Restoring default settings" in Lesson 1.

2 Make sure that AGaramond, Birch, Myriad Bold, Myriad Condensed Bold, and Myriad Roman fonts are installed on your system.

Windows only: *Because of the way Windows handles fonts, you must apply bold to Myriad Roman and Myriad Condensed to use Myriad Bold and Myriad Condensed Bold, respectively.*

3 Start Adobe PageMaker 7.0 and open the 08Chap1.pmd, 08Chap2.pmd, and 08Chap3.pmd files in the 08Lesson folder. Turn the pages in each publication to see how the book is designed. Later, you will look at the example files for the table of contents and index.

4 Close 08Chap1.pmd and 08Chap2.pmd. If you are asked if you want to save changes, click No. In 08Chap3.pmd, click the Maximize button to make the publication window fill the screen.

5 Set up the palettes you will need for this project. If the Control and Styles palettes are not visible, choose Window > Show Control Palette and Window > Show Styles. Close any other open palettes.

Creating a book list

The heart of this project is to assemble all the chapters into a book list that associates a number of separate publications as a unit. A book list makes it possible to generate page numbers, an index, and a table of contents across a set of publications you specify. In PageMaker, you create a book by generating a book list in any publication. You add each publication to the book list, and if you want the index and table of contents to be in separate publications, you add them to the book list as well.

The index and table of contents don't have to be in separate publications. You can generate the information and place it in one of the existing publications. For this book project, however, the graphic designer has designed and created a template file for the table of contents and another for the index. When you create the book list, you'll include those two (currently empty) publications.

You can create the book list in any of the publications that will be in the book. However, the book list must also be present in any publications from which you are generating a table of contents or index, so once the book list is created, you'll copy it to the table of contents and index publications for this book.

To create a complete book list that includes the index and table of contents, begin by using templates to create the empty files from which you will build these two publications.

1 Open 08TocTpl.pmt, the template for the table of contents. Because it is a template, it opens as an untitled document. Save this in the 08Lesson folder as 08Toc.pmd, and then close the publication. Next, open 08IdxTpl.pmt, the template for the index. Save it in the 08Lesson folder as 08Index.pmd, and then close the publication.

2 You can create the initial book list in any of the publications that will be part of the book. Therefore, it's OK to create it in the remaining open publication, 08Chap3.pmd.

3 Choose Utilities > Book.

PageMaker displays the Book Publication List dialog box. In the next steps, you will add the publications that are to be parts of the book and then arrange them in the correct order.

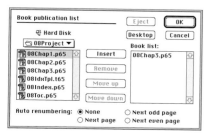

4 By default, the Book List on the right should include the current publication. If it isn't there, select 08Chap3.pmd in the left list, and then click Insert. Next you'll add the table of contents publication. In the left list, navigate to the 08Lesson folder if necessary, select 08Toc.pmd, and then click Insert to add it to the book list on the right. Now you will insert the index publication into the book list using a shortcut. In the list on the left, double-click 08Index.pmd.

5 In the left list, add 08Chap1.pmd and 08Chap2.pmd to the book list, so that the list includes the publications as shown below. You will arrange them in the correct order in the next step.

The order that the publications appear in the book list is important, because this is the order in which PageMaker numbers the pages. The publications should appear in the list with the table of contents first, the three chapters in order, and the index last.

6 In the book list, select 08Toc.pmd. If it is not the first publication in the list, click Move Up as necessary until 08Toc.pmd becomes the first publication. As necessary,

select other publications in the book list and click either Move Up or Move Down until the list matches the one shown below.

Before you close the Book Publication List dialog box, you need to tell PageMaker that the publications should be numbered consecutively and that each new chapter should begin on a right (odd-numbered) page. PageMaker will then add a blank page, if necessary, to the end of a chapter so that the next chapter begins on a right page. If you choose None as the Auto Renumbering option, PageMaker just uses whatever numbering you specified as the Starting Page # in the Document Setup dialog box for each publication.

7 Select Next Odd Page, and then click OK. PageMaker asks you if you want to renumber the publication now. Choose No.

You do not need to renumber the publication until you generate the table of contents, because the table of contents will add pages, and therefore will change the page numbers.

You'll need a copy of the book list in the table of contents and index files in order to generate their contents, so the easiest thing to do is to copy the book list to all the files in the book.

8 In 08Chap3.pmd, where you created the original book list, hold down Ctrl (Windows) or Command (Macintosh) and choose Utilities > Book.

That's all there is to it. PageMaker places a copy of the book list in every publication in the book list.

9 Save 08Chap3.pmd.

Adding index entries

Creating an index has four stages: inserting index entries into each publication in the book, looking the entries over and editing them if necessary, generating the index, and placing the index in the publication where you want it to be.

Wait until you have finished editing your publication before you add the index markers. If you make changes after you have added the markers, you run the risk of moving or deleting a marker as you edit, or of making an index entry inappropriate.

The mechanics of creating the index are relatively simple, but choosing the words and determining the structure of an index is a distinct discipline outside the scope of this book. In this lesson, we teach you how to add an entry and generate an index.

To add index entries, you should work in story editor so that you can see the index markers. The following steps take you through several different techniques for adding index entries to a publication.

Adding a simple page reference

When an index entry is spelled exactly the same as the text it refers to in the publication, creating an entry can be as easy as pressing a keyboard shortcut. When you want to customize an entry, PageMaker provides the Index Entry dialog box.

1 Select the text tool (**T**), click an insertion point in any paragraph on the first page of 08Chap3.pmd, and choose Edit > Edit Story.

In addition to using the Ctrl+E (Windows) or Command+E (Macintosh) keyboard shortcut while the text is selected, another way to open story editor is to triple-click the story with the pointer tool.

2 Choose Story > Display ¶ so that you can see the invisible characters in the story, including the symbols that mark index entries. The index marker symbol is a black rectangle with a white diamond inside (◘).

A quick way to insert an index entry is to select the text that should appear in the index, choose Utilities > Index Entry, and if the words in the Index Entry dialog box are correct, click OK. You begin by using Find to locate the phrase International Yacht Racing Union and then add it to the index.

3 Display the Find dialog box by choosing Utilities > Find or pressing Ctrl+F (Windows) or Command+F (Macintosh). To find the first phrase that you want to add to the index, type **International** in the Find What box, and click Find.

Find
Find what: International
Options: ☐ Match case ☐ Whole word
Search document: Search story:
⦿ Current publication   ○ Selected text
○ All publications   ⦿ Current story
○ All stories

(Find, Char attributes..., Para attributes... buttons)

4 When PageMaker finds the word International, close the Find window, and in story editor, select the rest of the phrase International Yacht Racing Union. To display the Index Entry dialog box, choose Utilities > Index Entry. The selected text appears as a first-level topic. Be sure that Page Reference is selected, rather than Cross-Reference, and click OK.

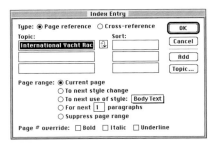

If you will be using the Find command often, you don't have to close the Find window. You can keep it open while you work in story editor.

You have just created an index entry for the selected phrase. In story editor, a marker symbol (❏) shows up to the left of the text you selected for the entry. This marker contains the indexing information that you entered in the Index Entry dialog box.

As you create more index entries, you may find it faster to open the Index Entry dialog box by using the keyboard shortcut: Ctrl+Y (Windows) or Command+Y (Macintosh).

Choosing the Page Reference option in the Index Entry dialog box adds to the index entry the page number on which the index marker appears. Later in this project, you use the Cross-Reference option to create entries that begin with "See…" and "See also…"

Customizing an index entry

In some cases, the words in the text aren't in the right form or in the right order for the index entry, so you need to take additional steps to create the entry you want.

You will create the next entry by typing text directly in the Index Entry dialog box, rather than by selecting text.

1 Go back three paragraphs to the one that begins **By the 1720s**. Click an insertion point anywhere in the paragraph, and open the Index Entry dialog box without selecting any text first. All the topic boxes are blank. Create a first-level topic by typing **racing boat to boat** in the top Topic box.

If you clicked OK now, you'd create a first-level topic entry with that text. But you decide that it should be a second-level topic entry instead.

2 Click the Promote/Demote button (↕) to move the entry down one level, and then type **yacht racing** as a first-level topic. Click OK.

You've created a main (first-level) index entry that says **yacht racing** and a second-level subentry that says **racing boat to boat**. If you are unfamiliar with the concept of first-level and second-level entries, you can examine the final index.

3 Open the 08IdxFin.pmd publication in the Final folder, and find the **yacht racing** entry.

Yacht racing is a first-level topic, and **racing boat to boat** and the other two indented entries under it are the second-level topics. PageMaker lets you create three levels of topic entries.

For basic first-level entries that don't need any editing, there's a good keyboard shortcut.

4 If necessary, use the Window menu to return to the story editor view of 08Chap3.pmd. In the paragraph just before the one you're in, which begins **Yacht racing began**, select the words **Charles II**. Press Ctrl+Shift+Y (Windows) or Command+Shift+Y (Macintosh).

That's all you have to do. PageMaker creates the index entry.

Indexing a range of pages

Now you will index a topic that is discussed in two sequential paragraphs. In PageMaker you can set up an index marker to refer to a range of paragraphs so that proper page numbers are generated even if the topic spans more than one page.

1 Choose Utilities > Find, type **Thames Tonnage rule**, select Current Story, and click Find. Notice that there are two paragraphs (the first one found and the subsequent paragraph) that discuss this topic.

2 Open the Index Entry dialog box. The selected phrase appears as a first-level entry, but it should be a second-level topic. Click the Promote/Demote button ( ) to change it to a second-level entry. Then type **Rating systems** above it as a first-level entry. Select For Next __ Paragraphs and type **2**. Click OK.

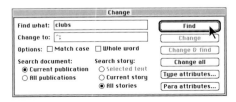

The For Next __ Paragraphs option is one way to index a topic across a page break. All pages where the specified paragraphs appear will appear in the index.

Indexing with the Find and Change commands

For the next indexing technique, you will use Find and Change to find a phrase and create an index entry for it. PageMaker doesn't really change the word, it only adds an index entry. You want to find all occurrences of the word **clubs** and create an index entry for each one. You can use the Change dialog box to do this quickly and easily.

1 In story editor, scroll to the beginning of the story, and click an insertion point in the title.

You want to use the Change option now, but you won't be able to open it if the Find dialog box is open.

2 If the Find dialog box is still open, close it, and choose Utilities > Change. Type the word **clubs** for Find What, type the characters **^;** for Change To, and then select All Stories. Click Find.

Note: The All Stories option will find matching text in any text block on any page, including the master pages.

The first occurrence is in the paragraph that begins **By the 1720s**. It's about the first racing clubs, which is relevant enough to index.

3 Click Change & Find to add an index marker and find the next occurrence of the word.

The second occurrence is also relevant.

4 Click Change & Find.

The third occurrence is in a paragraph that doesn't really say anything substantial about racing clubs.

5 Click Find Next to find the next occurrence of the word without adding an index marker to the current occurrence.

There are no more instances of the word **clubs** in the remaining text, so the Search Complete dialog box appears.

6 Click OK.

Next you want to find occurrences of the word **club** (rather than **clubs**) and index the occurrences as **clubs** where appropriate. The technique that you used in the last step—typing ^; for Change To—won't work here, because you want the index entry (**clubs**) to be slightly different from the word you're searching for. In the next steps, you will use two different techniques: You will type the entry, and you will choose the entry from a list of topics.

7 Click an insertion point at the beginning of the story. In the Change dialog box, type **club** for Find What, select the Whole Word and All Stories options. Click Find.

Note: *You can use the Change dialog box to find text without changing it, so that you don't have to switch to the Find dialog box.*

8 The first occurrence is one you want to index, so open the Index Entry dialog box. (The quickest way is the keyboard shortcut.) Click in the first-level topic box, and type **clubs**. Click OK to insert the index marker.

9 To find the next occurrence of **club**, click Find Next in the Find dialog box.

Instead of clicking Find Next, you can use the keyboard shortcut: Ctrl+G (Windows) or Command+G (Macintosh).

10 The next occurrence of **club** is not one for which you want to create an index marker, so click Find Next.

11 The third occurrence needs to be indexed. Open the Index Entry dialog box and click Topic. Choose the letter C for the Topic Section to display entries beginning with the letter C. Select **clubs,** and hold down Shift (Windows) or Option (Macintosh) as you click OK to close the dialog boxes.

12 In story editor, select the index marker and choose Edit > Copy.

You know you will be creating additional entries exactly like the one in the previous procedure. Because an index marker includes complete information for a single index entry, copying the index marker to the Clipboard lets you paste an entire copy of the same entry wherever you need it.

13 Find **club** again. When you find the next occurrence, click an insertion point before the word and paste the index marker you copied. Click Find, and paste another marker right before the next occurrence. After the fifth occurrence, you see the Search Complete dialog box. Click OK.

Indexing a proper name

In English, proper names appear in publication text with the first name first. However, they are indexed by last name. PageMaker can automatically change the order of a proper name so that it appears in the index by the last name.

1 Click an insertion point at the beginning of the story. Choose Utilities > Find to find the name **Dixon Kemp**.

You want to index this as **Kemp, Dixon**, but you don't have to reverse the name manually. PageMaker does it for you.

2 Press Ctrl+Alt+Y (Windows) or Command+Option+Y (Macintosh).

PageMaker adds the index marker.

3 To see how the index entry will look, select the marker that PageMaker just added to the left of Dixon Kemp (without selecting the name) and choose Utilities > Index Entry. The dialog box shows the index entry for the selected marker. Notice that the index entry reads **Kemp, Dixon** even though the text that you originally selected read **Dixon Kemp**. Click OK.

For the next index entry, you will find a name and then edit it in the Index Entry dialog box. This name is different—it includes

a title. The automatic name indexing you just used works with two-word names only, so you will use a technique that will let PageMaker index three word names by last name.

4 Click an insertion point in the first paragraph of the story. Choose Utilities > Find and locate the name **Sir William Perry**. In story editor, select the space between the words Sir and William, and replace it with a non-breaking space by typing Ctrl+Alt+spacebar (Windows) or Option+spacebar (Macintosh).

A non-breaking space will make the title and the first name index as one name, so that the automatic name indexing will work. You can use this technique with any three-word name, such as a name including a title or a middle name.

5 Select the name Sir William Perry and then press Ctrl+Alt+Y (Windows) or Command+Option+Y (Macintosh).

6 Select the index marker that you just created (without selecting the name), and open the Index Entry dialog box, either by using the keyboard shortcut or by choosing Utilities > Index Entry.

The dialog box shows the correctly indexed name—**Perry, Sir William**. You see a ^s in between the words **Sir** and **William**. This is the symbol for a non-breaking space that PageMaker displays in dialog boxes, so that you can distinguish it from a normal space.

7 Click OK.

Adding a cross-reference

A *cross-reference* is a kind of index entry that refers to another index entry instead of to a page number. In the following steps, you will create a cross-reference index entry that says **associations, see Clubs**.

1 Click anywhere in the text in story editor to deselect the index marker you just edited.

The location of the insertion point doesn't matter when you create a cross-reference, because a cross-reference does not refer to a page.

2 Choose Utilities > Index Entry and select Cross-Reference. Type **associations** as a first-level entry.

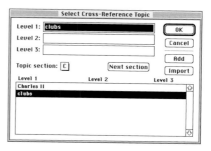

The options displayed in the bottom half of the dialog box change to those relevant to cross-references.

3 Select See. To make the word **see** appear in italics, select Italic for X-Ref Override. Click the X-Ref button.

In the Select Cross-Reference Topic dialog box you can choose from any existing topic in the index. This helps keep your topic list consistent. The list displays all entries beginning with the chosen letter of the alphabet.

To browse through existing topics, you can either click the Next Section button to see the entries for the next letter of the alphabet, or choose another letter for Topic Section to go directly to the desired section of the alphabet. You can use these techniques to browse through existing index entries for this project.

4 Choose C for Topic Section to see a list of entries in the current chapter that begin with the letter **C**.

To see all the index entries in all the publications in the book list, click the Import button.

5 Click **clubs** in the list of C entries, and then click OK.

6 Click OK. Save 08Chap3.pmd.

Previewing and editing the index

You can edit any entry by selecting its marker symbol in story editor and then opening the Index Entry dialog box. The information for the selected marker will appear. You can then make whatever changes you want. PageMaker offers you an even more convenient way to edit entries, however. You can create a preview of the index by using the Show Index feature and then edit any entry from within that listing.

1 In story editor, choose Utilities > Show Index.

PageMaker goes through all the publications in the book list for the currently active publication. When the search is complete, it displays the Show Index dialog box. The Index Section is set to A.

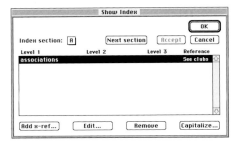

In the Show Index dialog box, you can see the cross-reference **associations, see clubs** that you just created.

Earlier, you added a cross-reference using the Index Entry command from the layout. You can also add a cross-reference from the Show Index dialog box, because a cross-reference isn't tied to a specific page. In the following steps you will add an entry that cross-references the topic **artificial materials** to the topic **synthetic materials.**

2 Click Add X-Ref. Type **artificial materials** for Level 1. Click X-Ref. Choose S for Topic Section, scroll to the bottom of the list, select **synthetic materials**, and then click OK. Click

OK to close the Add Index Entry dialog box. The new entry is visible in the list. Click OK to close the Show Index dialog box.

You'll open the Show Index dialog box again to edit another entry. Normally you would open Show Index just once to make many changes, but for this project you will open Show Index again to learn how to view only the index entries in the current publication, not throughout the entire book list.

3 Hold down Ctrl (Windows) or Command (Macintosh) as you choose Utilities > Show Index. Holding down Ctrl or Command opens Show Index with the entries in the current publication only.

The A section appears by default. The words **artificial materials** are selected, because they are the first entry for this letter.

4 Select **associations**, and then click Edit. In the Edit Index Entry dialog box, change **associations** to **organizations**, and then click OK. The Show Index dialog box automatically switches to the O section, where the edited cross-reference is visible. Click Accept, and then click OK to exit.

Note: *The Accept button lets you apply index changes you have made so far without having to click OK. However, you still have to click OK and choose File > Save to save the index changes to disk.*

Double-clicking an index entry is the same as selecting it and clicking Edit.

5 Close 08Chap3.pmd. When you are asked if you want to save changes, click Yes.

Generating an index

You will quickly create a fully formatted index using the index entries you have entered in this project. The sailing publication consists of more than one file, so you will use the Book command to index all of the publications together.

1 Switch to 08IdxFin.pmd to see how the finished index will look. If the publication window does not fill the screen, click the Maximize button in the right corner of the title bar to expand the window.

2 In the 08Lesson folder, open 08Index.pmd, the publication you created from the index template. If the publication window does not fill the screen, click the Maximize button in the right corner of the title bar to expand the window.

3 Choose Utilities > Book to confirm that this file contains an up-to-date book list, and then click Cancel to close the dialog box.

Note: *You can create an index for a booked publication only from a file that contains a book list. This file has a book list because earlier in this lesson you created a book list in 08Chap3.pmd and then copied it to all the other files on the list, including this one.*

4 Choose Utilities > Create Index. In the Create Index dialog box, be sure that Include Book Publications is selected.

If this option is not selected, PageMaker indexes only the current publication, not the whole book.

5 The Title option contains the text that will appear as the title of the index. For this project, you can accept the default of **Index**. If necessary, select Remove Unreferenced Topics.

In PageMaker, you can build a list of topics and reassign existing entries to different topics. As topic assignments change during a project, some topics may end up without references from any entries. Remove Unreferenced Topics ensures that topics without entries aren't included in the index.

In the next step, you will change the space that occurs between the entry and the first page number. The default is two spaces, but you change it to a nonbreaking en space. This prevents entries in which the number is on a line by itself.

6 Click Format. You will edit the Following Topic option. It is selected by default, so type a caret followed by a greater-than symbol (^>). In this dialog box, this is the code for an en space. Click OK to exit the Index Format dialog box, and then click OK again to generate the index.

Note: To see what the other codes mean, look in the online Help.

PageMaker compiles the information from all the index markers you created, and then displays a loaded text icon. You want to place the index in all three columns while leaving room for the index title, so you will use semi-automatic text flow to start each column part of the way down on the page.

7 Hold down Shift to change the loaded text icon to indicate semi-automatic text flow. Click at the intersection of the left edge of the first column and the guide at 3 inches. The index text flows into the first column from the guide to the bottom of the column.

8 Continue holding Shift as you click at the intersection of the left edge of the second column and the horizontal guide at 3 inches. Continue to flow index text into the third column the same way you did in the first two columns.

You want the index title to be above the three columns, so you'll simply reflow the title while keeping it threaded to the rest of the index.

9 Select the pointer tool and select the text block in the first column. Click the top windowshade of the first column to load the text icon. Starting where the left edge of the first column meets the guide at 1.375 inches, drag the loaded text icon across and down so that it spans the three columns and extends down past the guide at 2 inches.

Next, you will thread the remaining index text into three columns on the second page of the index.

10 With the pointer tool still selected, click the text block in the third column, and click the bottom windowshade handle of the third column.

11 On page 30 (the second page of this publication), starting in the first column at the horizontal guide at 1.375, drag to create a text block that fills roughly 1/3 of the column down from the top.

12 Click the bottom windowshade handle, and starting at the horizontal guide at 1.375, drag another text block roughly 1/3 the size of the column. Then, starting in the third column at the guide at 1.375 inches, click to

place the remaining text. If you don't have enough text left to do this, reduce the size of the first two columns.

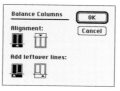

Depending on how carefully you placed the columns on page 2, they may be uneven, so you will use the Balance Columns plug-in to line up their bottom edges.

13 Select the pointer tool and select all three columns on this page.

14 Choose Utilities > Plug-ins > Balance Columns. Be sure the left icon is chosen for both Alignment and Add Leftover Lines. Click OK.

These two choices tell PageMaker that you want to adjust the bottoms of the columns rather than the tops and that if they can't be exactly the same length, the extra text should go on the left.

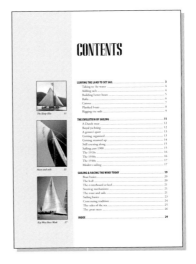

15 Save 08Index.pmd.

Generating the table of contents

PageMaker creates a table of contents by assembling the text from paragraphs that you designate. An easy and common technique is to set up a paragraph style that includes heading paragraphs in the table of contents. Using this method it is possible to build a table of contents without any manual intervention. In this project, you will include the text of the first-, second-, and third-level heads in the table of contents.

1 Open 08TocFin.pmd in 08Lesson/Final to see what you're about to create. If the publication window does not fill the screen, click the Maximize button in the right corner of the title bar to expand the window.

2 Open 08Chap3.pmd in the 08Lesson folder. Choose Type > Define Styles. Select Heading 1, click Edit, and click Para. Select the Include in Table of Contents option. Click OK twice to get back to the main Define Styles dialog box.

3 Select Heading 2, and repeat the process— click Edit, click Para, select Include in Table of Contents, click OK twice. Do the same thing for Heading 3, and then click OK to accept all the style changes. Save the chapter.

You have just specified that the text of all three heading levels in Chapter 3 should automatically be included in the table of contents. In the real world, you'd have to do the same thing for each of the other chapters, or better still, you would copy the Chapter 3 styles into the other chapters. In this project, however, this step has already been done for you in the other two chapters.

4 In the 08Lesson folder, open 08Toc.pmd, the empty file that you created earlier from the table of contents template. Take a quick look at the list of styles, and notice that they are the same ones that appear in your chapter publications.

Later on, you'll see that PageMaker creates some new paragraph styles for the generated table of contents text.

Now that the pages for this publication are final, you want to renumber the pages, making sure that each publication (chapters, TOC, and index) still begins on a right page.

5 In 08Toc.pmd, choose Utilities > Book, and in the Auto Renumbering section, click Next Odd Page (even if it is already selected—otherwise you won't be able to click OK). Click OK. Choose Yes when asked if you want to renumber the pages now.

PageMaker goes through all the publications in the book, updating the page numbering and adding blank pages where necessary to ensure that each publication begins on a right (odd-number) page. Now it's time to generate the actual table of contents.

6 Choose Utilities > Create TOC.

In the Create Table of Contents dialog box, the text in the Title box will appear as the title of the table of contents.

7 For this project, leave the default title of **Contents**. Be sure that Include Book Publications is selected.

You would deselect this only if you wanted to create a table of contents or paragraph list for just the current publication—not a common situation.

8 For Format, leave the default of Page Number After Entry.

9 For Between Entry and Page number, the ^**t** designates a tab between the entry and page number. You can use regular spaces instead, if you like, or you could use ^**m** to put in an em space. For now, leave the tab. Click OK.

PageMaker informs you of its progress as it goes through the publications looking for designated paragraphs. When it has completed the task, it presents you with an icon loaded with the newly generated text.

10 Click the loaded text icon in 08Toc.pmd near the top left corner of the page margins to place the generated text.

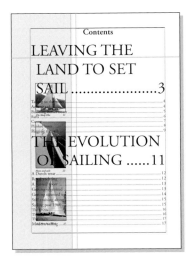

11 Save 08Toc.pmd.

Formatting the table of contents

Your table of contents text is in place, but the appearance isn't right. PageMaker created a new paragraph tag for each requested paragraph style, but it used the formatting of the source paragraphs as a default style definition. You will customize the look of the table of contents by editing the paragraph styles PageMaker automatically creates for a TOC.

1 Go to the first page of 08Toc.pmd, and look in the Styles palette. Notice that Page-Maker has added several new styles to the list. Each one begins with the letters TOC.

You begin by editing the paragraph style for the title.

2 In the Styles palette, hold down Ctrl (Windows) or Command (Macintosh) as you click the style TOC title. Click Char, and choose Birch as the font. Type **64** for Size, and set Case to All Caps. Deselect Bold, set the Track to Very Loose, and Horizontal scale to 105%. Click OK. Next, click Para in the Style Options dialog box. Set the Alignment to Left, Left Indent to **2.25**, the First Indent to **0**, and the Space After to **.65** inch. Hold down Shift (Windows) or Option (Macintosh) as you click OK to close all dialog boxes.

In the next steps, you define the other four styles that begin with TOC. The type specifications are expressed using the notation x/x, which is a shorthand method by which typographers and graphics designers describe type size and leading. For example, 12/15 means 12 point type on 15 points of leading.

3 In the Styles palette, hold down Ctrl (Windows) or Command (Macintosh) as you click TOC Heading 1. Click Char and specify **12/15** Myriad Condensed Bold. The Case is already set to All Caps, because Page-Maker picked up the attribute from the Heading 1 style in the chapters. Click OK, click Para, and specify **2.25** for Left Indent, **0** for First Indent, and **.2** for Paragraph Space Before. Click OK. Click Tabs, click the right-aligned tab icon (⬇), and then choose the dotted line for Leader. Type **6.74** for Position. Click the Position pop-up menu and choose Add Tab. Click OK twice to close both dialog boxes.

You will modify the next two styles using the same method you just used to edit the TOC Heading 1 style.

4 For TOC Heading 2, specify Char settings of **11.5/15** AGaramond Regular. Specify Para settings of **2.5** for Left Indent and **0** for First Indent. For Tabs, add a right aligned, dot-leader tab at **6.74**. Remember that you must choose Add Tab from the Position pop-up menu to record the new tab position.

5 For TOC Heading 3, change the Char settings to **11.5/15** AGaramond Regular. Specify Para settings of **2.5** for Left Indent and **0** for First Indent. Click Tabs and set a right-aligned, dot-leader tab at **6.74**.

The word **Index** is still not formatted correctly. It should look the same as the lines that have the TOC Heading 1 style applied to them. You will fix this in the next topic.

6 With the pointer tool selected, hold down the Shift key to constrain the movement to a single direction, and drag the text block so that the baseline of the title (**Contents**) rests on the guide at about 2 inches. If necessary, choose View > Show Guides.

7 Choose File > Save.

Making paragraph styles consistent

You're almost done. In the following steps, you will make the style for the index title — **TOC Index title**—the same as the TOC Heading 1 style. This is necessary because you are going to be generating the table of contents one more time, to update it. The number of pages in the table of contents changes as you apply formatting, and the new table of contents will reflect the changed numbers. If you change the definition of the TOC Index title style, the index title will be correctly formatted when the new table of contents is generated.

1 If necessary, drag the bottom window-shade handle of the text block down a little below the bottom margin so that you can see the large word **Index**.

2 Select the text tool (**T**), click in the last line, and look in the Styles palette to see that the line has the TOC Index title paragraph style applied to it. Notice the capitalization and spacing of the style name.

3 Click an insertion point in one of the lines that has the TOC Heading 1 style applied to it. Hold down Ctrl (Windows) or Command (Macintosh) as you click [No style] in the Styles palette to display the Style Options dialog box.

4 Type **TOC Index title** for Name, being careful to duplicate the capitalization and word spacing of the style name. Click OK, and then click OK again when asked whether you want to replace the style.

5 Choose File > Save.

You have now redefined the TOC Index title style to be exactly like the TOC Heading 1 style. When you regenerate the table of contents, everything will be formatted correctly.

Regenerating the table of contents

1 Choose Utilities > Create TOC.

2 Select Replace Existing Table of Contents, and click OK.

PageMaker generates a new table of contents and replaces the old text with the new table of contents text. The page numbers in the rest of the book have changed to reflect the changes you made.

Formatting the dot leaders and page numbers

The next problem is that the dot leaders of the bold TOC entries are too heavy. The obvious solution is to select the leader and apply different formatting, but if you try it, you'll see what actually happens.

1 Select a TOC Heading 1 leader without selecting the space that precedes it.

2 Apply 11.5-point AGaramond (not bold) to it.

The dot leader is still big and bold because it derives its formatting from the last character before the dot leader begins. However, you don't want to change the paragraph formatting of the TOC entry. To reformat any kind of tab leader differently than the characters

before it, you can add a space before the leader and format the space with the attributes you want for the leader.

3 Go to the first entry that has the TOC Heading 1 style applied to it, **Leaving the Land to Set Sail**. Select the text tool (**T**) and type a space immediately before the dot leader. Select the space you just typed, and use the Control palette in character view to apply 11.5-point AGaramond. Then choose Edit > Copy, because you want to use that space to format other leader tabs in the following steps.

4 The next TOC Heading 1 paragraph, **The Evolution of Sailing**, doesn't have a space before the dot leader, so after the word **Sailing**, paste the formatted space you copied in the previous step.

5 In the same way, paste the formatted space after the entries on the remaining TOC Heading 1 line and to the index title line.

Your table of contents should now match the sample file 08TocFin.pmd. You've completed the table of contents, and, in fact, you've completed the book. You'll hide the guides so that you can see the completed layout more clearly.

6 Choose View > Hide Guides.

7 Save 08Toc.pmd.

Printing the book

You can print a booked publication from any one of the publications within the book. You should first check the book list contained in the publication to be sure it's up to date.

1 In 08Toc.pmd, choose Utilities > Book, and check the list to be sure it contains 08Toc.pmd, 08Chap1.pmd, 08Chap2.pmd, 08Chap3.pmd, and 08Index.pmd, in that order. Click Next Odd Page, and then click OK. If PageMaker asks you if you want to renumber the pages, click Yes.

2 Choose File > Print. Make sure that a PPD appropriate for your printer is selected, if you have a PostScript printer. Otherwise, select the appropriate printer.

Note: You can also use the Export Adobe PDF command, as described in Creating an Adobe PDF version of the flyer on page 41.

3 Select Print All Publications in Book.

This choice is available to you because the publication that you're in has a book list in it. If the current publication doesn't contain a book list, this choice is grayed out. The other choices in the Print Document dialog box are the same as for a document that doesn't use a book list.

4 Select Print Blank Pages to print any blank pages that PageMaker may have added to make each publication begin on a right page.

This publication uses a paper size larger than Letter, so if your printer cannot print on paper larger than Letter size, you can automatically shrink it to fit the selected paper size.

5 If you want to print, click Paper, click Reduce to Fit in the Scale section, and then click Print. If you don't want to print, save the printing settings you specified by holding down Shift and clicking Done.

6 Close all open files, and quit PageMaker When asked if you want to save changes, click Yes.

Review questions

1 What are the benefits of combining publications into a book list?

2 How do you make PageMaker copy your book list into every file in the book list?

3 What is the fastest way to create an index entry from a word?

4 What's the easiest way to set up the entries in a table of contents?

5 What does it mean when a designer or typographer specifies type as 18/20?

Answers

1 A book list lets you automate the following tasks:

• Number several publications sequentially

• Generate a table of contents for multiple publications

• Generate an index for multiple publications

2 Hold down Ctrl (Windows) or Command (Macintosh) and choose Utilities > Book.

3 Select the word and press Ctrl+Shift+Y (Windows) or Command+Shift+Y (Macintosh). You can also open Story Editor, choose Utilities > Change, type the word for Find What and type ^; for Change To, click Find, and then click Change or Change & Find.

4 Set up a heading style to include all headings with that style in the table of contents. To do so, choose Type > Define Styles, select a heading style, click Edit, click Para, select Include in Table of Contents, and click OK for all dialog boxes.

5 It means the type should have a size of 18 points and a leading of 20 points.

Newsletter on the Web

Built-in support for both HTML and PDF in PageMaker 7.0 makes it easier to publish new or existing PageMaker files online. In this project you will prepare a back issue of a newsletter for the Web. You will add hyperlinks, or active areas, to the newsletter, so that your audience can navigate to different pages or Web sites. Then you'll export and view the newsletter in PDF and HTML, comparing how each format affects the production workflow and the readability of the publication.

In this project you create a World Wide Web page from an existing newsletter originally designed for print. The newsletter is in an archive of back issues that are now being distributed on the Web. You will add hyperlinks so that someone can navigate the publication on the Web, and then you will export it as Adobe PDF and as HTML to compare the capabilities of each format. You will also use Adobe PDF and HTML export options to enhance the on-screen readability of the newsletter.

In this project you will learn how to:

• Add and edit hyperlinks.

• Export a publication to Adobe PDF with the original layout intact.

• Identify areas of a publication that cannot be reproduced using HTML.

• Prepare text for HTML export by associating HTML paragraph formats with PageMaker paragraph styles.

• Prepare publication graphics for HTML export.

• Export a publication to HTML, approximating the original layout.

• Use a Web browser to preview the Web pages you created and saved on your hard disk.

This project should take you about 2 hours to complete.

Before you begin

1 Before launching PageMaker, return all settings to their defaults. See "Restoring default settings" in Lesson 1.

Note: Windows users need to unlock the lesson files before using them. For information, see "Copying the Classroom in a Book files" on page 4.

2 Make sure that the AGaramond, AGaramond Bold, Myriad Bold, Myriad Bold Italic, Myriad Condensed, Myriad Condensed SemiBold Italic, Myriad Roman, Poplar, Trajan, and Zapf Dingbats fonts are installed on your system.

Windows only: Because of the way Windows handles fonts, you must apply bold to Myriad Roman to use Myriad Bold; you must apply bold and italic to Myriad Roman to use Myriad Bold Italic; and you must apply bold and italic to Myriad Condensed to use Myriad Condensed SemiBold Italic.

3 Make sure that Acrobat Reader, Acrobat Distiller, and an Acrobat Reader-compatible Web browser are installed. Also, make sure you have enough RAM to run PageMaker, Distiller and Reader at the same time. You will use Reader and Distiller for the PDF section of the lesson.

Note: The RAM requirements above apply only when creating online documents. Viewing them requires much less RAM. HTML documents require only a Web browser to view them, and PDF documents require only Acrobat Reader.

4 Make sure that the PostScript driver provided with the PageMaker application is installed. On Mac OS, select a PostScript printer in the Chooser.

5 Start the Adobe PageMaker application.

6 Open 09Begin.pmt in the 09Lesson folder. If the publication window does not already fill the screen, click the Maximize button. Save the publication as 09Work.pmd in the 09Lesson folder.

What you see is the newsletter as it was originally printed. The publisher wants to make back issues of the newsletter accessible via the Web, rather than storing them and mailing them to readers. Of course, the design of the newsletter is not optimal for on-screen viewing, so it would be best to redesign the publications for the screen. The publishers, however, do not have the time or the resources to redesign several years of back issues. Instead, they will use features in PageMaker to make the newsletter easier to read on-screen in either PDF or HTML.

7 Set up the palettes you will need for this lesson. If the Hyperlinks, Styles, and Colors palettes are not visible, choose Window > Show Hyperlinks and Window > Show Colors. Drag the tab of the Hyperlinks palette onto the already combined Styles and Colors palette to combine all three. Close any other open palettes.

To prepare this publication for online distribution, you will first add hyperlinks to the publication to allow online navigation through the publication. After that, you will learn how to create HTML and Adobe PDF

versions of the publication, so you can compare them and evaluate the production requirements of each format.

Comparing HTML and PDF

PageMaker supports both HTML and PDF because the wide range of online publishing scenarios is not completely covered by either format. For example, some documents will only be read online, while others are meant to be printed after they are downloaded. HTML and PDF are complementary technologies that can cover most publishing scenarios between them. They can link to each other, and a PDF document can be embedded in an HTML page.

HTML, or Hypertext Markup Language, is the file format used by most of the pages on the World Wide Web. HTML is primarily a set of tags that describe the sequence of text and graphics and the location of hypertext links. Basic HTML is essentially one column of text with graphics that flow along with the text, as if they were characters themselves.

PDF, or Portable Document Format, is a cross-platform format that is popular on the Web. You can create PDF from any program that prints, so that you can author with software you already use. With Acrobat Reader it is easy to view PDF documents in a Web browser. PDF preserves the original typography, graphics quality, and layout precision of the original, and can include interactive forms and multimedia.

You can compare the different ways that the archived newsletter can appear online by viewing the final HTML and PDF versions of the newsletter, which are provided on the Classroom in a Book CD. To do this, you will use a Web browser to open files on disc instead of over the Web.

1 Start a Web browser. In the Web browser, open 09FnlPdf.pdf in 09Lesson/09FinPdf. The command you use to do this may vary depending on the browser, but it is usually File > Open File. If you don't see the 09FnlPdf.pdf file, you may need to choose All from a file format pop-up menu in order to see PDF documents. In many Macintosh applications, pressing Option as you choose File > Open File displays all file types. Or on either platform, it may be easiest just to drag the PDF file into the browser window.

This version of the newsletter was exported from PageMaker as a PDF document. It is identical to the original in every way.

2 In the Web browser, choose File > Open File, and double-click 09FnlHtm.htm in 09Lesson/09FinHtm. If necessary, click the Maximize button to enlarge the browser window.

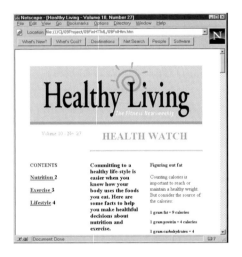

This version of the newsletter was exported from PageMaker using HTML options that approximate the original page layout.

If you are familiar with dragging between programs, and your browser supports drag-and-drop, you can simply drag HTML or PDF files from their folder window to the browser window.

Adding hyperlinks

Hyperlinks are one of the most significant differences between printed pages and Web pages. A Web page can contain hyperlinks to other Web pages or other parts of the same page. When you click a hyperlink, the Web browser takes you to the destination of the link. Hyperlinks can be invisible or appear as specially marked text or images on the page, depending on the page design and the viewing application. In PageMaker, the Hyperlinks palette makes it easy to create links. Hyperlinks you create will be active in your final document whether you export it to PDF or HTML.

One of the most important uses of a link is navigation. When a publication is on paper, navigating through it is simply a matter of physically turning pages. On the Web, you navigate with hyperlinks.

A hyperlink consists of two parts: an anchor (a destination) and a source (an object that jumps to an anchor). A source can jump to only one anchor, but an anchor can be a destination for more than one source.

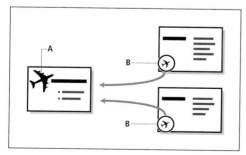

A. Hyperlink anchor (destination) **B.** *Hyperlink source (jump)*

Before you start creating hyperlinks, you may find it helpful to see how the hyperlinks will work when the publication is complete.

1 In 09FnlHtm.htm, scroll to the top if necessary.

2 Click the word Exercise. The browser takes you to the third page and its topic, Walking Your Way to Fitness.

3 Scroll to the bottom of the page and click **Return to Contents**. The browser takes you back to the first page.

Try out the hyperlinks to the other pages. After the following steps, the publication you are working on will have a complete set of hyperlinks just like the ones you just tried.

You will create hyperlinks in 09Work.pmd, which you saved earlier. You will then save two other versions of this publication: one that you export to Adobe PDF, and another that you will adapt for and export to HTML. Because the hyperlinks will be active in both formats, you will create them now, before you create the other versions of the publication.

Creating hyperlink anchors

Working with hyperlinks is easier if you develop hyperlinks in an organized way, so for this project you'll set up each page as an anchor, then you'll make a second pass through the document setting up sources that jump to the anchors.

1 Switch to 09Work.pmd. If the publication window does not already fill the screen, click the Maximize button. Select the text tool (**T**), and on page 1, highlight the text **CONTENTS**.

2 Click the Hyperlinks tab to display the Hyperlinks palette. Choose New Anchor from the Hyperlinks palette menu. Type **Contents**, and then click OK.

The new anchor appears in the Hyperlinks palette with an anchor icon next to it. The black symbol to the right of the anchor name indicates that the object to which this anchor is assigned is selected, and the outline around the icon indicates that the anchor is text selected with the text tool (as opposed to an entire text block).

On page 2, you will create an anchor using a faster method.

3 Go to page 2 and, with the text tool still selected, select the word **Nutrition** at the top of the page. Choose Edit > Copy. Click the New Anchor button (🔲), paste to create the name of the new anchor, and then click OK.

Clicking the New Anchor button is the same as choosing New Anchor from the palette menu.

4 Go to page 3 and, with the text tool still selected, select the word **Exercise** at the top of the page, and choose Edit > Copy. Click the New Anchor button, choose Edit > Paste, and then click OK.

5 Go to page 4 and, with the text tool still selected, select the word **Lifestyle** at the top of the page, and then choose Edit > Copy. Click the New Anchor button, choose Edit > Paste, and then click OK.

6 Save 09Work.pmd.

In the Hyperlinks palette, you can see that you have created an anchor for every page. Remember that an anchor is only half of a hyperlink—it's just the destination. You still need to create sources that jump to the anchors.

Creating hyperlink sources

Like anchors, you create sources using the Hyperlinks palette.

1 Go to page 1. With the text tool still selected, select the word **Nutrition** in the Table of Contents. You want this link to jump to the Nutrition anchor.

2 In the Hyperlinks palette, select the Nutrition anchor name in the palette (don't click the anchor icon), and then choose New Source from the Hyperlinks palette menu. Type **Contents to Nutrition**, and then click OK.

You can type any source name you want, but each name in the Hyperlinks palette must be different. For this project, the sources are named so that you can tell where they jump.

You will create the next source using a faster method.

3 With the text tool, select the word **Exercise**. You want this link to jump to the Exercise anchor, so in the Hyperlinks palette, click the anchor icon (![anchor icon]) next to the word Exercise. Type **Contents to Exercise**, and then click OK.

Clicking the anchor icon is the same as choosing New Source from the Hyperlinks palette menu with an anchor name selected in the palette.

4 Create a new source from the word **Lifestyle** on page 1 to the Lifestyle anchor in the Hyperlinks palette. Name it **Contents to Lifestyle**.

You've completed the hyperlinks that jump from the contents page to all of the sections in the newsletter.

Adding a source on a master page

Now you will add a way for people to get back to the contents page from any page. You will do this by adding a source that jumps to the Contents page.

Note: You can't add an anchor to a master page because an anchor is a destination on one specific page, and a master page item appears on multiple pages.

1 Go to the master page. Choose View > Show Guides. Select the pointer tool, choose File > Place, and double-click the 09ArtA.tif file in the 09Lesson folder. Click the loaded graphic icon below the page margin and between the vertical guides. Press the arrow keys to nudge the graphic so that it is centered in the space between the page margin, the page edge, and the vertical guides.

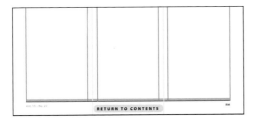

The graphic for the Return button is a TIFF image. You may be accustomed to using graphic formats such as GIF and JPEG for HTML Web pages. However, any graphic format PageMaker supports will convert to GIF or JPEG when you export to HTML. Regardless of the format you use, you must still consider how well the colors and resolution can be reproduced within the limita-

tions of GIF, JPEG, and Web browsers. For more information about how PageMaker converts graphics for HTML, see chapter 12 in the *Adobe PageMaker 7.0 User Guide.*

All graphic formats are supported when you export to Adobe PDF. Text and graphics in PDF are compressed for Web delivery.

2 With the button graphic still selected, click the anchor icon next to the word **Contents** in the Hyperlinks palette to create a source that jumps to the Contents anchor. Type **Return to Contents**, and then click OK.

A black icon appears to the right of the anchor name, indicating that the object to which this anchor is assigned is selected. The icons appear in one of two sizes: Large icons indicate a text link, and small icons indicate a graphics link.

3 Go to page 1, and save 09Work.pmd.

Because you added the Return to Contents button graphic and hyperlink to the master page, it will appear automatically on all of the pages which use the Document Master page. Because Page 1 contains the table of contents, however, the Return to Contents button and other master page items have been hidden on this page by deselecting the View > Display Master Items command.

Testing hyperlinks

You have completed all of the changes that make this a useful online publication. You can test the hyperlinks you created to make sure they work properly. You test hyperlinks using the hand tool.

1 Select the hand tool (🖑).

When you select the hand tool, all hyperlinks are outlined in blue. The blue outlines only appear in PageMaker, to help you identify hyperlinks as you test them.

2 Move the hand tool over the word **Nutrition** in the table of contents. The hand tool changes into a pointing hand, indicating that the word Nutrition is a hyperlink.

3 Click the word **Nutrition**. PageMaker takes you to the Breakfast Blunders section, and centers the anchor you created on that page.

You may not like the way the window centers around the anchor. You can change this behavior so that a destination page is always centered in the window after a hyperlink jump.

4 Choose File > Preferences > Online. Click to deselect the Center Upper-Left of Anchor when Testing Hyperlinks option. Click OK.

This preference doesn't affect how the hyperlinks are exported, it only affects how hyperlinks work when you test them in PageMaker.

5 Click the Return to Contents button at the bottom of the page. This time the destination page displays using the same view that was in effect the last time you viewed this page.

6 On page 1, click the word **Exercise**. After the Exercise page appears, choose Layout > Go Back.

The Go Back and Go Forward commands are another way to follow the trail of hyperlinks you've created in PageMaker. These commands can be useful when you are testing links and don't have them all built yet.

7 Save 09Work.pmd.

Adapting color for the Web

The newsletter was originally designed for inexpensive printing with two colors—black, and one spot color. You will change the second color to one that displays well on 8-bit monitors for viewing on the Web.

The second color originally used in this publication may not correspond to a color in the 216-color palette used by Web browsers, so to ensure predictability when this page is viewed on 8-bit monitors, you will edit the color to match a color in the online palette.

1 Display the Colors palette. Select PANTONE 138 CVU, and then choose Color Options from the Colors palette menu.

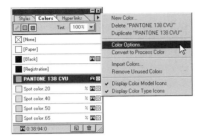

2 In the Color Options dialog box, choose Online from the Libraries pop-up menu.

The colors in this library are named after their position in the 216-color Web palette (before the dash) and their hexadecimal value, the way in which color is specified in HTML (after the dash). The color 183-FF9900 should be selected automatically as it is the closest match.

3 Click OK to close the Color Picker, and then click OK to close the Color Options dialog box.

The color name updates in the Colors palette.

4 Save 09Work.pmd.

Note: Although you may be able to find a color in the online browser palette that approximates the original color well, tints based on the spot color are variations which may not correspond to any color on the online palette. In this publication, the designer has chosen to let the browser dither the tints rather than spend the time finding a non-dithering alter-

native for every tint. Also, to fully adapt publication colors for 8-bit Web viewing, you must also respecify color in the original files of all imported color graphics (except photographs).

You can select a color quickly by typing the color name into the Color Picker.

Exporting to Adobe PDF

It won't take long to prepare a Web-ready Adobe PDF version of this publication. You have already created hyperlinks to help navigate the publication, so all you do now is add document information and export.

First you will save a new copy of the publication from which you will export to Adobe PDF. After this part of the lesson is complete you will return to 09Work.pmd and save another copy of the publication from which you will export an HTML version.

1 Choose File > Save As. Save the publication 09Work.pmd as **09PWork.pmd** in the 09Lesson folder. You will use 09PWork.pmd to create the Adobe PDF version, so keep it open.

When you export to Adobe PDF, PageMaker automatically starts Acrobat Distiller, which processes the file and produces an Adobe PDF version.

2 If you do not have enough free RAM to run Acrobat Distiller simultaneously with PageMaker, close all open applications other than PageMaker.

3 Choose File > Export > Adobe PDF.

Note: In Mac OS, be sure you have already selected a PostScript driver in the Chooser.

4 In the PDF Options dialog box, select OnScreen for PDF Style and Acrobat for the Printer Style. (The Acrobat printer style is created automatically the first time you export to PDF. For information on creating and editing PDF styles and printer styles, see chapter 12 of the *Adobe PageMaker 7.0 User Guide.*)

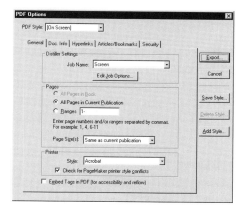

In this part of the lesson, you'll use the default settings in the PDF Options dialog box to create your Adobe PDF file. For most projects, these default settings are adequate. Later in the lesson, though, you'll look at the options that you can change if you need to change the file size or image quality, for example.

5 Click the Doc Info tab, and enter information for filename, subject, author and keyword. For Title, select and delete the file name. Type **Healthy Living** in the Title text box. For Subject, select and delete the file

name. Type **Volume 10 Number 27** in the text box. Leave the Author and Keyword entries *as is.*

Document information is often used to refine index searches in document collections. For this reason, you should always replace the file name with the document title. (Note this and Security are the only panels in this dialog box in which you can change information without defining a new PDF Style.)

6 Click Export.

7 In the Export PDF As dialog box, make sure the filename is 09PWork.pdf. Select the View PDF option (Windows) or View PDF Using option (Mac OS) if you want to open the newly created Adobe PDF file in Acrobat or Acrobat Reader rather than save it and open it at a later time. Click Save to save the PDF version into the 09Pdf folder in the 09Lesson folder.

PageMaker creates a PostScript file, and then starts Acrobat Distiller to convert the Post-Script into Adobe PDF. This may take a few minutes, depending on the speed of your computer.

Note: *On Mac OS, a window opens showing the progress of Distiller. The setting displayed in this window may not match those you selected in the PDF Options dialog box. Your PDF files will be created using the correct settings you specified.*

Acrobat or Acrobat Reader will launch auto-matically and display the Adobe PDF ver-sion of your file. Close this PDF file and Acrobat or Acrobat Reader when you have finished reviewing it. If the PDF file doesn't open automatically, navigate to the 09PDF folder and double click the 09PWork.pdf. Acrobat or Acrobat Reader will launch and open the newly created Adobe PDF file.

Viewing the PDF version in a Web browser

Now you'll see how the PDF file can be viewed in a Web browser. A Web browser uses the Acrobat Reader and the PDFViewer browser plug-in to display a PDF file. When you install Acrobat Reader, the installer automatically sets up Acrobat Reader and the plug-in.

Once again you will simulate Web viewing by using a Web browser to open the com-pleted file from your hard disk.

1 Start a Web browser. Choose File > Open File, and double-click 09PWork.pdf in the 09Pdf folder in the 09Lesson folder.

Note: *If you don't see the 09PWork.pdf file, you may need to choose All from a file format pop-up menu in order to see PDF documents. In many Macintosh applications, pressing Option as you choose File > Open File displays all file types.*

If a person chooses to print this document, the printed version will look just like the original.

2 Make sure the hand tool is selected in the Acrobat toolbar. Click the word **Nutrition**. The browser takes you to the Nutrition page.

3 Click the **Return to Contents** button at the bottom of the page.

4 On page 1, click the word **Lifestyle**. The browser takes you to the Lifestyle page.

This is a good time to test the PDF article you set up.

5 Move the hand tool over the first paragraph of the story. The hand tool turns into the article tool. Click the first paragraph.

The text you clicked is magnified to fit in the browser window.

6 When you have read to the bottom of the column, click that paragraph. Notice how Acrobat advances to the top of the next column where the article continues. Continue clicking forward in the story. To backtrack along the article, hold down Shift as you click. When you reach the end of the article, notice that your next click displays the entire page again.

If the text seems too large when you view an article, switch to Acrobat Reader, choose File > Preferences > General and lower the Max "Fit Visible" Magnification value. Any other changes you make to Acrobat Reader preferences will affect how a PDF displays in a browser.

7 Click Return to Contents.

8 When you are finished testing the PDF page, close the Web browser and Acrobat Reader.

9 Switch to PageMaker and close 09PWork.pmd if needed. If PageMaker asks you to save changes, click Yes.

Setting PDF Options

Earlier in this lesson, you created an Adobe PDF file using the Export Adobe PDF command and the Distiller default job options.

Depending on your publication and service provider requirements, you may sometimes need to customize the Distiller job options.

1 Choose File > Open, and open **09PWork.pmd** in the 09Lesson folder.

2 Choose File > Export > Adobe PDF to open the PDF Options dialog box. Save the file if necessary.

The PDF Options dialog box is where you control how content in the PageMaker file is converted—whether hypertext links are maintained, for example—as well as add PDF-based functionality such as security and document information.

3 Choose On Screen from the PDF Style pop-up menu because you are preparing a Web-ready PDF version of the newsletter.

A PDF style is a file that defines a particular set of PDF Options settings. You can choose between two predefined styles (On Screen and Print), you can define your own PDF styles, or you can use imported styles provided by colleagues.

Notice that after you choose On Screen for the PDF Style, editing almost any of the settings on any of the panels in the PDF Options dialog box, causes the PDF Style pop-up menu to revert to blank. The two default PDF Style settings—On Screen and Print—cannot be edited. However, you can use either as a basis for creating a custom PDF style, as you did in Lesson 7.

For information on printer styles, see chapter 12 in the *Adobe PageMaker 7.0 User Guide.*

Take a moment to check the range of options you can set in the PDF Options dialog box.

4 If needed, click the General tab.

The On Screen PDF Style uses the Distiller Screen job options (displayed in the Job Name pop-up menu) to convert the PageMaker document. The Distiller Screen job options are optimized to create Adobe PDF files appropriate for display on the World Wide Web or an intranet, or for distribution through an e-mail system. This option set produces the smallest PDF file size and optimizes files for byte serving.

5 To see the default values for the Distiller Screen job options, click Edit Job Options to open the Screen Job Options dialog box. This is the same dialog box, controlling the same options, as you will see in Distiller 5.0.

Notice that the Compatibility options is set to Acrobat 3.0, and the Optimize for Fast Web View option is selected. The Optimize for Fast Web view option compresses text and line art and restructures the file to pre-

pare for page-at-a-time downloading (byte serving) from Web servers. This makes for faster access and viewing when downloading the file from the Web or a network.

6 Click the Compression tab.

Color and grayscale images above 108 dpi are downsampled to 72 dpi. Distiller determines the best compression method and quality for color or grayscale images—JPEG is applied to 8-bit grayscale images and to 8-bit, 16-bit, and 24-bit color images when the images have continuous, smooth tones. ZIP is applied to 2-bit, 4-bit, and 8-bit grayscale images; to 4-bit color images and indexed 8-bit color images; and to 16-bit and 24-bit color images when the images have sharp color changes.

7 Click the Fonts tab. Notice that the Base fonts are embedded, and all embedded fonts are subsetted to reduce file size.

8 Click the Color tab.

The value of None in the Settings File pop-up menu means that information contained in the PostScript file is used to manage color. Unmanaged color spaces in the PostScript file are converted to RGB.

9 Click the Advanced tab.

Notice that Allow PostScript File to Override Job Options is selected, allowing Distiller to use settings stored in a PostScript file, rather than the current job options.

10Click Cancel to exit the Screen Job Options dialog box without making any changes and return to the PDF Options dialog box.

11 Click the Hyperlinks tab. Verify that the Internal Links option is selected to preserve the hyperlinks you just created.

The appearance of the links and the magnification are also set in this panel.

12 Click the Articles/Bookmarks tab. Verify that the Export Articles option is selected.

The tall columns of text on the pages of the newsletter in this lesson often don't fit on the screen at a readable size, because the newsletter was designed for print. As you follow a story from the bottom of one column to the top of another, you may find that you have to scroll up or down, making it tedious to read on screen. In PDF, you can make it easier for a person to follow a story by setting up each story as an *article*. In a publication that uses threaded stories, a PDF article automatically leads a person wherever the text goes, even if it jumps to other pages. Also, an article is automatically magnified to

fit the width of your screen so that a column of small type becomes easy to read and follow.

13 Click the Security tab to set options to limit access to Adobe PDF files and restrict features such as printing and editing. Because you are using the On Screen PDF Style, no security is applied to documents.

For complete information on the options in the PDF Options dialog box, see chapter 12 in the *Adobe PageMaker 7.0 User Guide*.

14 Click Cancel to exit the PDF options dialog box.

15 Choose File > Close, and close **09PWork.pmd** without saving any changes.

Preparing the HTML version

Many simple print publications translate well to HTML, but because there are significant differences between HTML and print, republishing print-oriented documents in HTML usually requires some modification. You can use PageMaker to adapt print-oriented publications for HTML without programming HTML code, but the capabilities of HTML still determine how faithful the conversion will be to the original design. Also, because PageMaker is capable of creating publications for print or online distribution, you can do many things in PageMaker that cannot be done using HTML. For these reasons, understanding the capabilities of HTML will help your publications work well on the Web. HTML may seem limiting from the point of view of print design, but from the point of view of online delivery, HTML provides many useful capabilities.

Page layout and HTML

Because a Web page can be viewed on any connected computer, HTML is designed to accommodate the wide range of different monitors that may be used to view it. A person can also change the size and shape of the window of the browser program in which they view an HTML page. Accordingly, the length of lines of text on a basic HTML page can change to adapt to the size of the window.

As a result, page size has much less significance in HTML than on paper, where the size of a page never changes. However, if you use certain HTML options to preserve page layout, you can "freeze" a particular page layout and page size on screen, at the expense of convenience on monitors that don't match the size you specify. Whether you are republishing formerly printed publications or designing new Web pages, preserving a PageMaker page layout is most effective when publications you export are designed using the grid features in PageMaker.

The simplest explanation of how HTML code works is that it describes how one object follows another in a sequence. Although special techniques can approximate page layout, basic HTML does not include two-dimensional information, such as page coordinates, and cannot describe overlapping foreground objects.

As you export the publication to HTML, PageMaker notifies you of layout elements that cannot be directly translated.

Typography in HTML

Type specifications that affect typographical density—such as tracking, word and letter spacing, and kerning—cannot be preserved in HTML. Browsers support only the most basic type specifications. The font and size are controlled by the Web browser and customizable by anyone, and line breaks are usually determined by the size of the window. By default, most browsers are set to display12-point Times Roman for body type and lists, and larger sizes of Times Roman for heads.

In addition, the following type characteristics are either controlled by or not supported by most Web browsers and won't be included when you export HTML from PageMaker:

- Font, type size, and leading

- Font width

- Strikethrough, outline, shadow, reverse, superscript, and subscript type styles

- Letter and word spacing, tracking, and kerning

- Spacing before or after a paragraph (other than standard spacing in HTML formats)

- Numerically specified paragraph indents

- Tab positions

HTML paragraph formats

Using HTML you can apply named *formats* to paragraphs. You apply a format based on the function of a particular piece of text, such as a heading, a regular paragraph, or a list. HTML formats are similar to the named styles in PageMaker in that the designer can change the appearance of a paragraph by applying a different format. However, a person using a Web browser can also change the appearance of an HTML format, to make it more readable on a specific monitor.

Because HTML styles are similar to PageMaker paragraph styles, adapting text to HTML is much easier if your publication text is structured using PageMaker paragraph styles.

HTML hyperlinks

As you have seen earlier in this project, hyperlinks are a great way to enhance a printed page for online use. You've already added hyperlinks to the publication earlier in this lesson, so that part of the conversion is complete.

Now that you know a little more about HTML, you will recognize aspects of the newsletter's design that you will change to make it work well in HTML.

Evaluating the publication for HTML

In the next sections, you evaluate the newsletter with HTML capabilities in mind and make the necessary changes. You'll start with the file you saved that includes the hyperlinks you added.

1 In PageMaker, open the publication 09Work.pmd. If the publication window does not already fill the screen, click the Maximize button. Save the publication as 09HWork.pmd in the 09Lessons folder.

2 Make sure guides are off. If necessary, choose View > Hide Guides.

Each section is marked by a large visual banner or headline that spans the top of the page. Later you will replace these PageMaker elements with graphics because they consist of overlapping text blocks and graphics that cannot be reproduced directly in HTML.

Pages 1, 2, and 4 use dotted horizontal rules which can be translated into HTML, but only as solid horizontal rules. PageMaker will convert these automatically.

All of the pages contain vertical rules between columns, which cannot be translated directly to HTML. You don't need to do anything about this; PageMaker will automatically delete them when you export.

Preparing the master page

PageMaker can export publication pages as one continuous HTML document. When you use this method, PageMaker inserts a rule between each page. However, there is already a rule across the top of each publication page which becomes redundant with the rule PageMaker automatically inserts. That rule is on the master page, so you will remove it before moving on to the regular pages.

1 Click the master page icon (📄).

2 Select the pointer tool, select the rule at the top of the page, and press Delete.

Preparing the bulleted lists for HTML

There are several bulleted lists in the publication, starting with one in the middle of the second column on the first page. Each line starts with a graphic bullet character and a tab character. The presence of a specific font is not guaranteed using HTML, so the bullet characters must be removed. Also, tab positions are not preserved in HTML, so leaving the tabs in may do more harm than good to the layout. You will use the Change command to remove both characters throughout the publication.

1 Go to page 1. With the pointer tool still selected, select the story containing the bulleted list in the second column, and choose Edit > Edit Story. Then choose Utilities > Change.

You will search for a sequence of characters that only appears where a line begins with a bullet and a tab. Different bullet characters are used throughout the publication, but you can find all of them in the same search pass by using a *wildcard* character that will find any character that otherwise fits the sequence.

2 Type ^p^?^t for Find What. This tells PageMaker to look for any character (^?) that has exactly a paragraph return (^p) before it and a tab character (^t) after it. Type ^p for Change To. This tells PageMaker

to leave the paragraph return intact, but remove the character and tab. Select the All Stories option.

3 Click Find. When you find one, click Change & Find. Repeat until the first line under **3 ways to stay motivated** is selected.

You don't want to replace the next three occurrences, because they are numbers, not bullets, so you will click Find Next instead.

4 Click Find Next repeatedly until the first line under **Exercise to energize** is selected. Click Change & Find repeatedly until the Search Complete message appears, and then click OK. Close the Change dialog box.

Finding and changing text throughout the publication has opened many story windows. You do not need to work in story editor for the next set of topics, so you can close all story windows.

5 Switch to any story window. Hold down Shift (Windows) or Option (Macintosh) as you choose Story > Close All Stories.

For a complete list of special characters you can use in the Find and Change dialog boxes, see online Help.

Editing the introductory paragraphs

In the original printed version of the newsletter, each section begins with an introductory paragraph formatted with large italic text. Later, when you export the publication to HTML, the paragraph style for the introductory text will be mapped to an HTML format that also uses large text. On the lower resolution of the computer screen, italic text is difficult to read, even at the larger size. You will edit the paragraph style to remove the italic formatting.

1 In the Styles palette, hold down Ctrl (Windows) or Command (Macintosh) as you click Body Text Intro. Click Char, deselect Italic, and then click Shift (Windows) or Option (Macintosh) as you click OK to close the dialog boxes.

2 Go to page 1, and save the publication.

Preparing page 1

A large TIFF image appears behind the text columns on page 1. HTML does not support overlapping foreground graphics, so if you export the page to HTML with this graphic in its current position, it will appear in the foreground next to another element—an undesirable result. It's better to remove it.

Note: It is possible to keep the graphic as an HTML background on the Web page, but an image with the dimensions of the current background graphic can significantly slow the display of the page. You can specify an HTML background in PageMaker, but an HTML background also tiles, or repeats, which may not be desirable in this case.

1 Select the TIFF image.

2 Press Delete.

Note: If you have trouble selecting the graphic, press Ctrl (Windows) or Command (Macintosh) as you click to select. PageMaker will bypass the topmost object and select the next object underneath.

Re-creating the banner on page 1

Now you will replace the logo banner at the top of the page, which was laid out in PageMaker. Because the banner uses large type sizes and many different fonts arranged in a highly designed manner, it cannot be translated directly to HTML in its current form. You can preserve its appearance by converting it to a graphic. PageMaker can export a graphic in any of several formats, but that technique won't work in this case because the banner exists in PageMaker as a mixture of text and graphics. Fortunately, PageMaker can quickly convert any page into an EPS file, and this is the method you will use to convert the many banner elements into a single graphic.

First you will move the issue information text out of the banner area. You want it to remain as text so that it can be found by people using search engines over the Web.

1 If the guides are not visible, choose View > Show Guides.

2 Select the pointer tool and drag the **Volume 10 Number 27** text down until its top edge snaps to the guide below the banner.

When PageMaker creates an EPS file, it uses the entire page area. The current page is too large, so you create a correctly sized page in another publication, from which you will export the EPS file. First you'll measure the area of the banner elements to determine the page size of the new publication.

3 With the pointer tool selected, draw a selection rectangle around the banner elements, including the horizontal rule. Make sure you do not select any elements below the rule, and choose Element > Group. In the Control Palette, note the values for H and W, which tell you the dimensions of the area you just selected. H should be approxi-

mately 16 picas, and W should be 45 picas. Make a note of these dimensions, and save 09HWork.pmd.

4 Choose File > New.

The default measurement system for new publications is currently set to inches. However, you can still specify the page size in picas.

5 Type a page size of **17p** by **45p**, or whatever value is just large enough to include the size you measured. Select Wide, and deselect Double-Sided. Set all margins to 0, and then click OK.

6 Choose File > Save As. Type **09Art.pmd** for a filename, and save it into the 09Lesson folder. Click Save.

7 Choose Window > Tile so you can see both publications. If necessary, in 09Art.pmd choose View > Fit in Window.

8 Click the window for 09HWork.pmd to make it the active publication. Go to page 1, select the pointer tool, and select the group of banner elements you grouped.

9 Select and hold the group of banner elements until you see the pointer change into an arrow, so that you see a screen image as you drag. Drag the grouped banner to 09Art.pmd, and drop it within the page.

10 Fine-tune the position of the banner elements so that all visible parts are within the page edge, particularly the sun rays poking through the top of the banner. If necessary, adjust the page size, but be careful—adding too much margin may cause the graphic to overlap another element on the final layout, but too small a page would crop the graphic.

11 Save 09Art.pmd.

Exporting and placing the EPS banner

Now you will generate an EPS version of the page you just created. Because an EPS file is similar to a PostScript file, you can export an EPS file from the Print dialog box in PageMaker.

1 In 09Art.pmd, choose File > Print. Choose Color General for PPD. Selecting a color printer ensures that color PostScript will be included in the new file. (Be sure the portrait option is selected if that option is present.)

2 Click Options. Select the Write PostScript to File option and the EPS option. Specify a name of **09Art.eps.** Click Browse (Windows) or Save As (Macintosh), send the file to the 09Lesson folder, and then click Save (Windows) or OK (Macintosh). In the Print Options dialog box, click Save.

3 Close 09Art.pmd. If PageMaker asks you if you want to save, click Yes. Switch to 09HWork.pmd, and click the Maximize button to make the window fill the screen. Select the pointer tool and delete the original grouped banner elements.

4 Choose File > Place. Double-click 09Art.eps in the 09Lesson folder. If PageMaker asks you if you want to replace a color, or include a complete copy of the graphic, click No in both cases. Click the loaded graphic icon at the top left corner of the page margins.

5 If necessary, select the crop tool (⌐) and crop the bounding box to closely fit the graphic. If the bounding box is too large, the graphic may be lost when you create the HTML file.

6 Drag the graphic up and left so that the top of the rectangle meets the top page margin, and the sun rays extend beyond the top page margin.

Because the banner is now included in the publication as a single graphic, PageMaker will be able to convert it for HTML.

7 Go to page 2 to get ready to edit it, and save 09HWork.pmd.

On the Macintosh, there is a faster alternative that can convert text and graphics to a single graphic. Select the elements and choose Edit > Cut (or Edit > Copy), choose Edit > Paste Special, and double-click the PICT option in the list.

Preparing page 2

Page 2 contains a headline (similar to the banner on page 1) that you must replace for the conversion to HTML to go smoothly.

There is also a frame containing text. PageMaker can export the frame as is, so you will leave it alone.

Note: The term frame *has a different meaning in PageMaker than it does in HTML. In PageMaker, a frame is a shape that can contain another object. In HTML, a frame is more like a pane—a way to divide a browser window.*

You will replace the headline graphic at the top of the page, just as you did on page 1. However, this time the EPS version has already been prepared for you. It was created by exporting to EPS as you did for page 1.

1 Select the pointer tool, and select the Breakfast Blunders headline, which is actually a group of separate text blocks. Do not select the word Nutrition, which you hyperlinked earlier, or the graphic beneath it. When you are sure that only the headline is selected, press Delete.

2 Choose File > Place. Double-click 09ArtB.eps in the 09Lesson folder. If PageMaker asks you if you want to replace a color or include a complete copy of the graphic, click No in both cases. Click the loaded graphic icon at the intersection of the left column guide of the second column and the first horizontal ruler guide down from the top.

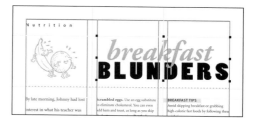

There is a graphic in the lower half of the page that resembles the top of a recipe card. This was drawn using the polygon tool in PageMaker, but PageMaker-drawn graphics cannot be exported so it must be replaced by a graphic that has already been prepared.

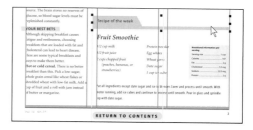

3 With the pointer tool still selected, select the Recipe of the Week graphic and press Delete.

4 Choose File > Place, and double-click the file 09ArtC.eps. If PageMaker asks you if you want to replace a color or include a complete copy of the graphic in the publication, click No in both cases. Click the loaded graphic icon at the intersection of the guides where the old graphic was positioned.

5 Go to page 3, and save the publication.

Preparing page 3

The table on this page was created in Adobe Table, a program included with PageMaker 7.0. PageMaker will automatically convert it to a graphic when you export, so you don't need to do anything to adapt the table to HTML.

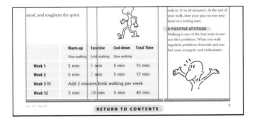

The only change you make on this page is to replace the large headline type the same way you replaced the banner and headline elements on page 1 and 2. Again, this graphic has been already been converted for you.

1 Select the pointer tool and select the **Walking Your Way to Fitness** headline, which is actually a group of separate text blocks and graphics. Make sure you do not select the Exercise text or the graphic beneath it. Press Delete.

2 Choose File > Place. Double-click 09ArtD.eps in the 09Lesson folder. If PageMaker asks you if you want to replace a color or include a complete copy of the graphic in the publication, click No in both cases. Click the loaded graphic icon at the intersection of the left column guide of the second column, and the first horizontal ruler guide down from the top.

3 Go to page 4 and save the publication.

Preparing page 4

All you have to do on this page is replace the headline elements with the single EPS replacement graphic. Again, this graphic has been already been converted for you.

1 Select the pointer tool and drag a selection rectangle around the In Balance headline, which is actually a group of separate text blocks and graphics. Make sure you do not select the Lifestyle text or the picture below the Lifestyle text. Press Delete.

2 Choose File > Place. Double-click 09ArtE.eps in the 09Lesson folder. If PageMaker asks you if you want to replace a color or include a complete copy of the graphic in the publication, click No in both cases. Click the loaded graphic icon at the intersection of the left column guide of the second column and the first horizontal ruler guide down from the top.

3 Save the publication.

Exporting to HTML

You have completed all of the manual adjustments to the publication. The rest of the conversion will be automatic. You will export the publication to HTML with settings that will specify how PageMaker will perform the conversion.

1 Choose File > Export > HTML.

The first thing you'll do is specify filenames and document titles for the HTML files. It is important to understand the difference between a filename and a document title.

The *filename* is the name of the HTML file as it appears on disk. For this reason, adhere to the standard file naming conventions that apply to the operating system that your Web server uses. If you publish through an Internet Service Provider (ISP), ask them what naming restrictions apply.

The *document title* is the name that appears in the title bar of a Web browser. You can use spaces in the name, and it does not have to conform to any file naming conventions.

2 Click Untitled1 in the HTML Document Title column.

In the HTML Document Title section, you specify the names of the HTML documents you want to create from the publication you are exporting. You have a choice here—you can export all of the publication pages as a single continuous HTML document, or you can separate the publication into a number of smaller HTML documents. Right now, the Export HTML dialog box indicates that all four pages will be assigned to the HTML document Untitled1. This is fine, but you will change the name of the HTML document.

3 Click Edit, and type **Healthy Living - Volume 10, Number 27** for the Document Title. Leave Assign PageMaker Pages selected, and then click Done.

You leave Assign PageMaker Pages selected because you want to divide this publication into HTML documents by page instead of assigning each text story to its own page.

Now you'll specify the filename of the HTML document.

4 Click Document and select the 09Html folder in the 09Lesson folder. Type **09HWork.htm** as a filename. Make sure Save Images Into This Folder is selected, and then click OK.

Setting export options

1 Click Options. Make sure that the Approximate Layout Using HTML Tables When Exporting Pages option is selected, and leave the Exported Page Width at 612 pixels.

The Approximate Layout Using HTML Tables When Exporting Pages option is what will preserve the three-column layout of the newsletter, including the text wrap and the banner and headlines that span each page.

Next you will map PageMaker styles to HTML formats. Keep in mind that HTML format names are standardized and that the font and size used by HTML formats are defined by the Web browser used to view the pages.

2 In the Style Assignments section of the Options dialog box, make sure that Preserve Character Attributes is selected. This will preserve the bold inline heads in the publication.

3 In the Style Assignments section of the Options dialog box, make sure that PageMaker styles are mapped to HTML formats as shown in the following table. In this table and in the Options dialog box, the PageMaker styles in your publication are listed on the left, and the HTML formats that currently correspond to them are listed on the right. To change the HTML format for which a PageMaker style is mapped, click the format name (Windows) or arrow next to the name (Macintosh) and choose the new format from the pop-up menu.

PageMaker style	HTML format
[No style]	Body Text
Body Text	Body Text
Body Text Intro	Heading 3
Body Text List	Body Text
Body Text Small	Heading 5
Contents	Heading 3
Footer	Heading 5
Headline	Heading 1
Numbered List	Body Text
Section Head	Heading 2
Sidebar Head	Heading 3
Sidebar Text	Heading 5
Subhead 1	Heading 4
Subhead 2	Heading 3

If you are familiar with HTML formats, you may notice that some style assignments made here are not the obvious ones. For example, HTML includes formats that automatically add bullets or numbers to lists. Although those types of lists exist in this publication, the corresponding HTML formats are generally not used in this publication because the indent amount for HTML

bullets and numbers is too great for the narrow print-oriented columns of this newsletter. If the newsletter publisher had the time and resources to redesign years of old issues for the Web, they would have created new, wider column widths that would have allowed the use of standard HTML bullet and numbering formats.

Also, some heading styles were assigned to body text. For example, the PageMaker style Body Text Intro was mapped to the HTML format Heading 3, because this was the large text in PageMaker that started each section.

HTML formats are named according to their purpose in the structure of a document, but for this publication they are used according to their appearance. Although this improves the appearance of the page in up-to-date graphical browsers, it will make the page harder to read in low-end browsers.

You can also work with HTML formats directly on the layout. Just choose Add HTML Styles from the Styles palette menu. This technique is usually most useful when you are creating a new, blank page that you will export to HTML. For republishing existing pages, mapping the original styles, as shown here, may be faster.

4 In the Graphics section of the Options dialog box, make sure that PageMaker Chooses, Use Short Name (8.3), and Downsample to 72 dpi options are selected, and then click OK.

5 You want to see how the HTML document turns out, so click the application icon and specify a Web browser in which you want to view the HTML pages when PageMaker is finished exporting. Then select View HTML.

6 Click Export HTML.

As the HTML is exported, a dialog box displays messages about the progress of the conversion and notes any page elements that cannot be exported.

7 When PageMaker is finished, it may display a dialog box listing elements that were not converted. Click OK to close the dialog box. The HTML version of the publication appears in the Web browser you specified.

Viewing the HTML page in a Web browser

In the Web browser, you can see how the HTML will be viewed over the World Wide Web, although it may appear differently in other browsers. Now you can test the hyperlinks you created, using your browser.

1 Click the word **Nutrition**. The browser takes you to the Nutrition article.

2 Click the **Return to Contents** button at the bottom of the page.

3 On page 1, click the word **Lifestyle**. The browser takes you to the Lifestyle article.

If you want the publication to be readable by the widest range of Web browsers, such as those that do not support the HTML tables that preserve page layout, you can export the HTML as a single column of text. This works best with publications already designed as a single column. In the HTML Export dialog box, open the Options dialog box and click to deselect Approximate Layout Using HTML Tables When Exporting Pages.

Comparing the final versions

The final step in Web publishing is to upload the publication to a Web server. This procedure varies depending on the publishing hardware, software, and other requirements, which are determined by your Internet Service Provider (ISP). Be sure to talk to your ISP for the exact steps required to publish your pages. In this project, you can examine how the final files appear on your hard disk after being exported from PageMaker.

1 In Explorer (Windows) or the Finder (Macintosh), open the folders 09Pdf and 09Html inside the folder 09Lesson, and arrange the folder windows so that you can see the files inside them.

The folder 09Pdf contains 09PWork.pdf (the PDF version you exported from the publication). Although it is only one file, it contains all the pages, text, and graphics in the publication. On a properly configured Web server, it will download one page at a time so that a person does not have to download the entire file to view a page.

The folder 09Html contains 09HWork.htm (the HTML version you exported from the publication) and all of the files linked to the publication. When you upload this page to a Web server for Web publishing, be sure you include all of the files in this folder.

You can compare the two versions in your Web browser. The HTML version should still be open, so just open the PDF version you exported earlier.

💡 If your Web browser supports multiple open windows, you can open a new browser window to compare the HTML and PDF versions side-by-side.

2 Start a Web browser. In the Web browser, open 09PWork.pdf in 09Lesson/09Pdf.

The HTML version resembles the original well and can be viewed without a plug-in. However, fonts and line breaks may not match the original because type specifications are largely determined by the way each individual Web browser is set up.

The PDF version is completely faithful to the original, particularly when printed, and the article threads make the document easier to read online.

In this project you adapted a previously printed publication for the Web, and exported it as PDF and HTML. You should now have a better idea of the strengths of each approach and how you might want to adapt your own publications for the Web.

3 When you finish examining the publications, close all open applications.

Adobe on the Web

If you have Internet access and a Web browser, be sure to visit Adobe's home page (http://www.adobe.com/).

You will find frequently updated information about Adobe products, free software and upgrades, tips and techniques from experts, links to other Web sites, and information about how to configure your Web browser to view Adobe Acrobat PDF files.

Review questions

1 When publishing on the Web, in which situations is it better to use PDF instead of HTML? In which situations is it better to use HTML instead of PDF?

2 How you create a complete hyperlink?

3 Where can you find colors that display well in Web browsers?

4 How can you turn a PageMaker page into an EPS file?

5 What are the two ways you can map PageMaker paragraph styles to HTML formats?

Answers

1 PDF can be a better solution for Web publishing when:

• You want to preserve a professional level of design and typography.

• The publication is likely to be printed at the receiving computer, particularly in color or at high resolution.

• You want the online version to match a printed original exactly.

• You want to be able to zoom in on the page without losing quality.

HTML can be a better solution for Web publishing when:

• You want the document to be viewable in browsers that do not support plug-ins.

• The publication uses a basic design which will translate easily to HTML.

2 First you create an *anchor*, or destination of the hyperlink jump, and then you create one or more *source*s that jump to the anchor.

3 The Online library in the Color Options dialog box contains the Web-safe palette of 216 colors.

4 When the computer is set up for a Postscript printer, choose File > Print, click Options, select Write PostScript to File, and then select EPS.

5 Choose File > Export > HTML, click Options, and map the styles using the Style Assignments table. This is most useful when you are republishing an existing publication. Or choose Add HTML Styles from the Styles palette menu. This is most useful when you are building a publication from scratch.

Lesson 10
PDF Web page

This project is a section of a multimedia online guide that you will export using the Portable Document Format (PDF), and compress to achieve small size and fast display in a Web browser or in Acrobat Reader. This project uses two kinds of links: Automatic links, which you create using PageMaker's indexing and table-of-contents features; and manual links, which you create using the Hyperlinks palette.

In this project, you will complete a partially built guide to a national park. The guide is designated for viewing in a Web browser. The designer has chosen to use PDF because of its high quality and simple workflow. To make the PageMaker publication interactive, you will use the Hyperlinks palette, adding jumps within the publication and to destinations outside the publication. Finally, you'll use the Export PDF command to print the publication as a PDF file.

In this project you will learn how to do the following:

• Use the Hyperlinks palette to create hyperlinks for a PDF publication.

• Generate an automatically hyperlinked table of contents and index.

• Add a hyperlink that appears on every page by adding it to a master page.

• Create a hyperlink between two PDF files.

• Create invisible hyperlinks using the shape tools in PageMaker.

• Set up one image as an image map, which can jump to different places depending on where you click.

• Link to a movie.

• Link to a URL on the World Wide Web.

• Export to PDF.

As you work, be sure to save the publication often.

Before you begin

As before, you will delete the existing PageMaker preferences or configuration file to return all settings to their defaults and make sure that lesson fonts are installed. Then you will open and inspect a final version of the document that you create in this project.

Note: Windows users need to unlock the lesson files before using them. For information, see Copying the Classroom in a Book files on page 4.

1 Before launching PageMaker, return all settings to their defaults. See "Restoring default settings" in Lesson 1.

2 Make sure that the AGaramond, AGaramond Bold, AGaramond Italic, Birch, Myriad Bold, Myriad Italic, Myriad Condensed Bold, Myriad Roman, Trajan, and Zapf Chancery fonts are installed on your system.

Windows only: Because of the way Windows handles fonts, you must apply italic to AGaramond to use AGaramond Italic; you must apply bold to Myriad Roman to use Myriad Bold; you must apply italic to Myriad Roman to use Myriad Italic; you must apply bold and italic to Myriad Roman to use Myriad Bold Italic; and you must apply bold to Myriad Condensed to use Myriad Condensed Bold.

3 Launch PageMaker and set up the palettes you will need for this lesson. You will be using the Hyperlinks, Layers, Styles, and Colors palettes. If they are not already open, choose Window > Show Styles, and Window

> Show Colors, Window > Show Hyper-links, and Window > Show Layers. Close any other open palettes.

💡 You may want to save screen space by combining the palettes. Just drag palette tabs to other palettes.

4 Make sure the QuickTime Frame import filter is installed: Press Ctrl (Windows) or Command (Macintosh) while choosing About PageMaker from the Help (Windows) or Apple (Macintosh) menu. (If necessary, you can install the filter from the PageMaker 7.0 CD using the Custom install option.)

5 Make sure that Acrobat Reader, Acrobat Distiller, and an Acrobat Reader-compatible Web browser are installed. Also, make sure you have enough RAM to run PageMaker, Distiller, and Reader at the same time.

Previewing the final version

To see what you'll be building, first view the completed PDF file in your Web browser.

1 Start your Web browser. Then switch to Explorer (Windows) or Finder (Macintosh), and open the 10Lesson folder. Arrange the folder window and the Web browser so you can see them both.

💡 In Windows, you can quickly arrange windows for drag-and-drop by clicking the taskbar with the right mouse button and choosing Tile Horizontally from the pop-up menu.

2 Drag 10Final.pdf from the 10Lesson folder to your Web browser window.

Note: *If the PDF file does not open properly in the Web browser, make sure Acrobat Reader is installed properly.*

The first page acts as an entrance to the project. You will get a sense of the general design of the guide by examining it. If necessary, click the Acrobat Fit in Window button to show the entire first page of the publication.

3 Click the Maximize button of the browser window to expand it to fill the screen. Click Continue on the guide's opening screen.

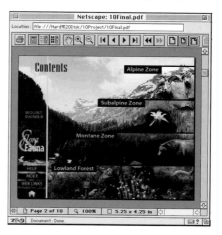

The second page is an illustration of the mountain with a superimposed diagram of the altitude zones of flora and fauna on the mountain. Along the left side of each page is a navigation bar with buttons that take you to other sections. The dividing lines between the entries are actually paragraph rules.

4 Click Lowland Forest.

The next four pages correspond to the altitude zones listed in the table of contents, starting at the lowest altitude. On these four pages, the navigation bar includes Previous Page and Next Page buttons.

Next page button
Previous page button

5 Click the Next Page button. Take a look at the page, then click the Next Page button again. Look at the next couple of pages and stop when you reach Alpine Zone.

The Alpine Zone page has no Next button as it is the final topic page. The last three pages are the index, help, and Web Links screens.

6 Click Help.

The Help button is on the navigation bar that appears on all topic pages. It was set up on a PageMaker master page, so you set up the jump only once. The Help screen describes how to navigate the publication.

7 At the bottom left corner of the page, click the Home icon.

You will build the links for all of these pages. Some links will be created automatically by PageMaker when you export to PDF.

You can open the PageMaker version of the completed publication so that you can use it as a reference as you work through the project. First you will close the Web browser because you will not need it until the end of the project. You will also close Acrobat Reader, which opened automatically to display the PDF in the Web browser.

8 Close the Web browser, close Acrobat Reader, and open 10Final.pmd in the 10Lesson folder.

Setting up the publication

The publication you use for this project has already been designed; your job is to complete it by adding the hyperlinks and exporting it to PDF. First you will open the partially completed publication.

1 Open 10Begin.pmt in the folder 10Lesson.

2 Choose File > Save As. Name the file **10Work.pmd** and save it into the 10Lesson folder. If the publication window does not already fill the screen, click the Maximize button.

If the page displays slowly, you can change the display resolution for images in the publication. This does not affect the quality of the final output.

3 Choose File > Preferences > General. Click Standard for Graphics Display, and click OK.

Remember to change the Graphics Display preference back to High Resolution when you require more detailed image display, such as when you are positioning elements precisely on top of images.

Using text and graphics as hyperlink anchors

The first step in this project is to manually create a number of hyperlinks by defining anchors (destinations) and sources (objects that jump to an anchor). You'll create text hyperlinks first, setting up anchors and then associating their sources with them. If you're unfamiliar with sources and anchors, review Lesson 9.

It's a good idea to create the anchor for this page while you're here, although you won't be using this anchor right away.

1 If necessary, click the Hyperlinks tab to display the Hyperlinks palette.

2 On page 1, select the text tool (**T**) and select the words **Mount Rainier**.

3 Choose New Anchor from the Hyperlinks palette menu. Type **Title Page** in the New Anchor dialog box that appears, and then click OK. The new anchor appears in the Hyperlinks palette.

You can type any name into the Hyperlinks palette, but each name in the Hyperlinks palette must be different. For this project, anchors are named after the title of the page where the anchor is located.

Now you will create an anchor on page 2 so you can get to it from page 1. This time you will create an anchor using a shortcut.

4 Go to page 2. With the text tool still selected, select the word **Contents**, and click the New Anchor button ( ) in the Hyperlinks palette. Name the anchor **Contents**, and click OK.

5 Choose Edit > Deselect All to deselect the words.

6 Select the pointer tool, and in the Hyperlinks palette, select the Title Page anchor name (don't click the icon). Choose Go to Title Page from the Hyperlinks palette menu.

The Go To command in the Hyperlinks palette menu is a quick way to go to the selected palette item. By default, PageMaker centers the anchor in the publication window. You will change this setting later.

7 Choose View > Fit in Window, even if it already appears selected in the menu.

Remember that an anchor is only half of a hyperlink—it's just the destination. To jump to the anchors, you need to create sources to the anchors.

8 With the text tool, select the word **Continue** in the middle of the title page.

9 In the Hyperlinks palette, click **Contents** (don't click the icon).

10 In the Hyperlinks palette, choose New Source from the Hyperlinks palette menu. Type **Title to Contents**, and then click OK.

11 Save 10Work.pmd.

For this project, the sources are named to describe where they jump. You now have a link that can take you from page 1 to 2. On the Hyperlinks palette, you can see that a source (such as Title to Contents) is always listed under the anchor that it jumps to (such as Contents).

Testing hyperlinks

You can now test the link to make sure it works properly.

1 Select the hand tool ($\text{\textcircled{?}}$). A blue outline appears around the Continue text where you created a source. Move the hand over the Continue text.

The hand changes to a pointing hand, indicating that it is over a hyperlink.

2 Click the text.

The publication jumps to the Contents page. The Contents text is centered on the screen, but this pushes part of the page past the edge of the window. You do not want the hyperlink anchor to be centered on screen after a jump, so you'll change the preference that controls this.

Note: The blue outlines you see when you use the hand tool do not appear when the publication is exported to PDF. In PDF, you design the appearance of a hyperlink source.

3 Choose File > Preferences > Online. In the Hyperlink section, deselect the Center Upper-Left of Anchor When Testing Hyperlinks option. Click OK.

This preference exists for those times when you have more than one anchor on a page and want to know which one you jumped to.

You will return to the title page so that you can try the link again. You haven't yet created a hyperlink source back to the title page, but PageMaker provides a command that lets you backtrack along pages in the order you viewed them.

4 Choose Layout > Go Back, and choose View > Fit in Window.

5 Click the word **Continue** to go to the Contents page again. PageMaker displays the Contents page using the view you used the last time you saw the page.

Adding a source on a master page

You can add a hyperlink source to a master page, which can save time when you want a hyperlink on every page that leads to the same anchor, such as a Help screen. You will do this by adding a source that jumps to the Contents page.

1 Choose the Flora and Fauna master page from the master pages pop-up menu by clicking the master-page icon with the right mouse button (Windows) or by positioning the pointer over the master-page icon and holding down the mouse button (Macintosh).

Note: When you click the master page icon, Flora & Fauna may already be selected, indicating that it is the master page applied to the current page. You still have to select it again to view and edit the Flora & Fauna master page.

2 Select the pointer tool, and select the Home graphic in the lower left corner of the page.

3 In the Hyperlinks palette, click the anchor icon () next to the Contents anchor. This is the same as choosing New Source from the Hyperlinks palette menu. Name the new source **Return to Contents** and then click OK.

Although you can add a source to a master page, you can't add an anchor to a master page because an anchor is a destination on one specific page, and a master page item appears on multiple pages.

Now you will create an anchor for the next page. You can make the anchor easy to identify by naming it after the page title. You will do this easily by copying and pasting the page title into its anchor name.

4 Go to page 3. Select the text tool (**T**), select the **Lowland Forest** title text, and choose Edit > Copy. Click the New Anchor button and paste the name you copied, and click OK.

5 Select the hand tool () and click the home icon. You just used the source you added to the master page to return to the Contents page.

6 Save 10Work.pmd

Setting up anchors for the rest of the publication

There is more than one way to create a large set of hyperlinks. You could continue working the way you have in this lesson so far, which is to create an anchor, a source to it, another anchor, and then another source. However, it is often better to create all the anchors first and then all the sources. If you set up publication anchors first, they all appear listed in the Hyperlinks palette, available for any sources you want to create. You'll use the latter method in this project.

You will be creating an anchor for each page, so it makes sense that each anchor should have the same name as each page title. You continue creating each source from each page title by copying and pasting each page title into its anchor name.

1 Select the text tool (**T**). Go to page 4, select the words **Montane Zone**, and choose Edit > Copy. Click the New Anchor button () in the Hyperlinks palette, paste, and click OK.

2 On pages 5 through 9, create anchors based on the title of each page, just as you did in the previous step.

Note: Remember to copy each page title separately for each source, because each name in the Hyperlinks palette must be unique.

3 Click the maximize button on the Hyperlinks palette and examine the new entries. If the palette minimizes, click the button again.

Each page now has an anchor associated with it. From now on, whenever you want to create a source, just click the anchor icon of the page to which the source will jump.

4 Save 10Work.pmd.

Completing the hyperlink sources

You have already set up a hyperlink from page 1 to 2. Now you will finish hooking up the navigation controls by setting up the Previous Page and Next Page buttons as

sources on the other pages of the guide. Finally, you will add sources to the Help, Index, and Weblink pages from the Flora and Fauna master page.

1 Go to page 3. Select the pointer tool, and select the right facing arrow graphic at the bottom left corner of the page. In the Hyperlinks palette, click the anchor icon for Montane Zone, and name the new source **Lowland to Montane**. Click OK.

2 Go to page 4 and select the right facing arrow at the bottom left corner of this page. In the Hyperlinks palette, click the anchor icon for Subalpine Zone, and name the new source **Montane to Subalpine**. Click OK.

Page 4 has both a Next Page and Previous Page button. You finished setting up the button to the next page, so now you will set up a button to the previous page by creating another source.

3 On page 4, select the left-facing arrow. In the Hyperlinks palette, click the anchor icon for Lowland Forest, and name the new source **Montane to Lowland**. Click OK.

At this point, you might notice that the right and left arrow sources for this page end up under different anchors, which can make it confusing to remember where to click to add a source. Just remember that the palette lists hyperlinks by anchor (destination). You always want to click on the anchor where you want the arrow to jump, not the anchor where the arrow is located.

You might also notice that the anchors appear in the Hyperlinks palette in the same order in which they are added. This is an advantage of creating all the anchors first in the same order as the pages in the publication. Anchors are easier to work with when you add them to the Hyperlinks palette in an organized manner, because you cannot rearrange them.

4 With the pointer tool still selected, continue setting up the Previous Page and Next Page arrows as sources on pages 5 and 6, as you did in the previous steps. When you create each source, remember to click the anchor icon for the anchor on the page where you want the source to jump.

5 Save 10Work.pmd.

6 Go to the Flora and Fauna master page by choosing it from the Master Page pop-up menu at the bottom left corner of the publication window.

7 Select the text tool (**T**) and drag to select the Help text at the left of the page. Click the Help anchor icon on the Hyperlinks palette, and name it **To Help**. Click OK.

8 Using the same method as in the previous step, create a source named **To Index** from the Index text to the Index anchor. Then create a source named **To Web Links** from the Web Links text to the To Web Links anchor.

9 Save 10Work.pmd.

Creating a source from grouped elements

Now you want the Flora & Fauna text (above the sources you just created) to jump to the title page. However, this text is made up of separate text blocks created in PageMaker. Fortunately, you can set up all of the objects as one source simply by grouping them.

1 Select the pointer tool, select the three text blocks containing the words **Flora & Fauna**, and then choose Element > Group.

2 With the group still selected, click the Title Page anchor icon in the Hyperlinks palette. Name the new source **To Title**, and then click OK.

3 Save 10Work.pmd.

The hyperlinks remaining to be done are those which lead to locations outside this publication, such as Web sites, and those which PageMaker can generate automatically, such as the table of contents and index.

Now that you've linked the Help, and Index text, all of the links on the master page are complete. Now you can test these links.

4 Go to page 1. Select the hand tool ( ), press Tab to hide all palettes, and click Continue.

5 Go to page 3, and click the right facing arrow to go to page 4. Click the left facing arrow to go back to page 3. Click the Help button and Index buttons.

6 Press Tab to display hidden palettes.

7 Save 10Work.pmd.

Completing the linked table of contents

PageMaker lets you mark paragraphs to be included in the table of contents. Inclusion in a table of contents is a paragraph-level attribute, so you can make it part of a paragraph style.

In this guide, you will set the Subhead style to be included in the table of contents. This causes each occurrence of Subhead to appear in the table of contents automatically. The Subhead style is used once on each page.

1 If necessary, click the Styles palette tab to display the Styles palette.

2 Go to page 3. Select the text tool, and click an insertion point in the words **Lowland Forest**.

You'll use a shortcut to edit the subhead style.

3 In the Styles palette, press Ctrl (Windows) or Command (Macintosh) as you click the Subhead style in the Styles palette. This opens the Style Options dialog box so that you can edit the style.

Style Options	
Name: **Subhead**	**OK**
Based on: **No style**	**Cancel**
Next style: **Same style**	**Char...**
next: Same style + face: CorvinusSkyline + size: 24 + leading: 24 + color: Deep Purple + track: normal + flush left + space after: 0p7.2 + incl TOC + hyphenation	**Para...**
	Tabs...
	Hyph...

4 Click Para. Select the Include in Table of Contents option at the bottom of the dialog box. Press Shift (Windows) or Option (Macintosh) as you click OK to close all dialog boxes.

You won't see a visible change to the text, because all you did was tell PageMaker to include paragraphs of that style in the table of contents when you generate it later.

5 Save 10Work.pmd.

Generating the table of contents

You are ready to generate the table of contents. If you like, take a look at page 2 in the 10Final.pmd publication to see how the TOC should look when finished. Select the pointer tool and click any of the headings to see how they are positioned. The headings were laid out in advance as frames which

were threaded in advance to keep the story together, acting as placeholders for the hyperlinked table of contents generated later. In 10Work.pmd, the frames are already positioned and threaded, so all you have to do is generate the table of contents.

1 If you switched to 10Final.pmd, switch back to 10Work.pmd.

The final PDF file will include a map page that points out important places in the national park. The map is currently in a separate file, but it contains index entries you want in the final PDF file. Although you are not creating the index yet, automatic hyperlinks work best if all desired publications are in the book list the first time you generate hyperlinks, so you will add the map file now.

2 Choose Utilities > Book. In the file list on the left side of the Book Publication List dialog box, select the file 10Map.pmd in the 10Lesson folder and click Insert to add it to the book list. Click OK.

3 If the publication window does not already fill the screen, click the Maximize button. Go to page 2, where you will place the Table of Contents you are about to generate.

4 Choose Utilities > Create TOC. Delete the word **Contents** from Title and leave it blank. Select Include Book Publications. For Format, select the No Page Number option, and then click OK.

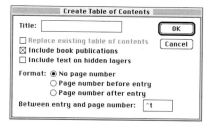

PageMaker creates a text story containing the new table of contents. As with any other placed story, you can position a table of contents anywhere, but as you saw in the final publication there are already four threaded frames set aside for the table of contents in this project. You will place the table of contents into the bottom frame. Because the frames are already threaded, the headings will climb through the four frames from bottom to top just like the actual biological zones on the mountain.

5 Click the loaded text icon on the X in the frame near the bottom left corner of the page as shown.

The word **Contents** appears—not the same Contents page title you deleted from the Create Table of Contents dialog box, but the subhead from the Contents page. You will remove it soon. The other headings flow through the frames in the order they were threaded, from bottom to top.

6 With the pointer tool still selected, select any frame and choose Edit > Edit Story to open the story editor. If paragraph returns are not visible, choose Story > Display ¶.

The triangle icons in the text are hypertext markers attached to text which PageMaker generated automatically.

Now we'll edit this contents list to include only our main topics: Lowland Forest, Montane Zone, Subalpine Zone, and Alpine Zone.

7 Click the style name TOC Subhead to the left of the word **Contents** to select the entire paragraph, and then press Delete.

8 In the same way, delete the paragraphs containing the words **Help**, **Index**, and **Web links**. Make sure you delete the triangle icons that accompany those words.

9 When you are finished, close story editor.

The page should appear as shown below.

PageMaker has automatically set up these table of contents entries as hyperlinks. You can test them to see if they work.

10 Select the hand tool (☝) and click any heading. After PageMaker jumps to the page, you can return to the TOC page by clicking the Home icon.

Note: Hyperlinks generated by the table of contents feature do not appear on the Hyperlinks palette.

11 Save 10Work.pmd.

Creating a multiple-source image map out of one graphic

Since you added the table of contents, a person can now use Page 2 to jump to the other pages. However, you don't have to build a table of contents using text. You can also use graphics. You will complement the text table of contents you created by also building graphic links on page 2, so that a person does not have to click on text.

The mountain image behind the table of contents contains several pictures that can function as graphic links to the same sections marked by the text. You would normally set them up as sources by selecting each of them, but in this case they can't be selected separately because they are all part of a single Photoshop image. However, you can still create multiple sources for a simple image by drawing invisible shapes over the image in PageMaker.

Before you create these links, you'll create a new layer that contains all the links you are about to draw. This makes it easier to find, lock, and hide the next set of links you create, which you will make invisible.

1 Click the Layers palette tab or choose Window > Show Layers. Click the New Layer button (▣), name the layer **Hidden Links**, and then click OK. For the next step, make sure the Hidden Links layer remains selected in the Layers palette.

You will lock the Default layer so that you know all of the objects you are about to draw end up on the Hidden Links layer, and so you don't accidentally select other items.

2 In the Layers palette, select the Hidden Link layer so that new elements appear on it. In the Default layer, click the lock column. A pencil icon appears to indicate that the default layer is locked.

Now you will set the default stroke and fill color for the link sources you are about to create. You will temporarily set them to be visible while you edit them. After you complete them, you will make them invisible.

3 Choose Edit > Deselect All to make sure no objects are selected. If the command is dimmed, no objects are selected. In the Colors palette, click the Stroke icon, and click Paper. Then click the Fill icon, and click None.

4 Select the rectangle tool (☐), and draw a shape over the fern picture within the Lowland Forest zone. With the square still

selected, create a new source from the shape to the Lowland Forest anchor in the Hyperlinks palette. Name it **Contents to Lowland**.

If you find it difficult to position the shape because the background image is too coarse, choose File > Preferences > General and select High Resolution for graphics display.

You can create a source using any shape tool. For this lesson, you will use the rectangle tool for all of the shapes on this page.

5 With the rectangle tool still selected, draw a shape over the bear picture within the Montane Zone. With the rectangle still selected, create a new source to the Montane Zone anchor in the Hyperlinks palette. Keep the shape within the zone; don't overlap the Lowland Forest zone. Name it **Contents to Montane**.

6 Draw a shape over the flower in the Subalpine Zone. With the rectangle still selected, create a source from the shape to the Subalpine Zone anchor in the Hyperlinks palette. Name it **Contents to Subalpine**.

7 Draw a shape around the mountain goat, and create a source from the shape to the Alpine Zone anchor in the Hyperlinks palette. Name it **Contents to Alpine**.

You don't want these white rectangles to be visible, so now you will make them invisible. Because you locked the other layer, you will be able to select all of the shapes on the Hidden Links layer at once without affecting the rest of the publication.

8 Choose Edit > Select All. In the Colors palette click the Both button and click None. Choose Edit > Deselect All.

Note: From this point, if you want to select and edit the shapes, remember that they are currently invisible. You will have to lock the Default layer and draw a selection rectangle around the area where a shape is located.

You'll now unlock the Default layer so that you can work on the other sections.

9 In the Layers palette, click the pencil icon in the lock column of the Default layer to unlock it.

10 Save 10Work.pmd.

11 Select the hand tool ( ), and test any of the invisible sources you just created.

Linking to a movie

You can include multimedia elements in a PDF file. To take advantage of this feature, you will add a QuickTime movie to this guide. As with most video formats, movie performance is usually less than satisfactory over the Internet. However, when publishing a PDF on a CD, movies work quite well.

You'll select the large bear image on the page and replace it with a QuickTime movie. PageMaker actually imports only a single frame of a movie. However, when you export a publication to PDF or HTML, the exported file automatically includes a hyperlink to the full movie. The exported file and the movie need to be in the same folder.

Note: For cross-platform compatibility (necessary on the Web), a movie must be in the flattened QuickTime format. Its name mustn't exceed eight characters, and must be followed by the extension .mov.

1 Go to page 4. With the pointer tool selected, click in the middle of the large bear to select it.

2 Choose File > Place. Select Bear.mov in the 10Lesson folder. Make sure Replacing Entire Graphic is selected, and click Open (Windows) or OK (Macintosh).

Note: If Replacing Entire Graphic is dimmed, you need to install the QuickTime Frame import filter from the PageMaker 7.0 CD (using the Custom install option).

3 In the QuickTime Frame Import dialog box, leave the first frame of the movie displayed, and click OK.

PageMaker replaces the bear image with the movie's first frame (the same image). (Because PageMaker imports only a single frame of the movie, you can't test the movie until you create the PDF file.)

4 Save 10Work.pmd.

Creating URL anchors

A person reading this guide can find additional information on related Web sites. You'll add those Web sites as anchors in the Hyperlinks palette using several methods.

1 Go to page 9, and choose New URL from the Hyperlinks palette menu. Type **http://www.aqd.nps.gov/natnet/wv/ biodiv.htm** and then click OK.

2 In the PageMaker publication, select the text tool (**T**). Taking care not to select any characters other than the words (such as the paragraph return), drag to select the two words **Biological Diversity**.

3 In the Hyperlinks palette, click the globe icon for the URL you just created. Name a new source called **To Biodiversity page**, and then click OK.

4 Save 10Work.pmd.

Importing URL anchors

You can also import a list of URLs into the Hyperlinks palette, such as a browser's Bookmarks file. In this project, a URL you need is already available from a file.

1 Choose Import URLs from File from the Hyperlinks palette menu, select the file 10URL1.htm in the 10Lesson folder, and then click Open. The URLs in the file appear in the Hyperlinks palette after the existing URLs.

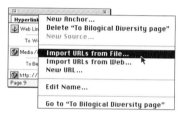

If you want to see the contents of the 10URL1.htm file, you can open it in a text-editing application.

2 With the text tool still selected, click an insertion point after the words Biological Diversity, and then press Return or Enter. Type **Endangered Species**, and then select the words you just typed.

3 Click the globe icon for the URL that ends in **/es.htm**. Name a new source called **To Endangered Species page**, and then click OK. Deselect the text.

4 Save 10Work.pmd.

If you have an active Internet connection, you can import URLs directly from a Web page by choosing Import URLs from Web from the Hyperlinks palette menu and typing the location of the page containing the URLs.

Dragging URL anchors

If your browser and your operating system support drag-and-drop between programs, you can also drag and drop URLs directly into a PageMaker publication. You can also drag URLs in from other programs that support drag-and-drop. When you drag a URL into a PageMaker publication, it is automatically added to the Hyperlinks palette as an anchor. The URL you will use is in a Web page stored in the 10Lesson folder, so you will open the Web page.

1 Select the text tool (**T**). Click an insertion point after the words **Endangered Species**, and then press Return or Enter. Type **Watchable Wildlife**, and then select the words you just typed.

2 Open a Web browser. Arrange the folder window and the Web browser windows so that you can see the contents of both.

3 Using Explorer (Windows) or the Finder (Macintosh), drag the file 10URL2.htm from the 10Lessons folder into the Web browser window.

4 If 10Final.pmd is open, close it. Position the Web browser window and the PageMaker publication window so that you can see the text in both windows.

In Windows, you can quickly arrange windows for drag-and-drop by clicking the taskbar with the right mouse button and choosing Tile Horizontally from the pop-up menu.

5 Switch to the Web browser, and drag the link **Watchable Wildlife** and drop it on the words Watchable Wildlife which you highlighted in PageMaker. Take care to drag the link right away without selecting the text—if you simply click, you'll open the link instead. On the Macintosh, if you don't drag the link immediately a pop-up menu will appear.

The new source and anchor are automatically added to the Hyperlinks palette.

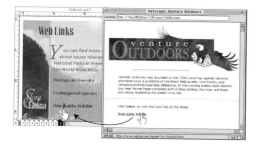

Note: If you only see the first part of the link in PageMaker, the link may be wrapping to a second line in the Web browser. Some Web browsers do not let you drag more than one line of text. Try making the browser window wider to fit the entire link on one line.

6 In PageMaker, click the maximize button so that the publication window fills the screen.

7 With the text tool still selected, click an insertion point in the text you just linked, and choose Edit > Select All. In the Styles palette, click WWW Links. This style visually identifies text that links to the Web. Formatting text does not affect its hyperlinks.

8 Select the pointer tool and select the text block containing the Web links.

9 Save 10Work.pmd.

If your Internet connection is active, you can test URL hyperlinks the same way you would any other kind of hyperlink.

Note: The URL anchors in this publication were current at the time of publication, but may have changed. If you have trouble connecting to these URLs, double-click them in the Hyperlinks palette and type any working URL you want.

10 Select the hand tool (🖑) and position it over the words Biological Diversity. The hand tool changes to a pointing hand with a letter W, indicating that it is over a Web link. Click the words **Biological Diversity**. The page appears in your Web browser. If PageMaker asks you to find a Web browser, locate one on your computer.

PageMaker only asks for a browser the first time you connect to a Web URL.

You can change the Web browser PageMaker uses in the Online Preferences dialog box. Choose File > Preferences > Online.

11 Close the Web browser and switch back to PageMaker.

Adding index entries

This guide will include an index generated by PageMaker. Like the table of contents, PageMaker can automatically create hyperlinks from index entries so that a person can go to an index entry by clicking it.

Some entries have already been added to the index. You will complete the index by adding a few entries yourself.

1 Go to page 4. Select the text tool (**T**), and select the words **black bears** near the end of the article. Choose Utilities > Index Entry.

2 Make sure **black bears** is the entry in the top of the Topic column, and then click OK. You've just added that text to the index.

3 With the text tool still selected, select the word **movie** near the bottom right corner of the page (taking care not to select spaces), and choose Utilities > Index Entry. Click the

Promote/Demote button ( ) to move the **movie** entry to the second level, type **black bears** as a new first-level entry, and then click OK.

4 Save 10Work.pmd.

Generating the hyperlinked index

To include the index in the publication, you must generate it. The index will automatically include links to the separate map publication that you included in the book of publications you set up when you generated the table of contents earlier.

1 If necessary, choose View > Show Guides.

2 Go to page 8, the page where you will place the index you will generate. Choose Utilities > Create Index. Delete the Title and leave it blank. You will include index markers in the separate Map.pmd file, so make sure Include Book Publications is selected, and click OK.

When PageMaker finishes processing, the loaded text icon appears. Placing an index is just like placing a text story from a word processor.

3 Check to make sure Layout > Autoflow is selected. Position the loaded text icon at the guide intersection where the Control Palette reads **6p** for X and **5p3** for Y. Click to flow the index into the columns. The index includes many more entries than the ones you added, because the publication was partially indexed before you opened it.

You have completed building the multimedia publication. Before you export it to PDF, you can test the automatically generated index hyperlinks with the hand tool.

4 Select the hand tool (🖑). The cursor changes to a pointing hand when positioned over the hyperlinked index entries.

In PageMaker you will simulate as much as possible the way the publication will look in PDF, by hiding all palettes and turning off the blue outlines that mark the hyperlinks automatically generated by PageMaker.

Note: Hyperlinks generated by indexing do not appear on the Hyperlinks palette.

5 Press Tab to hide all palettes, and choose View > Hide Guides.

6 Choose File > Preferences > Online. Deselect the Outline Link Sources When Hand Tool is Selected option, and then click OK.

7 On page 8, click the *black bears* entry. PageMaker jumps to the correct page.

8 Save 10Work.pmd

Exporting to PDF

The final step in building the guide is to create a PDF file from it. Not only can PageMaker export to PDF directly, it also provides a high degree of control over how the PDF is created.

When PageMaker exports to PDF, it sends the publication to Acrobat Distiller in a process much like printing. The PDF version of the publication that Distiller produces will take up much less disk space than the original publication but will still be viewable at high quality across platforms, by using the Acrobat Reader.

Note: If the amount of memory installed in your computer is not much more than the amount recommended for PageMaker, free up memory by closing all other applications except PageMaker.

1 Choose File > Export > Adobe PDF. Save the file if necessary. If PageMaker asks you if you want to include other publications in the book or if you need to save the publication, click Yes in both cases.

Note: In Mac OS, be sure you have a PostScript driver selected in the Chooser before choosing File > Export.

2 In the PDF Options dialog box, select On Screen for PDF Style. Verify that Acrobat is selected for Printer Style. You will use the default settings for all the panels except the Doc Info panel in this dialog box.

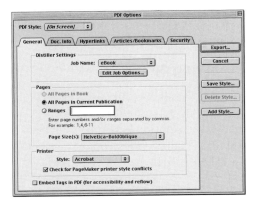

For information on the options available in the various tab panels of the PDF Options dialog box, see chapter 12 in the *Adobe PageMaker 7.0 User Guide.*

3 Click the Doc Info tab to change the filename, subject, author, and keyword information. For Title, select and delete the file name. Type **Mount Ranier Guide** in the Title text box. For Subject, select and delete the file name. Type **Fauna and flora of**

alpine, subalpine, montane, and lowland forest zones in the text box. Leave the Author and Keyword entries *as is.*

Document information is often used to refine index searches in document collections. For this reason, you should always replace the file name with the document title, for example. (This and Security are the only panels in which you can change information without defining a new PDF Style.)

4 Click Export.

5 In the next dialog box, select the View PDF option (Windows) or View PDF Using option (Mac OS) if you want to open the newly created Adobe PDF file in Acrobat or Acrobat Reader rather than save it and open it at a later time. Then click Save to save the 10Work.pdf file in the 10Lesson folder.

PageMaker automatically starts Acrobat Distiller and processes the PDF file. Processing may take a few minutes. Depending on your settings, Acrobat opens the PDF version of the publication in Acrobat or Acrobat Reader. If the PDF file doesn't open automatically, locate the 10Work.pdf file in the 10Lesson folder, and double click to open it in Acrobat or Acrobat Reader.

When you select On Screen for PDF Style, Distiller uses the Screen job options. The Distiller Screen job options are optimized to create Adobe PDF files appropriate for display on the World Wide Web or an intranet, or for distribution through an e-mail system. This option set produces the smallest PDF file size and optimizes files for byte serving.

The default settings for these options use Acrobat 3.0 compatibility to ensure maximum efficiency over the Internet. However, Acrobat 3.0 PDF documents may not open properly in versions of Acrobat earlier than 3.0.

The Base 14 fonts are embedded; all fonts are subsetted.

Hyperlinks are preserved, as are articles and bookmarks.

No security is applied to the Adobe PDF file.

Note: *On Mac OS, a window opens showing the progress of Distiller. The setting displayed in this window may not match those you selected in the PDF Options dialog box. However, your PDF files will be created using the correct settings you specified.*

For more information, see Exporting to Adobe PDF on page 274 in Lesson 9 and chapter 12 in the *Adobe PageMaker 7.0 User Guide*.

Viewing the PDF in a Web browser

You can view the completed PDF version of the guide in a Web browser.

1 If you still have the PDF file open in Acrobat Reader, close the PDF file. Also, close Acrobat Distiller (if necessary) and PageMaker, because you will longer need those programs for this lesson.

2 Start your Web browser.

3 Switch to Explorer (Windows) or the Finder (Macintosh), and open the folder on your hard disk that contains the PDF file you just created. Arrange the folder window and the Web browser window so you can see both. In Windows, you can click the taskbar with the right mouse button and choose Tile Vertically from the pop-up menu.

4 Drag 10Work.pdf from the 10Lesson folder window to your Web browser window. To make the browser window fill the screen, click the Maximize buton.

5 Click Continue, and then click any other hyperlinks in the publication.

6 Click the zoom tool (🔍) and click text. PDF allows page magnification, and anti-aliases type so that type displays smoothly at many sizes.

You've successfully added hyperlinks to a publication, and you've converted a publication to a PDF document that you can publish on the Web.

Review questions

1 In what order do hyperlink anchors appear in the Hyperlinks palette?

2 How do you link to another file, such as a PDF document?

3 How do you make a hyperlink source appear in the same position on more than one page?

4 What is the difference between Acrobat Distiller and Acrobat Reader?

Answers

1 Hyperlink anchors appear in the order that you create them. They cannot be rearranged in the Hyperlinks palette.

2 Choose New URL from the Hyperlinks palette menu and type the URL of the file where it will exist on the volume where you will publish the PDF.

3 Put the hyperlink source on a master page.

4 Acrobat Distiller is like a software version of a printer, but instead of creating printed pages, it creates PDF pages. Acrobat Reader is used by compatible Web browsers to display PDF pages in a Web browser window, or it can display PDF pages on its own.

Index